Crisis & Communion

The Remythologization of the Eucharist— Past, Present, and Future

JOHN R. MABRY

apocryphile press
BERKELEY, CA

apocryphile press
BERKELEY, CA

Apocryphile Press
1700 Shattuck Ave #81
Berkeley, CA 94709
www.apocryphile.org

Printed in the United States of America

ISBN 0-9747623-8-5

This book is dedicated to
the core members of the
Festival of the Holy Names:

Lawson Barnes
Barbara Frey
Christine Sinnott
John Sullivan
Karyn Wolfe

We done a grand thing.

Other books by John R. Mabry

God As Nature Sees God: A Christian Reading of the Tao Te Ching
Heretics, Mystics & Misfits
Tao Te Ching: a New Translation
The Little Book of the Tao Te Ching

Contents

Acknowledgements

This manuscript has had a long and arduous birth process! It began as my doctoral dissertation (of the same title), and I am grateful to my dissertation committee for their hard work on my behalf: Dr. Paul Schwartz, Dr. Mara Keller, Dr. Brendan Collins, and Dr. Dorothy Donnelly.

I am also indebted to my friend and former spouse, Karyn Wolfe, for her support and input. Thanks also to everyone who ever took part in a Festival of the Holy Names service, especially the core members who put their heart and soul into the project: Lawson Barnes, Christine Sinnott, John Sullivan, Barbara Frey, and Karyn Wolfe, to whom this volume is dedicated. I couldn't have done it without you! (And a special "thank you" to Lawson, Christine, and Karyn for proofreading the dissertation.)

I am likewise indebted to numerous authors, whose works were essential to this one, especially Marjorie Procter-Smith and Janet R. Walton, Joanne Carlson Brown and Rebecca Parker, William R. Crockett, Horton Davies, Nancy A. Hardesty, Gary Macy, and Rosemary Radford Ruether. Thank you for teaching me.

In preparing this manuscript for publication I would also like to thank Dr. Janeen Jones and the Rev. Nancy Bancroft for their comments and proofreading, and Dr. Flavio Epstein for his encouragement and support.

Introduction

The Eucharist needs to change. The Christian church[1] is undergoing a crisis that is threatening its very existence, a crisis rooted in issues of power and identity that are most explicitly voiced and perpetuated in our liturgies. Studies report that mainline churches such as the Presbyterian Church (USA), the Episcopal Church, and the United Methodist Church are losing members at an alarming rate.[2] Many people of conscience regard Christianity as irrelevent or even a hindrance to humanitarian progress, and women in increasing numbers are giving up on their childhood faith as sexist and inflexible.

Feminist theologians have been debating for three decades whether women should stay in the church and fight for change or abandon it as irredeemable, while mainline and Roman Catholic social scientists have for years worried over declining statistics in church membership and growth. And while there have been many books of speculation, many reports, and countless conferences on spirituality and church renewal, the crisis is not abating, but rather increasing.

Young adults who have been reared in postmodernism are deeply distrustful of bureaucracy, hierarchy and dogma in any form. The liturgical forms and rituals do not speak their language, nor do they impact their daily lives. Words like "atonement" and "blood sacrifice" are meaningless if not offensive. Issues that genuinely matter to them, such as freedom, peace, and justice, are painfully missing from the institutional churches' liturgical agendas. Among such young people the irrelevance of the church is almost a given.

Women of all ages have been similarly marginalized and are just in the last couple of decades awakening *en masse* to this fact. While women of every denomination are fighting for their right to take an equal place beside men in ordained ministry and academics, many Roman Catholic women are "opting out" of the institution and forming their own worship communities, called "Women-Church," which exist partly as a means of protest, and partly out of the desperate need for a form of worship that does not betray or insult women. For Women-Church collaborators, sitting through an ordinary service at their local parish is excruciating, since the very language of the liturgy reinforces sexist stereotypes and imperialist views of the world.

While young adults of Generation X (roughly 20-40 years of age) are likely to be drawn to traditional elements of worship such as chanting, incense, ritual, etc., they are exceptionally eclectic and have little tolerance for body-spirit dualities, militaristic metaphors, or exclusive proclamations ("ours is the only way to God, etc."). Xers have no tolerance for the politics of religious institutions or for liturgical celebrations that seem, at best, irrelevant, or at worst, at odds with their core values.

Our liturgies are in desperate need of reform—especially, I believe, the liturgy of the Eucharist. From the liturgies of the Roman Catholic Church to the Lord's Supper celebrations of Evangelicals, our Eucharistic rites themselves contain sexist language, support spirit-over-body and heaven-over-earth dualities, and promote an ecclesial manifest destiny that many people of conscience even within our churches find intolerable. Feminist theologian Elizabeth Schüssler Fiorenza writes that "the Eucharist has become the ritual symbolization of the structural evil of sexism."[3] Helen Wright concurs, saying that "for more and more women, the Eucharistic celebration is becoming an experience of segregation and alienation."[4]

One woman I talked to for this project worried whether or not she could continue to call herself a Christian at all if she had to accept uncritically the teachings of her church. Many women remain silent rather than recite offensive parts of their church's liturgy, since they cannot speak the creeds or other sections in good conscience.[5]

This dilemma is tragic, since we as Christians are defined and shaped as a people by the celebration of our central ritual, the Eucharist. The Eucharistic prayer contains the history of salvation, our source of nourishment and nurture in the present, and our hope for the future. How we celebrate the Eucharist defines who we are as individual Christians and as Christian communities. With very few exceptions,[6] this ritual of blessing and sharing bread and wine has been celebrated by all Christians in every time and place, from Baptists to Russian Orthodox, Pentecostals to Plymouth Brethren, Calvinists to Roman Catholics, Mennonites to Lutherans. All feast at the Eucharistic table.

The word "Eucharist" comes from the Greek *eucaristeo*, which means "I give thanks." Gratefulness and thanksgiving were originally the purpose of the rite. For this reason, the 1979 Episcopal *Book of Common Prayer* calls the Eucharist "The Great Thanksgiving." Roman Catholics call it the "Mass," a name which derives from the conclusion of the service in Latin: "Ite, missa est" ("Go, it is over"). To many Protestants, the "Lord's Supper" is the title of choice, while the Orthodox call it the "Divine Liturgy."

It is supposed to be a time of joy, of "communion" or "co-inherence"[7] with God and with each other. Yet because the theology imbedded in its text and the language in which it is couched are in many cases several hundred years old, this ritual often does not produce the desired result.

Until the Eucharistic ritual speaks to us in words that are philosophically tenable and socially relevant, few will have reason to join or return to our altars. The bread that we consecrate there must be the kind of food that people in our time are hungry for. In order to provide an invitation to thanksgiving for *all* the peoples of the earth who find meaning in the story of Jesus, the Eucharist needs to change.

A Changeable Feast

The idea of "changing" the Eucharist seems preposterous—even blasphemous—to some. When I asked one Episcopalian how the Eucharist needed to change, she seemed offended and said, "I can't think of any way at all. The Eucharist isn't the issue: it's in a real sense *all* we've got. The very fact that we think it has to change is a *baaaad* sign." Another man, a Catholic, responded similarly, adding, "People across the theological spectrum can agree that the Eucharist is useful and valuable *as is* and it has lasted unchanged in its essentials for some 1950 years."

History reveals the absurdity of this last comment. As we shall see in Part One, in every age, every ensuing crisis met by the church has changed its understanding of what this very important ritual actually means. For centuries, Christians have argued, fought wars, and issued proclamations of damnation upon each other over questions such as "exactly *how* is Christ present in the Eucharist?" The history of these arguments reveals how often complementary and conflicting opinions co-exist, often within the same faith community. For though the actions of this rite—the taking, blessing and distribution of bread and wine—have been retained,[9] the meaning ascribed to these actions has never stopped evolving in the imaginations of its participants.

Even at the beginning of the Christian movement, before the testimony of the biblical record, there was no clear consensus on the meaning of the rite. The later patristic writers, though their theological discourses are voluminous, rarely discussed the Eucharist directly, but usually referred to it in passing while addressing other concerns. As Gary Macy contends, they

> ...did not sit down and carefully work out a consistent understanding, nor did they compare notes with their fellow theologians and bishops to see if everyone was teaching the same thing. The result is, of course, that when one places these random thoughts side by side, one is faced with a number of common themes, but no common theology. What the fathers of the early church bequeathed to their followers was not a theology of the Eucharist, but a pluralism of themes out of which any number of theologies could develop.[10]

What happened during these first few centuries of the church's life was the emergence of various theological "threads," independent traditions concerning the Eucharist, which throughout the next two millennia can be found weaving in and out of the church's life. Though most "threads" began as singular understandings, before long, Eucharistic practice often saw two or more "threads" woven through a prayer, culminating in the complex and multivalent prayers with which we are familiar today.

Many of these threads are indeed complementary. Some others might be seen as contradictory, while some are built on differing assumptions of what the crucifixion and resurrection actually mean. But all of the threads we shall discuss—whether they have been subsumed by other threads, evolved beyond recognition, or been forgotten altogether—have at one time or another in the church's history been regarded as orthodox ("correct teaching").

The theologies that define these threads typically arose in response to various crises encountered by the church. Generations of Christians, faced with new political and spiritual challenges, shaped their understanding of their ritual meal in order to help them meet their challenges, creating new threads of tradition, and reinterpreting old ones, giving them new life, new hue, and new meaning.

In Part One of this book, we will look closely at the formation of these threads, and at the crises that precipitated them. It is here that we shall see that Eucharistic remythologization is not some modernist, relativist aberration, but part of the normative life of the evolving organism we call the church.

Exploring the Current Crisis

Crisis in the church is not simply an artifact of history. Our churches continue to struggle with how to make our faith congruent with our lives in a contemporary culture. The language and theology of our liturgies are frequently at odds with how we see the world around us. They are philosophically antiquated, which, in the history of the Eucharist, is an intolerable situation (as we shall see). Christians everywhere are asking themselves and their liturgists: How can we affirm the goodness of the earth, when our liturgies lead us only to heaven? How do we proclaim an end to sexism, when our liturgies insist on referring to all people as "men?" How can women fully understand themselves as created in the image and likeness of God, when all God language is masculine? How can we declare God's salvation for all people and exclude wedding liturgies for same-sex partners? How can we affirm people's basic worth, when our liturgies tell us that we are "miserable offenders" or "not worthy to eat the crumbs" that fall from God's table?

Until our liturgies are made congruent with a contemporary, essential, and inclusive understanding of the Gospel, the integrity of the Gospel suffers. So long as our rituals are not in sync with our sermons we will be perceived as lazy at best—or at worst, duplicitous. Something must be done.

In this book we shall examine the issues involved in this crisis in detail, drawing upon the experience of feminist and liberation theologians, the insights of Generation X, and the personal experience of both clergy and laity interviewed for this book.[8] We shall hear the voices of those who have for centuries been silenced, and invite the experience of women and oppressed peoples to influence, and sometimes lead, our exploration.

Myth, Ritual, and Change

While the idea that the Eucharist has changed—and must change—might be upsetting to some Christians, to scholars of myth and ritual it is predictable. The idea that the sacraments were "handed down by Jesus" in their complete and present form is itself a myth, and one that the church can no longer afford to entertain.

Many scholars have debated in this century over which comes first, the myth or the ritual. According to mythologist Th. P. Van Baaren, however, this is a chicken and egg situation. Myth and ritual are inseparable, and as a result the stories told about Jesus were amplified, romanticized, and re-interpreted, in tandem with the evolution of the Eucharistic rite. This is as it should be: in the church's succeeding eras, different aspects of the Jesus story spoke to people's imaginations,[11] and people in different eras were in need of very different meanings.

By myth, I do not mean to suggest a denial of historicity or truth; instead, I use the term as mythologists use it, to denote "a story which makes sense of people's lives,"[12] which is always true in one or more ways. To deny the historicity of the person of Jesus of Nazareth is foolish—but what the church has believed about Jesus has evolved along with the Eucharistic rite.

Myths and rituals do not arise from a vacuum, of course, but as folklorist Raymond Firth writes, they arise "in response to a situation of challenge, where justification of an event has to be secured if status or more material benefit is not to be lost."[13] For the earliest Christians, the material benefit they most needed was their very survival. For later Christians, maintaining the status quo was of the greatest import, and the church's self-concept as well as its understanding of the person of Jesus changed accordingly.

The earliest Christians, for example, would have been mystified by the doctrine of the Trinity, yet the development of such a doctrine was deemed necessary to avoid heresy in the centuries following. Th. P. Van Baaren writes that when a myth and reality are out of sync what results is,

> ...either religious behavior which is not adapted to the real situation, or an effective form of behavior taking no account of religion. In this conflict-situation between mythical and worldly reality one force must give in and change, or disappear. The character of myth is opposed to disappearance, but not...to change. The reality of this world is only rarely open to sufficiently fundamental change; therefore in cases of conflict, as a rule it is the myth which will change.[14]

Thus, myth—and its sibling, ritual—seems to have an "instinct" for survival, and as long as a people can derive meaning from it, it will remain active, though its interpretations may (indeed, *must*) change, often drastically. As we shall see, Christian history is no stranger to this process. In every age the church has met new challenges, and its story about who Jesus is and the celebration of its central rite have shifted accordingly to meet the need.

Where Are We Headed?

This of course begs the question, "How does the Eucharist need to shift now?" This is the real problem addressed in this book. The discoveries of the Liturgical Movement in the past fifty years have inspired such conformity across denominational lines that a Eucharist at a Roman Catholic church today is little different than the celebration at the United Church of Christ down the road. While this phenomenon has done an enviable job of promoting ecumenical unity, it has also fed the popular notion that the Eucharistic rite is a monolithic and unchanging liturgical entity that one must swallow whole, as-is, or not at all. History reveals the error of this perception; reason reveals that the blasphemy might not be in the "changing" of the rite, but in resistance to change. Categories of thought that formed Eucharistic theology in ages past are no longer applicable, yet the church has been slow to explore and embrace new avenues. For instance, although Aquinas' interpretation of

Aristotle was timely and sophisticated, we no longer understand the world in Aristotelian terms. The church has yet to embrace contemporary philosophies and has much work to do exploring its faith in terms relevant to contemporary society. The necessity of our doing this is obvious: if the church refuses to speak a comprehensible language, it will be discarded as irrelevant, or cherished as little more than a quaint relic.

But the church, if it is truly what it has always proclaimed itself to be, the body of Christ on Earth and a living testimony to God's faithfulness, cannot tolerate irrelevance. The danger of irrelevancy is tied up in a much greater struggle faced by the church the world over, a dilemma equal to the dangers faced by the church throughout its long history, and one that needs to be brought to light both intellectually through the church's teaching, and liturgically through its rites.

Unfortunately, the natural evolution of the Eucharistic prayer has been retarded by a number of factors that keep the prayer from speaking to these issues. The advent of the printing press, the liturgical uniformity imposed by various institutional churches, and the development of systematic theologies that have not kept pace with secular philosophies have kept most Eucharistic prayers mired in fifteenth- and sixteenth-century theological categories.

Beautiful as the language or form of these prayers may be (or may have been), the pain and misunderstanding they precipitate today call us to re-evaluate them. One Anglican I interviewed said that although he was a traditionalist he didn't believe in using the 1662 *Book of Common Prayer* because the Eucharist is not a museum piece. Just so.

It seems to me that liturgical change should be a natural and inevitable process. And indeed, in times when the Eucharistic prayer was an oral tradition, change happened frequently and easily, as early Christians interacted with God and the world around them. Change, in fact, is at the very heart of liturgy. Marjorie Procter-Smith writes,

> ...Metanoia, conversion, transformation...[are] central to the liturgy because the primary action of liturgy is dialogue. Liturgy is a dialogue with God, an encounter with the one who calls us into community with one another. And as an inevitable result of that encounter, we are changed. Change is always the result of genuine dialogue with another per-

> son, since we cannot enter into such dialogue without being open to the perspective of someone other than ourselves. But when the genuine encounter is with God, a profound transformation is called forth.[15]

Real attention to spiritual life in community and to the needs of others requires us to change and grow liturgically. This must not happen as a forced mandate, but as the natural process of listening to each other and responding compassionately to shape our common worship to meet an ever more inclusive vision of the church. While the crises of the past have been responded to theologically and liturgically, the current crisis of domination and marginalization continues for many. It is my opinion that we are still not listening, and that the issues involved need to be stated in such a way that all peoples of the church may hear and respond.

Since the liturgies of the Eucharist have become more static than can ever be good for the health of the church, the third and final section of this book will be devoted to some suggested "ways ahead" for changing the Eucharistic liturgy to help meet our needs as contemporary Christians.

To explore these ways ahead, I was aided in my search by The Festival of the Holy Names, a worshipping community mostly comprised of Gen Xers (with a couple of Baby Boomer mentors along the way) that served as a ritual laboratory in one form or another for five years. Drawing from the Festival's experience, Part Three is a guide to "conscious" exploration of people's needs, and may serve as a primer for communities to begin their journeys toward liturgical innovation. We shall explore the Eucharist's potential for inciting us to social justice, as well as several other contemporaneously relevent interpretations. As Horton Davies writes, "The Eucharist, as a central symbol of the Christian religion, is an enacted parable with an almost inexhaustible set of meanings. The modern world is beginning to realize in a very realistic way the implications of the Eucharist for human justice in a world that flaunts it."[16]

We will also discuss the use of inclusive language and the problem of dualistic categorization. We shall walk a delicate tightrope between tradition and innovation, and though we shall come to few, if any, absolute answers, we shall raise many useful questions along the way.

In short, this book is a call to liturgical transformation. Part One will show that such transformation has historical precedent and that it is, in fact, inevitable. In Part Two we shall see that change in how we celebrate the Eucharist today is imperative. Part Three provides a discussion of how that change might occur, with analysis of the theological and social challenges such a proposal raises, and offers concrete suggestions for moving the church forward from a state of crisis to a state of grace.

PART ONE

The History of Eucharistic Remythologization

Biblical Traditions and The Early Church

It began with an act of remythologization. A group of friends met on the eve of the Passover to celebrate God's faithfulness to them with the bounty of the earth. Their Rabbi began the meal in the traditional manner: taking bread in his hands, he blessed the Creator, Sovereign of the Universe, who brings forth bread from the earth. He broke the bread and passed it to his friends. Then, in a moment of inspiration, he added something that was not in the liturgy. Looking at the broken crust of bread in his hands, he surprised them all by saying, "This is my body."

His friends were stunned. Their teacher had been acting very strange of late, dwelling on his impending death and possessed of a tired melancholy. Peter's hand had frozen halfway to his mouth at his teacher's cryptic utterance. What did he mean by that? Peter's mind reeled with the possible implications of the words. He felt a stab of fear in his gut. The sacred meal would never be the same.

Thus begins the Eucharistic rite, which has held its place at the center of Christian worship through nearly two millennia of tumultuous political change, theological debate, and radical reform. The traditions surrounding the Eucharist arise from a number of distinct, though complementary sources. Primary is the Judaic practice of celebrating sacred meals to welcome the Sabbath and as an annual reminder of the covenant between God and Israel. Beyond this, Jesus used this tradition in a parabolic manner to illustrate key ideas throughout his ministry. Finally, there are the biblical records of the Last Supper. In the next few pages we shall examine the earliest traditions associated with the Eucharist, Jesus' initial use of table fellowship as a teaching device, the Judaic tradition of the early church, and the Hellenistic tradition of the early church.

The Brachot Thread: Thanksgiving and Community

The earliest Christians were Jews, for whom the observance of a sacred meal was infused with great symbolic meaning and was an important aspect of religious life. Belief in Jesus as the Messiah did not mitigate the practice of their native faith until much later when Paul began to challenge the inherent "Jewishness" of Christianity. The Acts of the Apostles, St. Luke's record of the early church, records that the apostles and their followers continued to worship in the synagogue. Hatchett describes the pattern of a typical Sabbath evening that Jesus and the disciples would have known well:

> Following the liturgy of the word at the synagogue, participants came home, performed ritual ablutions, and then shared conversation over wine before coming to the table to eat. Assembling at the table, participants thanked God over the bread: "Blessed be God, King of the universe, who brings forth bread from the earth." The bread was then broken and distributed, providing the means for eating from common dishes...
>
> After the meal the diners shared a cup of wine which was first blessed by the *pater familias* who called upon the group to stand: "Lift up your hearts," and asked their permission to give thanks in their name: "Let us give thanks to the Lord our God." God was then blessed as creator, sustainer, and redeemer, in relation to the particular day or occasion, and prayer was offered for the community of Israel, usually in petitions with an eschatological overtone. The wine was blessed by blessing God: to "bless" in Hebrew is the equivalent of to "thank," to name the Name of God, to associate with the revelation of God...[1]

The recitation of the prayer of blessing, the *Brachot*, over the bread (and on more festive occasions the wine) would have been the normative act of celebration for Jesus and his followers. For the Jews this practice of table-fellowship carried deep symbolic significance, of which Jesus made profound and extensive use during his ministry. To sit at table with someone was to testify to one's acceptance of them, one's unity with them. To eat a meal with someone (especially a sacred meal such as the Sabbath or Passover) was to recognize that your fellow diners were in good standing with God and the community, and also to communicate to them the blessing pronounced in the prayers. Jesus frequently scandalized his religious contemporaries by making a habit of sharing meals with "outcasts and sinners":

> And as he sat at dinner in Levi's house, many tax collectors and sinners were also sitting with Jesus and his disciples—for there were many who followed him. When the scribes of the Pharisees saw that he was eating with sinners and tax collectors, they said to his disciples, "Why does he eat with tax collectors and sinners?" When Jesus heard this, he said to them, "Those who are well have no need of a physician, but those who are sick; I have come to call not the righteous but sinners."[2]

For Jesus, none were excluded from God's love and the benefits of religious community. Those whom the religious leaders of the time scorned, were in fact, in Jesus' eyes, those most in need of friendship and support.

Most contemporary scholars are in agreement that Jesus' primary message was "the proclamation of the future reign of God."[3] This was not unusual in his time; the eschatological mythology of the "kingdom of God" was a popular topic for preachers of the period. What was so profound about Jesus' teaching, however, was his insistence that the kingdom is already here and is hidden beneath our own noses: "The Kingdom of the Father is spread out upon the earth, and people do not see it" (Thomas 113). Jesus' "realized eschatology" is expressed in his many parables, in which he makes ample use of the language and imagery connected with the popular mythology of the eschatological feast. Both canonical and pseudepigriphal writings make explicit reference to a mythical eschatological meal which will be shared by all. In Isaiah 25:6-8 we read,

> On this mountain God's hosts will make for all peoples a feast of rich food, a feast of well-aged wines, of rich food filled with marrow, of well-aged wines strained clear. And God will destroy on this mountain the shroud that is cast over all peoples, the sheet that is spread over all nations;

> God will swallow up death forever. Then God will wipe away the tears from all faces, and the disgrace of the peoples he will take away from all the earth, for the Holy One has spoken.

Thus, when Jesus healed the centurion's servant, and said of this gentile, "I tell you, many will come from East and West and will eat with Abraham and Isaac and Jacob in the kingdom of heaven, while the heirs of the kingdom will be thrown into the outer darkness, where there will be weeping and gnashing of teeth,"[4] it is easy to see why the religious leaders, the "heirs of the kingdom" in Jesus' story, might be scandalized.

Paul, in perhaps the earliest of scriptural references to the Eucharist, expands upon Jesus' theme: "The cup of blessing that we bless, is it not a sharing in the blood of Christ? The bread that we break, is it not a sharing in the body of Christ? Because there is one bread, we who are many are one body, for we all partake of the one bread."[5]

Although the Jewish Christians in Jerusalem continued to be skeptical about whether Christianity may be appropriate for peoples other than the Jews, Paul seems to have truly gotten Jesus' point when he says,

> For in Christ Jesus you are all children of God through faith. As many of you as were baptized into Christ have clothed yourselves with Christ. There is no longer Jew or Greek, there is no longer slave or free, there is no longer male and female; for all of you are one in Christ Jesus. And if you belong to Christ, then you are Abraham's offspring, heirs according to the promise.[6]

Whatever else we may say about the Apostle Paul, it is clear that he takes Jesus' charge that "we all be one" very seriously. In his epistle to the Corinthians, he gives a primitive description of the last supper (which we shall consider shortly), and then chastises the Corinthians for not treating each other with equal consideration:

> To begin with, when you come together as a church, I hear that there are divisions among you; and to some extent I believe it. Indeed, there have to be factions among you, for only so will it become clear who among you are genuine. When you come together, it is not really to eat the Lord's supper. For when the time comes to eat, each of you goes

> ahead with your own supper, and one goes hungry and another becomes drunk. What! Do you not have homes to eat and drink in? Or do you show contempt for the church of God and humiliate those who have nothing? What should I say to you? Should I commend you? In this matter I do not commend you! ...Whoever, therefore, eats the bread or drinks the cup of the Lord in an unworthy manner will be answerable for the body and blood of the Lord. Examine yourselves, and only then eat of the bread and drink of the cup. For all who eat and drink without discerning the body, eat and drink judgment against themselves.[7]

As Crockett points out, this last passage has been traditionally interpreted in an individualistic manner, that the communicant should be "right with God" lest God strike them dead upon partaking of the elements! Yet the context of Paul's admonition is clear: eating in an unworthy manner is for him the very antithesis of individualistic concern—it refers explicitly to how a community lives out the Gospel they proclaim, whether the meal is truly shared, and whether it is truly a celebration open and available to all.

This community aspect of the Eucharist finds its strongest support in these very early glimpses, as well as in some of Jesus' discourses in the Gospel of John.[8]

Fortunately, the Thanksgiving and Community thread did not die out with Jesus. Early Christians, especially of the second century, although embarking on threads of their own, continued to be influenced by this, Jesus' own thread. They partook of the bread and wine to celebrate God's goodness in creation, God's faithfulness, and the Community God had made of them, adding special thanksgivings for the gift of Christ Jesus. The *Didache* Eucharistic prayer is an example of this "carryover" (see Appendix A).

The Last Supper Traditions

The accounts of the Last Supper given by the evangelists and Paul are frustratingly fragmentary and are, in fact, irreconcilable. The Gospels record four accounts of the Last Supper, and Paul adds his own to the mix in his first epistle to the Corinthians. The synoptic Gospels (Matthew, Mark, and Luke) give differing accounts of the meal itself—and the institutional narrative found in these Gospels (where Jesus institutes the Lord's Supper by saying "This is my body...this is my blood") is absent from John's account. What the synoptics agree on is that the last supper took place in the context of the Passover celebration, which the Gospel of John denies. Where the synoptic accounts differ is on the exact words spoken by Jesus, revealing two distinct oral traditions circulating amongst the churches at the time of their writing.

The Judaic Thread: Mark and Matthew

The first two accounts we shall consider form the Judaic thread. The Gospels of Mark and Matthew are both written from a Judaic perspective, are intended for a Jewish audience, and interpret their events in Judaic terms. So doing, they were self-consciously attempting to interpret the Christ event in terms of their own culture and tradition. Their accounts are as follows:

> **Mark 14:22-24:** While they were eating, he took a loaf of bread, and after blessing it he broke it, gave it to them, and said, "Take; this is my body." Then he took a cup, and after giving thanks he gave it to them, and all of them drank from it. He said to them, "This is my blood of the covenant, which is poured out for many."
>
> **Matthew 26:26-28:** While they were eating, Jesus took a loaf of bread, and after blessing it he broke it, gave it to the disciples, and said, "Take, eat; this is my body." Then he took a cup, and after giving thanks he gave it to them, saying, "Drink from it, all of you; for this is my blood of the covenant, which is poured out for many for the forgiveness of sins."

These two accounts are the most similar to each other in structure, and it is generally agreed that Matthew used Mark as one of his primary source texts (as did Luke, but he was writing for a different audience).

Notable in both of the accounts above is the use of the term "my blood of the covenant" in reference to the cup. For Jews, the word covenant has explicit and universally recognized significance. It refers to the Mosaic covenant, the bond between God and the people Israel instituted on Mount Sinai following the exodus from Egypt:

> And Moses wrote down all the words of God. He rose early in the morning, and built an altar at the foot of the mountain, and set up twelve pillars, corresponding to the

> twelve tribes of Israel. He sent young men of the people of Israel, who offered burnt offerings and sacrificed oxen as offerings of well-being to God. Moses took half of the blood and put it in basins, and half of the blood he dashed against the altar. Then he took the book of the covenant, and read it in the hearing of the people; and they said, "All that God has spoken we will do, and we will be obedient." Moses took the blood and dashed it on the people, and said, "See the blood of the covenant that God has made with you in accordance with all these words." Then Moses and Aaron, Nadab, and Abihu, and seventy of the elders of Israel went up, and they saw the God of Israel. Under his feet there was something like a pavement of sapphire stone, like the very heaven for clearness. God did not lay his hand on the leaders of the people of Israel; also they beheld God, and they ate and drank.[9]

This is the institution of the covenant meal in the Sinai wilderness that the Jews continue to celebrate at the feast of Passover. The "blood of the covenant" was clearly understood, as every Jew at the time made sacrifices at the temple in Jerusalem in accordance with the Mosaic Law. In light of this, Jesus' use of the term "*my* blood of the covenant" must have been slightly unsettling for the disciples, since they would naturally connect the "blood of the covenant" with the temple sacrifices and a substitutionary payment for sin.

The disciples had been warned that Jesus' death was impending. However much they may have been in denial of this inevitable event, Jesus' allusion to his own blood as operative as "the blood of the covenant" must have been a chilling notion. Whether or not these were the precise words spoken by Jesus at the Last Supper, what is important is that the early Jewish believer chose to interpret his death in the terms with which they were the most familiar and comfortable, that of cultic sacrifice. This theology is most explicitly developed in the anonymous Epistle to the Hebrews:

> Therefore he had to become like his brothers and sisters in every respect, so that he might be a merciful and faithful high priest in the service of God, to make a sacrifice of atonement for the sins of the people. Because he himself was tested by what he suffered, he is able to help those who are being tested. Therefore, brothers and sisters, holy partners in a heavenly calling, consider that Jesus, the apostle

> and high priest of our confession, was faithful to the one who appointed him, just as Moses also "was faithful in all God's house."[10]

Eventually, these early Christians came to understand Jesus' blood sacrifice as the perfect sacrifice after which no more were necessary, and of which all the earlier (animal) sacrifices were but foreshadowings:

> For Christ did not enter a sanctuary made by human hands, a mere copy of the true one, but he entered into heaven itself, now to appear in the presence of God on our behalf. Nor was it to offer himself again and again, as the high priest enters the Holy Place year after year with blood that is not his own; for then he would have had to suffer again and again since the foundation of the world. But as it is, he has appeared once for all at the end of the age to remove sin by the sacrifice of himself. And just as it is appointed for mortals to die once, and after that the judgment, so Christ, having been offered once to bear the sins of many, will appear a second time, not to deal with sin, but to save those who are eagerly waiting for him. Since the law has only a shadow of the good things to come and not the true form of these realities, it can never, by the same sacrifices that are continually offered year after year, make perfect those who approach.[11]

As Crockett explains, this concept of sacrifice was applied to the Christians' sacred meal as well:

> According to this perspective, those who share in the Eucharistic cup have a share in the fruits of Jesus' death interpreted on the analogy of a cultic sacrifice... The fruit of Jesus' sacrificial death is the renewal of the covenant relationship between God and humanity, which was first established on Sinai, and is now renewed by Jesus' death.[12]

It is interesting to note that even in this most Jewish of interpretations, there is a pronounced Platonism involved, as evidenced by the Hebrews passage. "...The law has only a shadow of the good things to come and not the true form of these realities," supplied by Christ's sacrifice. Thus, even from the very first, Christianity was understood only in the context of a multiplicity of cultural ideas, even in Judea itself.

The Judaic thread is one of the oldest and most enduring. Because there is so much scripture (especially the Judaic Gospels and Hebrews) that interprets Jesus' death in cultic sacrificial terms, the church has inferred much, including the Eucharist, in this light. Although its influence waned after the third century and is known hardly at all in the East, it will re-emerge (as we shall see) in the late Middle-Ages in the West as the Sacrifice thread.

The Hellenistic Thread: Paul and Luke

Another thread of tradition is represented by Luke and Paul, the two "Hellenizers" of the Christian message. Both these writers are hoping to make Gentile converts, and so interpret the events of Jesus' life (including the Last Supper) in terms that are relevant to non-Jewish audiences.

Their accounts of the Last Supper are strikingly similar:

> **Luke 22:19-20:** Then he took a loaf of bread, and when he had given thanks, he broke it and gave it to them, saying, "This is my body, which is given for you. Do this in remembrance of me." And he did the same with the cup after supper, saying, "This cup that is poured out for you is the new covenant in my blood.
>
> **1 Corinthians 11:23-25:** The Lord Jesus...took a loaf of bread, and when he had given thanks, he broke it and said, "This is my body that is for you. Do this in remembrance of me." In the same way he took the cup also, after supper, saying, "This cup is the new covenant in my blood. Do this, as often as you drink it, in remembrance of me."

There are several distinctive features of this tradition. First, the covenant spoken of by Jesus is a "new covenant." Second, Jesus instructs the disciples to do this "in memory of me." Both of these features are exclusive to Paul and Luke, and it is important that we look at each of them.

In both cases, Jesus speaks of a "new covenant," which is different from the Law. The theme of freedom from the Law is expounded upon at length elsewhere in Paul's writings, and clearly has significance for those Christians who have never been under the "old" covenant. The new covenant would have reminded the early Christians of a passage from Jeremiah:

> The days are surely coming, says the Holy One, when I will make a new covenant with the house of Israel and the house of Judah. It will not be like the covenant that I made with their ancestors when I took them by the hand to bring them out of the land of Egypt—a covenant that they broke, though I was their husband, says the Holy One. But this is the covenant that I will make with the house of Israel after those days, God says: I will put my law within them, and I will write it on their hearts; and I will be their God, and they shall be my people. No longer shall they teach one another, or say to each other, "Know the Holy One," for they shall all know me, from the least of them to the greatest, says the Holy One; for I will forgive their iniquity, and remember their sin no more.[13]

This emphasis on "new covenant" is reminiscent of the eschatological focus of Jesus' common meals. For in declaring that this meal is the "new covenant" Jesus alludes to this "coming kingdom" for which the Jews so eagerly waited. In the Last Supper, he declares that the "kingdom" is now present and in their midst; the "new covenant" was being enacted before them, operative upon his death.

According to Luke, Jesus and his disciples were celebrating the feast of Passover, during which they would have been recounting the faithfulness of God to the community of Israel in their rescue from bondage to Egypt. In the midst of a meal designed to remind them of God's saving action in the past, Jesus surprised them all by telling them, at the sharing of the wine, to "do this, as often as you drink it, in remembrance of me." This must have been a shocking statement for the disciples, for Jesus was inserting himself into their history of salvation. But what Jesus had done was to say that his eventual death and promised resurrection would become as much a part of the disciples' religious heritage as the crossing of the Red Sea.

Certain scholars, especially H. Lietzmann and G. Bornkamm, made much of the theory that there are many similarities between the Last Supper and the Greek tradition of holding memorial feasts for the dead. If this is true—and they do make a convincing case[14]—it is very fitting that the formula "do this in remembrance of me" is found in the Hellenistic Eucharistic tradition of the early church, for whom such statements would hold native significance.

Other Biblical Material

Other biblical material on the Supper is scarce. John gives a long Eucharistic discourse in chapter six, but gives no account of the institutional narrative itself, confining his account to the washing of the disciples' feet and the betrayal of Judas. One might be able to construe some of the post-resurrection accounts of Jesus eating meals with his disciples as Eucharistic in nature, but the textual evidence is inconclusive. Many current theologians (such as Episcopal Bishop John Shelby Spong) believe that it was in the breaking of bread together that the disciples recognized Jesus' continued life and presence among them, and that the myth of the resurrection was an expression of this experience.[15] The best example of this kind of interpretation can be found in Luke's account of the two disciples on the road to Emmaus:

> ...Two of them were going to a village called Emmaus, about seven miles from Jerusalem, and talking with each other about all these things that had happened. While they were talking and discussing, Jesus himself came near and went with them, but their eyes were kept from recognizing him. ...And beginning with Moses and all the prophets, he interpreted to them the things about himself in all the scriptures. As they came near the village to which they were going, he walked ahead as if he were going on. But they urged him strongly, saying, "Stay with us, because it is almost evening and the day is now nearly over." So he went in to stay with them. When he was at the table with them, he took bread, blessed and broke it, and gave it to them. Then their eyes were opened, and they recognized him; and he vanished from their sight (Luke 24:13-31).

Although this passage is ripe for Eucharistic interpretation, it has always been used in a supplementary way, and has never been used as the basis for an independent tradition.

It is from these two early threads—the Judaic and the Hellenistic—that the early Christian church formed their further theologies of the Eucharistic meal, though the Judaic and Hellenistic traditions were to eventually dominate the Church's understanding in the West and the East, respectively. But to understand how the traditions developed, it is necessary to also trace the development of Christian worship.

Worship in the Early Church

In the sharing of their common meal, the followers of the crucified Jesus continued to find comfort and community in gathering together, but any formal and distinctively Christian liturgy was slow to develop. Bridge and Phypers speculate that "in all probability there was wide diversity of practice. Spontaneous material and liturgical form probably co-existed side by side."[16] The book of Acts records that soon after the resurrection, the followers of Jesus began to meet on Sundays, which they termed "the Lord's Day," in honor of the day Christ arose from the grave. It is probable that elements from the synagogue liturgy were fused with an extemporaneous Eucharistic prayer when the church gathered on Sundays in small groups. There is no written record of a Eucharistic prayer until the second century. While Acts records that the early Christians "...devoted themselves to the apostles' teaching and fellowship, to the breaking of bread and the prayers" (Acts 2:42), and the apostle Paul records the institutional narrative (quoted above), we must speculate as to the actual performance of the rite at this early date.

What we can glean from Paul's Epistle to the Corinthians was that the Eucharist originally took place in the context of a full meal, just as its progenitors, the Passover celebrations and Sabbath suppers, were full meals. Soon, however, the *agape* or "love feast," as the communal meal came to be called, separated from the Eucharistic prayer, until the practice of sharing a full supper died out completely in the fourth century.[17]

Justin Martyr, writing in the mid-second century, provides us with our first coherent glimpse of an early Christian service in which the Eucharist had already been separated from the proper meal:

> On the day which is called the day of the Sun we have a common assembly of all who live in the cities or in the country, and the memoirs of the apostles or the writings of the prophets are read, as much as there is time for. Then, when the reader has finished, the one presiding provides, in a discourse, admonition and exhortation to imitate these excellent things. Then we all stand up together and say prayers, and as we said before, after we finish the prayer, bread and wine are presented. He who presides likewise offers up prayers and thanksgiving, to the best of his ability, and the people express their assent by saying "Amen,"

> and there is the distribution and participation by each one in those things over which thanksgiving has been said, and these are sent, through the deacons, to those not present. The wealthy, if they wish, contribute whatever they desire, and the collection is placed in the custody of the president, and he helps the orphans and widows, those who are needy because of sickness or any other reason, and the captives and the strangers in our midst; in short, he takes care of all those in need.[18]

Already we can see a form of worship taking place that is familiar to us even today. Most interestingly, Justin's description sees the presider as offering the Eucharistic prayer extemporaneously, evidence that in the second century there was a great deal of variation in the celebration.

Though Justin speaks of "the presider," and Paul gives a list of ministries extant in the church in his time, there is at this time no developed system of clergy. Macy states that there "seems to have been a good deal of freedom about who presided at the liturgy. There is some evidence that in the very beginning the prophet in the community presided....The earliest celebrations of the liturgy were truly community celebrations, and there seems that there was no clear distinction between those who led the liturgy and those who did not. More accurately, no one led the liturgy; everybody seems to have worshipped together."[19]

With all of these untrained (and many, no doubt, unlearned) presiders giving prayers "to the best of their ability," it is inevitable that those to whom the church looked as leaders (elders or bishops) would eventually want to provide a model prayer to help those whose level of ability may have proved detrimental to the worship experience.

The Eucharistic liturgy recorded in *The Didache* ("The Teaching") is just such a model. An early second century "church handbook," it contains instructions for church government, initiation, and to some degree, celebration. The liturgy provided is very interesting, in that it does not contain an institutional narrative and uses the Jewish prayer form modeled above. It makes reference to Christ—for whom God is thanked—as being the "bread of life," and "the holy vine of David":

> Now about the Eucharist: This is how to give thanks: First in connection with the cup:
>
> "We thank you, our Father, for the holy vine of David, your child, which you have revealed through Jesus, your child. To you be glory forever."
>
> Then in connection with the piece [broken off the loaf]:
>
> "We thank you, our Father, for the life and knowledge which you have revealed through Jesus your child. To you be glory forever.
>
> "As this piece [of bread] was scattered over the hills and then was brought together and made one, so let your church be brought together from the ends of the earth into your kingdom. For yours is the glory and the power through Jesus Christ forever..."
>
> After you have finished your meal, say grace in this way: "We thank you, holy Father, for your sacred name which you have lodged in our hearts, and for the knowledge and faith and immortality which you have revealed through Jesus your child. To you be glory forever.
>
> "Almighty Master, 'you have created everything' for the sake of your name, and have given people food and drink to enjoy that they may thank you. But to us you have given spiritual food and drink and eternal life through Jesus, your child.
>
> "Above all, we thank you that you are mighty. To you be glory forever.
>
> "Remember, Lord, your Church, to save it from all evil and to make it perfect by your love. Make it holy, 'and gather it together from the four winds' into your Kingdom which you have made ready for it. For yours is the power and the glory forever. Let Grace come and let this world pass away. Hosanna to the God of David!"[20]

The *Didache*'s Eucharistic prayer is a fascinating document, for it reveals just how closely early Christian worship continued to be modeled on Jewish practice. The prayer above is simply a series of Thanksgivings for Jesus. It contains no Institutional narrative, nor does it (surprisingly!) contain any of the sacrificial emphasis found in the Judaic tradition of Mark-Matthew. It is, in fact, most representative of Jesus' own tradition of table-fellowship in the context of a common meal. It echoes Jesus' own concerns for unity, especially in the beautiful passage that speaks of "these grains that were scattered upon the mountains" being brought together to form one loaf. As Macy explains, "The early Christians spoke of the Eucharist as forming the community of believers, that the Eucharist both celebrated and affected the life of faith and love to which Christians dedicated themselves in the ceremony of sharing the life of the risen Lord."[21]

This is reminiscent of Jesus' words in the Gospel of Matthew: "For where two or three are gathered in my name, I am there among them" (Matt. 18:20). For the Christians of the second century, the "body of Christ" referred to themselves as being called together from the ends of the earth to be one people. This understanding was to exert influence even after other interpretations had largely supplanted it, for as St. Cyprian (d. 258) would write,

> ...The very sacrifices of the Lord demonstrate that the Christian unanimity is bound to itself with a firm and inseparable charity. For when the Lord calls bread made from the union of many grains His Body, he indicates our people whom He bore united; and when He calls wine pressed from the clusters of grapes and many small berries and gathered in one His Blood, He, likewise, signifies our flock joined by the mixture of a united multitude.[22]

Thus, at this early stage, some Christians still understood Christ's words of institution figuratively, as pertaining not to the offerings of bread and wine that were used to give thanks, but to the communicants themselves as a gathered body of believers.

The earliest of Christians tolerated a great deal of diversity in their understanding of the Eucharist. It had not yet come to be understood as a "sacrament" but was a carryover from the Jewish mealtime prayers using bread and wine to give thanks. Jesus was understood to be among them wherever and whenever two or more followers were gathered. Thus the early church carried on Jesus' own mealtime ministry to some extent, eschewing differences between themselves and striving to be a community of liberation and support as Jesus had taught them. But soon, scandals, persecutions—and, surprisingly, the greatest difficulty of all: acceptance—would rock the early church and change forever its attitudes and celebrations.

The Undivided Church

Persecution and the Eschatological Thread

As the Christian movement began to grow, it invariably met with a great deal of opposition. As Robert Linder describes it:

> Early persecutions were sporadic and local. The first intensive effort by the state to eliminate Christians came after the burning of Rome during the reign of the Emperor Nero in 64 CE. Nero made the Christians the scapegoats for the disaster and they were savagely tortured and burned at least in and around Rome. Empire-wide persecutions came periodically in the third and early fourth centuries. Untold numbers of Christians died heroically for their faith; only relatively few recanted.[23]

Under this extreme duress, the Christian community drew upon Jesus' promise that the end of the world was imminent and that the eschatological Kingdom would dawn within the apostles' own lifetimes:

> And he will send out his angels with a loud trumpet call, and they will gather his elect from the four winds, from one end of heaven to the other... Truly I tell you, this generation will not pass away until all these things have taken place. Heaven and earth will pass away, but my words will not pass away. But about that day and hour no one knows, neither

> the angels of heaven, nor the Son, but only the Father. For as the days of Noah were, so will be the coming of the Son of Man (Matthew 24:31, 33-37).

Apparently ignoring the fact that "this generation" did in fact "pass away" before the promised consummation of history, the persecuted church began to look forward with renewed vigor towards a time when their suffering would end and their cause be vindicated. Therefore, while the early church continued to focus on the realized eschatology of Christ in their midst in the Eucharist, they also celebrated the coming feast of the Community (Kingdom) of God. For them, the Eucharist became both a proclamation of the reality of Christ in their midst and a foretaste of the messianic feast when all that they pray for comes to pass. This feast is part of a rich Jewish tradition which holds that at the consummation of history, "God will provide a great feast or banquet, and those who share in the blessings of eschatological salvation will sit down at table and eat and drink in the presence of God."[24]

Consider especially this portion of Luke's last supper account:

> [Jesus] said to them, "I have eagerly desired to eat this Passover with you before I suffer; for I tell you, I will not eat it until it is fulfilled in the kingdom of God." Then he took a cup, and after giving thanks he said, "Take this and divide it among yourselves; for I tell you that from now on I will not drink of the fruit of the vine until the kingdom of God comes" (Luke 22:15-18).

Enigmatic as this saying is, it nonetheless directly links the last supper traditions with the eschatological emphasis proclaimed by the early church. The early Christians understood Jesus to be talking about his approaching death, that this would be his last meal until he ate again in the Community/Kingdom, in the presence of God. But these words are rich with the eschatological language so familiar to the disciples, implying that in sharing this feast they were, in fact, dining with Jesus at the eschatological meal. They were being given a foretaste that would feed their souls until all the world could sit down at the table of the Son of Man.

This eschatological orientation is clearly evident in the prayer quoted above from the *Didache*, as well as in the Eucharistic prayer provided in the *Apostolic Tradition of Hyppolitus* from the early third century:

> We render thanks to you, O God, through your beloved child, Jesus Christ, whom *in the last times* you sent to us as a savior and redeemer and angel of your will; who is your inseparable Word, through whom you made all things, and in whom you were well pleased. You sent him from heaven into the virgin's womb; and conceived in the womb, he was made flesh and manifested as your Son, being born of the Holy Spirit and the Virgin. Fulfilling your will and gaining for you a holy people, he stretched out his hands when he should suffer, *that he might release from suffering* those who have believed in you (Emphasis mine).

Note the emphasis on the present as the "last times" and the promise to end suffering. After the Institutional narrative, the prayer continues:

> Remembering therefore his death and resurrection, we offer to you the bread and the cup, giving you thanks because you have held us worthy to stand before you and minister to you. And *we ask that you would send your Holy Spirit upon the offering of your holy church, that gathering it into one, you would grant to all who partake of the holy things to partake for the fullness of the Holy Spirit* for the strengthening of faith in truth, that we may praise and glorify you through your child, Jesus Christ, through whom be glory and honor to you with the Holy Spirit, in your holy church, *both now and to the ages of ages.* Amen (Emphasis mine).[25]

This prayer, rich in eschatological portent, affirms the early church's belief that they were living in the last days, that their suffering was great, and that the coming of the "Kingdom" was imminent. The portion of the prayer following the institutional narrative is an early form of what would later develop into the *epiclesis*, beseeching God to gather the church together and to manifest the "Kingdom" in the community gathered in the present, ending with a dual affirmation of God's glory both now and in the future.

In proclaiming the coming "Kingdom" as pre-figured in their own community, the early Christians strove to live with each other in the same spirit of unity, harmony, and love that would be shared by all the redeemed in the "Kingdom" of God. The church became the "little Kingdom" that would eventually overcome the world. Sadly, this optimism, which was born of the external pressure of persecution, was to be thwarted by the church's own internal struggles.

Gnostics and the Incarnationalist Thread

Though the Christians were terribly persecuted, the threat of persecution did not deter other religious groups from appropriating Christianity's rich mythic elements. The kaleidoscope of sects falling under the umbrella of Gnosticism found in the story of Christ a useful metaphor for their philosophies, causing a great deal of panic and confusion among the orthodox Christian ranks.

One teaching that the many varieties of Gnostics held in common was the belief in a radical dualistic split between matter and spirit. Gnostics held that the flesh and all things material were evil, the creation of a wicked demiurge, Yahweh, the God of the Hebrews.

In one Gnostic cosmology,[26] Sophia (recognized in the Jewish scriptures as God's Holy Wisdom, whom we shall explore at length later) somehow "slipped out" of the Pleroma, the dwelling of the Godhead. Hoping to regain her place through imitation, she gives birth to a lesser deity, a demiurge, known as Yaldabaoth (the Hebrew God Yahweh). Yaldabaoth creates the world, and having gained a taste of divine power, contrives to keep Adam and Eve enslaved forever.

For the Gnostics, the earth was a prison-planet ruled by an evil tyrant. The soul would continue to reincarnate in this insufferable vale of tears until the power of Yaldabaoth and his evil angels (the "archons") could be broken.

Meanwhile, the "true" God, observing these events from the Pleroma, decided to help humankind, which, though helplessly trapped in matter, nonetheless contained a spark of divinity longing to rejoin the Godhead, if only it could escape the body and the earth. Thus, the highest God sent the serpent to the garden to help Adam and Eve in their plight. Acting on the serpent's wise counsel, the pair ate of the fruit of the knowledge of good and evil, and their eyes were opened to their incarceration. But before they could eat of the other tree which would break the archons' power, Yaldabaoth interceded and succeeded in keeping them captive, though no longer ignorant of their plight.

In the fullness of time, the true God from the top of the Pleromic hierarchy sent the Christ to teach humanity how to break the power of the archons once and for all, and to woo Sophia back into the Pleroma. Christ, in the Gnostics' view, was neither God nor human. Being a divine, angelic being, the Christ could not contaminate himself by actual contact with matter. This obscenity was avoided by merely *seeming* to be human. Far enough down the divine totem pole to live as a spiritual being amongst creatures of flesh, Christ nonetheless had no corporeal nature of his own, but took on the appearance of flesh in order to teach against the archons and thereby to liberate humanity.

While there are many versions of this myth, this one will suffice to illustrate the many characteristics of Gnostic theology as a whole. There were many Gnostic sects at the time of Christ, and they lost no time in appropriating the Christian mythos to illustrate their beliefs. Even during the apostles' lifetime, Gnostic interpretations of the Jesus story were felt to be a threat to the fledgling church. As Bridge and Phypers point out, Gnosticism "denied the creation, the incarnation, the atonement, the resurrection of Christ and the redemption of the body. Further developments of it into the area of ethics lead either to extreme asceticism or to extreme permissiveness."[27]

Ironically, the writings of the Apostle John, which so vehemently denounced the Gnostic heresy, simultaneously employed imagery that lent itself easily to a Gnostic interpretation. The Jesus of John's Gospel is entirely unlike the Christ of the synoptics. John's Jesus is a ghostly homiletist who made grand claims for himself, whereas the synoptics portray Jesus as a very human soul who consistently avoided any claims of divinity for himself, and even shunned celebrity. John's Jesus walks through walls after the resurrection, and yet in the very same account, he has Thomas putting his hand in his side to testify as to his corporeality:

> When it was evening on that day, the first day of the week, and the doors of the house where the disciples had met were locked for fear of the Jews, Jesus came and stood among them and said, "Peace be with you." After he said this, he showed them his hands and his side. Then the disciples rejoiced when they saw the Lord. Jesus said to them again, "Peace be with you. As the Father has sent me, so I send you." When he had said this, he breathed on them and said to them, "Receive the Holy Spirit. If you forgive the sins of any, they are forgiven them; if you retain the sins of any, they are retained." But Thomas (who was called the Twin), one of the twelve, was not with them when Jesus came. So the other disciples told him, "We have seen the Lord." But

> he said to them, "Unless I see the mark of the nails in his hands, and put my finger in the mark of the nails and my hand in his side, I will not believe." A week later his disciples were again in the house, and Thomas was with them. Although the doors were shut, Jesus came and stood among them and said, 'Peace be with you." Then he said to Thomas, "Put your finger here and see my hands. Reach out your hand and put it in my side. Do not doubt but believe." Thomas answered him, "My Lord and my God!" Jesus said to him, "Have you believed because you have seen me? Blessed are those who have not seen and yet have come to believe" (John 20:19-29).

In contrast to the Gospel of John, the Johannine epistles contain none of this ambivalence, and are resolute in their defense of Jesus' incarnation:

> We declare to you what was from the beginning, what we have heard, what we have seen with our eyes, what we have looked at and touched with our hands, concerning the word of life—this life was revealed, and we have seen it and testify to it, and declare to you the eternal life that was with the Father and was revealed to us—we declare to you what we have seen and heard so that you also may have fellowship with us; and truly our fellowship is with the Father and with his Son Jesus Christ (1 John 1:1-3).

Since there was very little developed theology in the Christian church in the first couple of centuries, any belief that sounded plausible was a candidate for interpretation. Thus it was that the Apostles felt so strongly about the Gnostic threat. It relegated their God to the status of "pretender to the throne" of heaven, and made Jesus out to be an apparition bent on celestial espionage. This was so contrary to their experience that John, Peter, and Paul all forcefully attacked the heresy. Those who came after them would do the same, for nearly four hundred years.

What made the Gnostics' version so threatening is that they had developed a powerful and detailed Christology: an understanding of who Jesus was and what his mission was about. The church only had the stories of Jesus and the lives of their communities. No systematic theologies had been developed. There was no authoritative teaching regarding the nature of Christ or the meaning of his mission. Even the testimonies of the epistle-writers seemed to be at odds as to what salvation meant and how it was achieved.[28]

Naturally, the elders of the church began to shape its worship in an effort to reinforce the teachings they considered essential to "true" Christianity. One of the primary issues was the incarnation, which affirmed the Jewish belief in the goodness of Creation and the holiness of the body. Thus an "incarnational" thread began to wind its way through the history of the Eucharist.

The incarnational thread drew upon the Last Supper traditions where Jesus identifies the bread and wine as his body and blood. Christians began to see the Eucharist as an enacted "parable," wherein the mystery of the Incarnation is re-enacted in the sharing of the meal.

Of course, with no clear Christology at this time, exactly what the Incarnation meant to the early Christians is also questionable. Ultimately various heresies forced the church to define its Christology in dogmatic terms, but at the time when the Gnostic struggle was first making itself felt, it was unclear exactly what Jesus' relationship to the Father actually was.

Adoptionism was clearly an option. This position stated that the Holy Spirit descended upon Jesus at his Baptism, and at that point he became the "Son of God." Thus Jesus "became" divine, and was not God "all along." Another option was, in John's words (and according to the Johannine school at Ephesus), that "the Word became flesh and lived among us," in which Jesus was seen as the incarnation or embodiment of *Sophia*, Holy Wisdom, which was Hellenized into the masculine *Logos*. This is evidenced by Paul's assertion that Jesus was "the first-born of all Creation" and many other New Testament references which parallel Wisdom passages from the Hebrew Scriptures.

In any case, whichever Christology was used, Christians were eager to affirm that

> Jesus really had come in the flesh, really had suffered and died, really had been physically resurrected. Underlining this was the fact that the Eucharist was celebrated with material elements. The bread and wine, so expressive of body and suffering (and thus so repulsive to the Gnostics) so really represented the essential facts of the incarnate Christ and his cross that they could be described in synonymous and interchangeable terms with Christ's body and blood.[29]

Thus, an incarnationalist approach to the Eucharist would have made sense. If the Holy Spirit "came upon" Jesus at his baptism and made him holy, thus did the Holy Spirit "come upon" the bread and wine and make it likewise. If "the Word was made flesh and lived among us" in history, then the Word is made flesh again in the sacred meal. Thus Justin Martyr writes,

> We do not receive these things as common bread or common drink; but as Jesus Christ our Savior being incarnate by God's Word took flesh and blood for our salvation, so also we have been taught that the food consecrated by the word of prayer which comes from him, from which our flesh and blood are nourished by transformation, is the flesh and blood of that incarnate Jesus.[30]

It is Irenaeus (130-200 CE) who is credited with first formulating clearly the Incarnationalist thread. As John D. Zizioulas explains,

> Irenaeus faced the...Gnostic...contempt for the material world...by referring to the tradition present in the writings of Ignatius of Antioch: the Eucharist is the "antidote against death" and therefore the source of immortality and eternal life. Irenaeus fought the Gnostics by stressing that the material world is a direct product of the one and only God, the Father, and that matter is good. In the same way he stressed that history and time are also good and constitute the ground and the context of the exercise of human freedom, which is an indispensable condition of spirituality. Adam was created by God and was placed in the material world, in the course of time and history, in order to reach full communion with God by acting freely and creating decisive events *(Kairoi)*, that is, history.[31]

The incarnationalist approach seems to have done its job. It has successfully safeguarded the doctrine of the incarnation for succeeding generations. Unfortunately, this was done at a cost that could not have been forseen at the time: for it began the shift in the locus of the "Body of Christ" from the community to the elements.

Formerly, the Body of Christ was understood to be present in the community, meeting to pray with a holy meal, but after the introduction of this thread, it was the everyday elements of bread and wine that were beginning to be seen as the vehicle (or the "host") of Christ's presence. While the early Christians could then say, "Not only is the Eucharist...a means of thanking God for creating the world with all things that are in it...it is also a vivid reminder of the reality of the incarnation,"[32] they had at the same time crossed a symbolic threshold from which the church has never returned.

The Metabolist Thread

Once the rite had become in many places a re-enactment of the "mystery of the incarnation" for the benefit of those potentially swayed by Gnostic teachings, Christians began to speak of a "change" happening in the elements during the recitation of the Eucharistic prayer. While the earliest Christians sought only a change of heart, and therefore a change in the nature of human community through the ritual, third-century Christians increasingly saw the bread and wine themselves as the locus of divine activity. What was initially simple table fare became, during the course of the rite, possessed of the same spiritual nature as Jesus following the resurrection. By the fourth century this notion of "change" (*metabolé*) taking place in the elements was part of commonplace theological writing.[33]

Precisely when this change in the bread and wine occurs, however, has long been a subject of some debate. According to Ambrose, it is the recitation of the words of Jesus at the Last Supper that affects the bread and wine. When the presider says "This is my body," it is by the power of the Word (through the Holy Spirit) that the bread in fact becomes possessed of its divine character. Likewise with the wine. It is this view (that the "change" occurs at the exact point of the recitation of the Institutional narrative) that has since gained prominence in the West.

Ambrose (339-397 CE) writes powerfully about the power of the Word as a transformative agent:

> The Lord commanded, the heaven was made. The Lord commanded, the earth was made. The Lord commanded, the seas were made. The Lord commanded, every creature came to be. You see then how effective is the word of Christ. If, then, there is so great a power in the word of the Lord Jesus that things which were not began to exist, then how much more effective, that those things which were existing, and are changed into something else! The heaven was not, the sea was not, the earth was not, but hear David as he says, "He spoke and they were made, He commanded and they were created" (Psalm 148:5). Therefore, to answer you,

> there was not the body of Christ before the consecration; but after the consecration, I tell you, it is then the body of Christ. He spoke and it was made, He commanded and it was created. You existed, but you were an old creation. After you were consecrated, you began to be a new creation.[34]

Ambrose elsewhere explains that "when the time comes for the venerated sacrament to be accomplished, the bishop no longer uses his own words, but uses the words of Christ. So the word of Christ accomplishes this sacrament."[35]

At the same time Ambrose was writing in Milan, Cyril, bishop of Jerusalem, testifies to a different tradition in asserting that it is the *epiclesis*, the prayer that invokes the Holy Spirit upon the elements (and often upon the gathered assembly as well), that affects the change.[36]

The *epiclesis* developed from a feature of the eschatological thread, specifically from the prayer that God would "gather his church from the ends of the earth" into a single body. The roots of the *epiclesis* can be seen as far back as the *Didache*:

> Remember, Lord, your Church, to save it from all evil and to make it perfect by your love. Make it holy, and gather it together from the four winds into your Kingdom which you have made ready for it. For yours is the power and the glory forever. Let Grace come and let this world pass away. Hosanna to the God of David!

Gradually this prayer asked for the Holy Spirit to act upon the assembled community, to fill them and to make of them the Body of Christ. In the liturgy contained in the *Testamentum Domini*, the modest *epiclesis* merely asks that the communicants may be made one with God and filled with the Holy Spirit.[37]

From there it is a relatively short leap to invoking the Holy Spirit in the same prayer to likewise transform the elements of bread and wine. Not necessarily tied to the Last Supper traditions, many early Eucharistic prayers emphasize the *epiclesis* to the total exclusion of the Institutional Narrative. In the Liturgy of St. Mark (fourth century) the *epiclesis* beseeches God to "fill the sacrifice with the Holy Spirit" but no mention is made of the "sacrifice" becoming the "body" and "blood" of Christ.[38]

Another ancient prayer of the same period (third-fourth centuries), contained in the *Euchologium of Sarapion of Thmuis*, is also unusual in its use of "body and blood" imagery. This prayer asks that "God's Word may come upon the bread and chalice so that they may become the body of the Word and the blood of truth."[39]

What is so striking about these examples is that in the rush of theological development—in which the idea that a change occurs in the elements caught on very quickly—there is a decided lack of consensus of what, precisely, the elements change *into*. While "the body and blood" of Christ were clearly the preferred identifications, even these took on manifold interpretations, with many ancient writers assigning their own, often surprising, correspondences. For Ignatius of Antioch (35-107 CE), the bread became "faith" and the wine "truth."[40]

Likewise the fragmentary prayer of *Der-Balyzeh*, as late as the sixth century, has the following, and quite peculiar, epiclesis:

> God of truth,
> let your holy *Logos* come upon this bread,
> that the bread may become the body of the *Logos*,
> and on this cup,
> that the cup may become the blood of truth...[41]

In the first few centuries after its founding, one of the church's most fertile periods of theological innovation, churches were still free to discover what the Body (and blood) of Christ meant *for them*, and it is quite clear that differing communities found meaning in a variety of ideas, especially in regard to the change of plain bread and wine into sacraments. The discovery of such diversity of interpretation can come to many contemporary Christians as something of a revelation. This is especially so since for the majority of these early churches, celebrating the Eucharist in a way that made sense to them rarely cast doubts upon a community's orthodoxy, but instead spoke loudly of the vitality of the people's life of faith.

Platonism and the Divinization Thread

For many Christians it was important that their faith be reasonable, coherent, easily communicated, and that it could withstand the attacks of its critics. Such a faith needed to have cultural relevance to have any appeal, and, accordingly, Christians from the time of Paul onward began to view the life of Jesus in terms of the philosophical conventions of the day.

With the advent of the metabolist perspective, Christians were faced with the dilemma of celebrating one thing (bread and wine) that they perceived to be something else entirely (in most cases, the body and blood of Christ). This was not as difficult as it might seem, since people in the ancient world were much less confused about the relationship between the symbol and the signified than we are today. As Crockett explains,

> A symbol in ancient society is not primarily a pointer that represents something apart from the symbol. In ancient society, a symbol participates in that which it represents, so that it can almost be said to be that which it represents... In antiquity, the symbol is the presence of that which it represents and mediates participation in that reality.[42]

The later debates between those who held "realist" views of the Eucharist (the elements have literally changed into flesh and blood) and "spiritualist" views (the elements *merely* symbolic) would have seemed silly to the early Christians. For them, the dominant philosophy of Platonism provided a ready vocabulary to describe what was occurring in the consecration of the elements. Christianity had never been a stranger to Platonism, of course; the writings of both John and Paul are replete with Platonic twists. But from the time of Justin Martyr (100-165 CE) onwards, Christianity was to be radically reinterpreted in Platonic terms, and at the same time the Eucharist would once again be radically re-mythologized.

Justin was a gentile convert who began his career as a philosopher. After trying on many doctrines for size, he finally seized upon Platonism as the highest truth, until he debated an elderly Christian. Justin was converted, though he did not renounce his Platonism. Justin began to teach theology dressed as a Greek philosopher, creatively interpreting the Christian Gospel in the language of Platonic metaphysics. As a result, he not only created a systematic theology that satisfied his own need for a reasonable faith, but also provided a vocabulary by which other thinkers of his day could make sense of the strange Levantine cult he had adopted. It provided "a ready-made and respectable tradition which gave academic justification and impressive clarity to what was really a very recent religious movement."[43]

This re-visioning of the Gospel in Platonic terms proved to be decisive for the future of Christianity, and from the second and third centuries until the middle ages, Platonism was to be heralded by the church as inspired. Many of the early church's greatest theologians were Platonists; among them were Athenagoras, Aristides, and Origen. Socrates was even thought of as a "virtuous pagan" who was a Christian without knowing it.

Plato perceived that there must be another, more real, world that lends this world its shape. Objects in this world are mere shadows, signs, or symbols for realities in this other world. Plato called this higher reality the World of Forms, where reside the perfect, archetypal ideas in which physical objects of our world participate, and which they reflect. For instance, in the World of Forms there exists the Idea of "horse," which all physical horses in our world reflect and participate in, albeit in an imperfect way. Thus a horse in our world is not separate from the Idea of "horse" in the World of Forms, for we only recognize this animal as a horse in the first place because of its participation in the larger reality of "horseness" in the other world. The two are not separate or distinct, but inform and participate in one another.

Thus, for the Christian Platonists—which was soon to mean most if not all Christians—the mystery of the Eucharist was easily comprehended in a similar way. There was the reality they perceived in our world (bread and wine), which is informed by and participates in the body and blood of Christ in that other World. By partaking of the earthly elements of bread and wine, Christians understood that they were receiving the benefits of that heavenly reality in which they participated—the divinized, resurrected body of Christ.

Having a grasp of the importance of Platonic philosophy on Christian theology at this point, let us turn to a discussion of the "true reality" of the resurrected Body of Christ that was being celebrated in the Eucharist.

As we have seen in our analysis of the Eschatological Thread, the early church navigated its persecutions by looking forward to the messianic feast, pre-figured in the Eucharistic meal. As its persecutions continued, however, and Christ's return was delayed, the church began looking backwards at the story of Christ for its inspiration and encouragement. This it found in the Resurrection.

Later to be termed the "Christus Victor" theory of the atonement, this tradition aided the early church by asserting that "suffering is a prelude to triumph and is in itself an illusion."[44] In this tradition, Jesus is painted as "the conquering hero," recalling the Jews' anticipation of a militant messiah, but transporting the drama of the conflict to a more cosmic scale. Jesus sets himself up as bait for Satan, who "seeks to devour human beings."[45] When Jesus dies and is swallowed by death, he has craftily gained access to Satan's stronghold, the underworld. There, on his home turf, Satan is confronted with the messiah in all his glory. Satan is utterly overwhelmed, and his power broken forever.

It is easy to see how such a myth might be attractive to those undergoing extreme persecution. To them such a theology said,

> Be patient, something good will come of this. The believer is persuaded to endure suffering as a prelude to new life. God is pictured as working through suffering, pain, and even death to fulfill 'his' divine purpose. When suffering comes it may be looked upon as a gift, and the believer will ask, Where is God leading me? What does God have in store for me? In this tradition, God is the all-powerful determiner of every event in life, and every event is part of a bigger picture—a plan that will end with triumph.[46]

Naturally, this view was to have its effect on the Eucharist. Like its antecedent, the Eschatological Thread, the Divinization Thread offers a promise and a foretaste of a future and coming redemption. However, it is not the messianic feast as such to which the meal points, but to a universal regeneration, a "general resurrection" of the cosmos.

In the Resurrection, the body of Jesus was transfigured and divinized. For the Christians of the fourth century, Christ's resurrection was a "down payment" on the eventual transfiguration of the entire created order. Christ's mission came to be understood in terms of God, through Christ, "assuming" the fallen created order into Godself, and beginning to reconcile what was lost. Just as for Paul, we who were enemies of God are now not just God's slaves, but joint-heirs with Christ (Romans 5). The Church saw the fallen created order joined irrevocably to its Creator in the Incarnation, and believed the Resurrection set into motion a process of redemption, of "divinization." This process would eventually transform not only humanity, but the universe itself into the blessed Community of God, where the "Cosmic Christ" reigns in the heart of all things. What was broken by sin is, through the goodness and graciousness of God, not simply being healed, but embraced utterly and transfigured by divinity into something ineffably glorious.

The Eucharist thus became both the celebration and the means of this transfiguration. As Davies says, "the purpose of the liturgy, as of the Christian religion, is to sanctify, even to deify, humankind, bringing transfigured Christians to the Christ of the Transfiguration. Through the bestowal of grace in the liturgy, humanity is raised to the supernatural order and therefore into sharing the divine existence, light and glory."[47]

This position, of course, requires the acceptance of the full divinity of Christ to make any sense, and as such it soon became the plumbline interpretation of orthodox teaching. As Hilary, bishop of Poitiers in France, wrote in the fourth century:

> If the Word has indeed become flesh, and we indeed receive the Word as flesh in the Lord's food, how are we not to believe that He dwells in us by His nature; He, who, when He was born as man, has assumed the nature of our flesh that is bound inseparably with Himself, and has mingled the nature of His flesh to His eternal nature in the mystery of the flesh that was to be communicated to us? All of us are one, because the Father is in Christ and Christ is in us.[48]

Thus, in the incarnation, the Word united itself irrevocably with the Created order, not, as St. Athanasius says, "by conversion of the Godhead into flesh but by taking of humanity into God,"[49] renewing and setting into motion the full divinization of the cosmos in the Resurrection. The Eucharist, once the consecration has been enacted, becomes possessed of this same resurrected and redeemed matter. "As human nature was transformed by its union with the Word (through the action of the Spirit), so the Eucharistic elements are transformed in order that we too may be transformed and saved from corruption."[50] When the Eucharist is eaten, this redemption is assumed by the communicants, and the work of the divinization of their lives—spiritual, intellectual and material—is promoted and continued.

This idea was to become essential to Orthodox teaching. The spirit of the believer receives from the Spirit of God the beginnings of its redemption. But the body cannot be saved by the spirit, only by flesh like itself. An ancient Orthodox axiom is, "God cannot save what God does not assume." In assuming flesh and blood, God thereby is capable of redeeming it, and of sharing divine life with creatures of flesh and blood. Thus, in order for our souls to be saved, they must be infused with the Holy Spirit; for our bodies to be saved (and by extension, the created order as a whole) they need to be infused with the resurrected body of Christ in the Eucharist. As Gregory of Nyssa was to write in the late fourth century, "Just as a little leaven...makes the whole lump like itself, so the body which was made immortal by God, by passing entire into our body, alters and changes it to itself."[51]

That such importance was ascribed to the physical nature is evidence that at this stage the Gnostic antipathy towards the flesh had not yet been appropriated by the church, and that the body was still seen as a holy gift of God.

Thus, when hopes failed for an impending apocalypse, the martyrs' hopes became set upon the long "working out" of grace, transforming the created order, and on the promise of resurrection. In Platonism, a philosophical framework was discovered to revitalize the fallen hopes resulting from Christ's delay and the scattershot oppression suffered by the early church. In the resulting theology, Christianity took on a more transcendent tone than its parent religion, Judaism, had ever claimed, and championed a cosmology as cosmic and universal as the prevailing philosophies of the day. It was this philosophical sophistication that was to win for the church such able theologians as Justin and Origen, and which can arguably be said to be responsible for Christianity's growing intellectual credibility in the second through fourth centuries.

Acceptance and the Mystery Thread

The latter half of the fourth century brought about rapid changes that would have made the Christian church virtually unrecognizable to believers of just a hundred years previous, for with the advent of the Emperor Constantine (d. 337 CE), Christianity was to suffer the greatest threat to its survival since the great persecutions: acceptance. Although Constantine did not make Christianity the official state religion as commonly believed,[52] he did consider himself to be a convert, and raised the bishops of the church to a grand status within the Roman Empire. He erected the enormous basilicas of Saints Peter and Paul, and rewarded conversion with political favor. The resulting swelling of ranks in Christendom changed the face of the church considerably. Small communities of deeply committed and faithful people were replaced with the imperial spectacle encouraged by the swarms of nominal converts, who sought to find in Christianity the lost splendor of the old Roman religion and the social vogue attached to the new cult.

In this period Jesus came to be seen as the militant "Emperor of the World," "trampling down death by death"[53] in his triumphant resurrection, reflecting Constantine's military and political victories and embodying Plato's "Philosopher King." Accordingly, the church became, as Davies puts it, "Christianity on parade, with vast congregations meeting in large churches not only recognized by, but approved by the society surrounding it. Now it was hierarchically celebrated, with the leaders entering in solemn processions in distinctive garb."[54]

During the fourth century the churches became financially viable institutions, and clergy became increasingly full-time and professional in their approach to their vocations. The Eucharist took on the spectacle of imperial pageantry, turning into an event at which large groups of worshippers were merely "spectators," rather than full participants in the liturgy.

This was accompanied by a shift in the attitude of the more sincere believers that the church had been "sold out," and that the very precious gift that God had given them in their communities was being destroyed by the Church's cancerous acceleration and its assimilation of the popular pagan culture. Accordingly, there was a knee-jerk effort by the faithful to preserve the holiness of their faith, manifesting in a desire to protect and maintain the mystery they had previously felt in connection with the Eucharist. Fortunately, such a reaction synchronized nicely with the needs of the new "converts." The many new adherents also brought into the church much that they held to be valuable in their pagan practices.

As a result, many of the actions associated with rituals in the Greek "mystery religions" began to crop up in the Eucharistic liturgy, incorporating the "appearances and disappearances of the celebrant, veiling and unveiling of the elements, opening and closing of the doors, and various gestures connected with the sacrament."[55] The Eucharist became, as Ernst Benz writes, "an elaborate, complicated mystery play."[56] Dean Inge claims that the church owed to the mystery religions the "notions of secrecy, of symbolism, of mystical [fraternity and sorority], of sacramental grace, and above all, the three stages in the spiritual life: ascetic purification, illumination, and *epopteia* (supreme bliss) as the crown."[57]

Although this no doubt added to the popular appeal of the "new" cult, Luis Boyer believes that the "Christianization" of the mystery religions was "more or less unfortunate, because it tended, contrary to the hopes of its own promoters...to obscure our appreciation of the creative originality, and therefore, everlasting validity, of the great vision of Christianity."[58] The shift towards a "mystification" of the Eucharist was indeed a far cry from the common meals shared by Jesus with the disciples. In its favor it must be said that in the complicated and dramatic rite there is found "the whole mystery of salvation, the Incarnation, the death and resurrection of the Logos, his glorification, and the outpouring of the Holy Spirit, and its climax in the descent, the appearance, and the divine presence of the resurrected Christ, who enters the congregation as "King of the universe borne invisibly over their spears by the angelic hosts."[59]

Accordingly, the clergy began preaching sermons that emphasied fear and awe towards the Eucharist. As Meyendorf says,

> The faithful responded by abandoning communion, and thus the community was split into a communicating elite and the majority of others. No longer an act of "communion," the reception of communion became an act of personal devotion. Thus the traditional notion of the Eucharist as a meal, as fellowship, began to break down, to be replaced by a different understanding, where this active participation was not so essential.[60]

What for the earliest Christians was a meal that emphasized God's immanence and proximity was transformed into a pageant that emphasized God's transcendence and imperial splendor, evoking fear and trembling instead of the ecstacy of freedom previously enjoyed by Christians. This impulse towards hoarding the mystery of the rite eventually banned the uninitiated not only from participating in the Eucharist, but even from observing it.

The rite became divided in two parts, the "Mass of the Catechumens" came first, and consisted of the Readings, the sermon and the prayers, and is analogous to the Liturgy of the Word in the West. Anyone was welcome to attend this portion of the service, and attendance was required for those who were preparing for baptism (the catechumens).

At the close of this part of the service, the priest cries, "The doors, the doors." This happened just before the singing of the Nicene

Creed because the Creed was considered a secret formula. Having excluded everyone but the initiates, those "privy to the mysteries," the service continues with the "Mass of the Faithful," which is analogous to the later Western Liturgy of the Table.

The liturgies in use by the Orthodox churches today retain this terminology, although the unbaptized are no longer "shooed out" of the church. They are denied communion, but unlike their counterparts of the fourth century, they are at least welcome to witness the liturgy. The "mystery tradition" is strong in all of the liturgies that developed in this period of the Byzantine empire. Myendorf describes its later development:

> The Byzantine tradition...saw the development of that peculiarly Eastern phenomenon, the iconostasis. A development of the primitive chancel barrier, it now became a real wall, covered with icons. This emphasized, in the Byzantine mind, the "mystery" element of the Eucharist. Moreover, the Eucharist was not something to be seen through physical eyes, but to be received as food. The mystery was seen through the program of icons on the walls, and particularly on the iconostasis, with their images of Christ and the saints.[61]

The Orthodox liturgies currently in use, the Liturgy of St. John Chrysostom and the Liturgy of St. James, have retained much from this thread and come down to us with only minor accretions, being the oldest continuous thread of tradition extant today. They are testament to the power of humanity's urge towards transcendance and the necessity of mystical religion.

The Western Church

The West and the Sacrifice Thread

While the Divinization Thread would come to dominate the Eucharistic theology of the Eastern churches, the West took a very different turn. As the idea of the bread and wine actually "becoming" the body and blood of Christ (the Metabolist Thread) gained ground, it was a short leap to the Eucharist becoming a sacerdotal, sacrificial ritual, where these "spotless and bloodless victims" are offered to appease God. Once the clericalism and the distancing took effect after Christianity's acceptance into the mainstream of religious life, it is not surprising that the general populace's familiar ideas of sacrificial worship—the norm in pagan society as much as in Judaic—began to surface in the church's understanding of its own "sacrifice."

Sacrificial language had already been long associated with the rite. In the very early Eucharistic liturgy of Hippolytus, the oblation of the first fruits is mentioned. As Thurian notes, "Bread and wine are offered, but also milk and honey, water, oil, olives, fruit and flowers."[62] This usage is not connected to sin offerings, but to the ancient Judaic thank offerings which we have already discussed above in the *Brachot* thread, and it is fair to say that if the early Christians thought of the Eucharist as a sacrifice at all it was as a sacrifice of praise and thanksgiving. Irenaeus offers the meal "in order that they be not ungrateful."[63]

Likewise, Origen in the later third century continues the *Brachot* thread, writing, "We are not people with ungrateful hearts; it is true we do not sacrifice....to such beings who...are our enemies; but to God who has bestowed upon us an abundance of benefits...we fear being ungrateful. The sign of this gratitude towards God is the bread called Eucharist."[64] Thus it was the entire rite, not simply the bread and the wine (or the flowers or the milk or the honey) that constituted the sacrifice of praise.

After several centuries, however, Christians began to speak of the Eucharist as a different kind of sacrifice. As Macy writes, "the language originally reserved to discussions of animal sacrifices was applied metaphorically to the supper as a reminder of the saving offering of Jesus' own life and of the similar pledge which each Christian makes in the celebration of the ritual meal."[65]

This "sacrifice" language first begins to appear explicitly in the writings of Saints Cyril and Ambrose in the late third century. Cyril described the Eucharist as "that sacrifice of propitiation, for the common peace of the churches, for the stability of the world, for emperors, for armies and auxiliaries, for those in sickness, for the oppressed."[66] Even more to the point, Ambrose set down a Eucharistic prayer which reads, "Remembering his most glorious passion and resurrection from the dead, and ascension into heaven, we offer you this spotless victim, reasonable victim, bloodless victim, this holy bread and this cup of eternal life."[67]

Thus the locus of the offering was narrowed from the whole assembly to the "bloodless, spotless and reasonable victim"[68] in the form of bread and wine. And, as Bridge and Phypers point out, "since it is legitimate to speak of the tokens or signs as if they are what they signify, 'thus does the Church...offer him (i.e. Christ) to God'."[69] This sacrificial thread began to see the Eucharist as a re-presentation of Christ's death as a propitiatory sin-offering to the Creator "in the tradition of the sacrifices of the Old Covenant with the people of Israel, of which it is a fulfillment, in so far as it is a sacrament or actualization of the unique and perfect sacrifice of Christ on the cross."[70]

The theology of this sacrificial thread presupposes a different soteriology from that of the Divinization thread. In the West the Christus Victor theory of the atonement (which still is the predominant view of the Eastern churches) was supplanted by the

"Satisfaction" theory, which was most definitively articulated in the eleventh century by St. Anselm. Anselm writes that "everyone who sins ought to pay back the honor of which he has robbed God and this is the satisfaction which every sinner owes to God."[71]

But humankind is tainted and cannot pay the debt. Thus, as Brown and Parker write,

> Only by the death of God's own Son could God receive satisfaction.... God's demand that sin be punished is fulfilled by the suffering of the innocent Jesus... God is portrayed as the one who cannot reconcile "himself" to the world because "he" has been royally offended by sin, so offended that no human being can do anything to overcome "his" sense of offense. Like [King] Lear, God remains estranged from the children God loves because God's honor must be preserved... It is to free God that the Son submits to death, sacrificing himself...out of overwhelming love for the two alienated parties: God and the human family.[72]

Sometimes known as the "penal" theory of atonement, this view emphasizes Christ's crucifixion and death as the crucial event in salvation history, rather than the resurrection. Far less abstract than the divinization theory, this theology would have been much more easily grasped and assimilated by pagan converts in the "barbaric" West for whom animal sacrifice was a more familiar context in which to understand the Eucharist than neo-Platonism.

This view found biblical support not only in the Judaic Eucharistic thread of Matthew and Mark, but more explicitly in the epistle to the Hebrews: "For the bodies of those animals whose blood is brought into the sanctuary by the high priest as a sacrifice for sin are burned outside the camp. Therefore Jesus also suffered outside the city gate in order to sanctify the people by his own blood."[73] According to this epistle, the animal sacrifices of the ancient Jews were but foreshadowings of the crucifixion:

> Since the law has only a shadow of the good things to come and not the true form of these realities, it can never, by the same sacrifices that are continually offered year after year, make perfect those who approach. Otherwise, would they not have ceased being offered, since the worshipers, cleansed once for all, would no longer have any consciousness of sin? But in these sacrifices there is a reminder of sin

> year after year. For it is impossible for the blood of bulls and goats to take away sins.
>
> Consequently, when Christ came into the world, he said, "Sacrifices and offerings you have not desired, but a body you have prepared for me; in burnt offerings and sin offerings you have taken no pleasure. Then I said, 'See, God, I have come to do your will, O God' (in the scroll of the book it is written of me)."
>
> When he said above, "You have neither desired nor taken pleasure in sacrifices and offerings and burnt offerings and sin offerings" (these are offered according to the law), then he added, "See, I have come to do your will." He abolishes the first in order to establish the second. And it is by God's will that we have been sanctified through the offering of the body of Jesus Christ once for all. And every priest stands day after day at his service, offering again and again the same sacrifices that can never take away sins. But when Christ had offered for all time a single sacrifice for sins, "he sat down at the right hand of God," and since then has been waiting "until his enemies would be made a footstool for his feet."[74]

Augustine echoes this view when he writes, "Before the coming of Christ, the flesh and blood of this sacrifice were foreshadowed in the animals slain; in the passion of Christ, the types were fulfilled by the true sacrifice; after the ascension of Christ, this sacrifice is commemorated in the sacrament."[75]

In the middle ages there arose some confusion about precisely in what way the Eucharist is a sacrifice: is it merely a commemoration of Christ's one and only sacrifice upon Calvary, or is Christ in some way sacrificed again in the ritual? The official teaching of the Western church is clear: the Eucharist is merely a re-presentation of a once and for all sacrifice accomplished by Christ on the cross, and as such, "if Jesus was offering his life to God, then his self-offering can be regarded as in some sense continuing, and the idea can be developed that in the Eucharist, Christ, through his body which is the church, is somehow re-presenting the sacrifice of his life to the Father."[76] This was the view of Theodoret, bishop of Cyrus in the fifth century when he wrote, "We do not offer another sacrifice, but accomplish the memorial of that unique and saving one...so that in contemplation we recall the figure of the sufferings endured for us."[77]

This was the official teaching of the Western church throughout the middle ages. As Thomas Aquinas would write,

> For two reasons is the celebration of this sacrament called the sacrifice of Christ. First...the celebration of this sacrament is a definite image representing Christ's passion, which is his true sacrifice.... Second, in respect of the effect of Christ's passion. By this sacrament we are made sharers of the fruit of the Lord's passion. Hence in a Sunday secret prayer it is said, "Whenever the commemoration of this sacrifice is celebrated the work of our redemption is carried on."[78]

However fast the church's teachers were to hold to this position, it was not enough to satisfy the popular imagination. This, in turn, could not help but influence the church's practice. As with other sacrifices, this one came to be thought of by the people as efficacious in a special way each and every time the ritual was performed. Pope Gregory I testifies to this in the late sixth century:

> The sacrifice alone has the power of saving the soul from eternal death, for it presents to us mystically the death of the only-begotten Son. Though He is now risen from the dead and dies no more, and "death has no more power over him" (Rom 6:9), yet, living in Himself immortal and incorruptible, He is again immolated for us in the mystery of the holy Sacrifice. Where His Body is eaten, there His flesh is distributed among the people for their salvation. His Blood no longer stains the hands of the godless, but flows into the hearts of His followers. See, then, how august the Sacrifice that is offered for us, ever reproducing in itself the passion of the only-begotten Son for the remission of our sins. For, who of the faithful can have doubt that at the moment of the immolation, at the sound of the priest's voice, the heavens stand open and choirs of angels are present at the mystery of Jesus Christ.[79]

In the popular imagination, the consecrated elements gradually took on a magical aura. During the Dark Ages, when relics and other mystical paraphernalia were proliferating, there was an increasing fascination with the Eucharist's magical efficacy. Thus, in the religion of the common people, the Mass was given "the value of a sacrifice independent of the sacrifice of Christ on the Cross."[80]

As Crockett explains, the people began to see the Mass as

> ...a new Calvary...as a sacrifice somehow added to the Cross. This also became linked in the later Middle Ages with a theology of the "fruits" of the Mass. This is related to a kind of quantitative thinking that attributes a limited "worth" to each Mass. In this case, two Masses are better than one. This led to a dramatic increase in the number of masses celebrated and "private" masses were offered for all kinds of individual needs.[81]

Indeed, in the late Middle Ages, there were

> ...votive Masses of the twenty-four patriarchs or elders; of the fourteen, fifteen, and more "holy helpers"; of the seven joys and sorrows of Mary; votive Masses against sicknesses, including one against pestilence, one of Holy Job against syphilis, of St. Christopher against sudden death, one each of Saint Roch and Saint Sebastian against pestilence, one of Saint Sigismund against fever; votive Masses for special requests: in honor of the Archangel Raphael or of the Three Magi for a safe journey; a Mass to keep away thieves and to recover stolen property, a Mass before a duel or ordeal, one against Hussites and Turks and against witches; the seven-day, thirteen-day, or thirty-day Masses of emergency, which had to be offered by one priest for seven, thirteen or thirty days respectively, at the end of which interval guaranteed liberation from sickness and distress was expected, and in addition the three Masses of Saint Nicholas for needs.[82]

Many of these concepts were present in some form from the church's beginning, yet they were always balanced with other imagery. Only gradually—and only in the West—did the Sacrifice Thread come to dominate the church. It is still the primary orientation of Western Christianity, both Catholic and Protestant. From a "sacrifice of praise and thanksgiving," to a virtual re-playing of events on Golgotha, the sacrifice thread has a long and complex history. But in the late medieval period, it was ready to be turned inside out by new controversy.

Transubstantiation and the Realist Thread

As the West continued to celebrate the Eucharist as a presentation of Christ's sacrifice on the Cross (whether as a memorial or, later, as a sacrifice recurring with each and every celebration), the ecclesial aspect of the rite was largely forgotten. Whereas for Paul and the Eastern Church, it is the entire liturgy which mediates grace, and by partaking of the holy elements the assembled believers themselves become the "Body" of Christ, in the West the focus is squarely upon the elements.

With the locus of Christ's presence thus pinpointed in the bread and the wine, late medieval Christianity would become obsessed with the question of precisely *how* Christ was present in the elements. As stated above, the relationship between symbol and signified was not a concern to the patristic writers. Whereas in the Classical world, the symbol and the signified were co-inherent, with the symbol participating in and mediating the reality signified, the Middle Ages saw the dissolution of such a presumption. The effect of this loss was an insecurity regarding the "reality" of Christ's presence in the Eucharistic elements.

The West was to deal with this issue by dividing into three broad threads of tradition. The first is the Realist Thread, in which Christ is felt to be "actually, physically" present in the bread and the wine. In reaction to this arose two other threads: the Real Presence Thread maintained that while Christ is not physically present in the elements, he is nonetheless mystically present; while proponents of the Spiritualist Thread held that Christ is present only in the gathered community, the elements being void of any but "merely symbolic" significance.

The first to formulate a specifically Realist perspective was Paschasius Radbertus, a monk and abbot of the Corbie monastery in Northern France in the ninth century. For Radbertus, nothing short of a realistic understanding of Christ's presence was acceptable. As he wrote in his treatise *On the Body and the Blood of the Lord*,

> ...and since he willed to remain, though under the figure of bread and wine, we must believe that after the consecration these are nothing else at all but the flesh and blood of Christ... And that I may speak more marvelously, [this flesh] is in no way at all distinct from that which was born of Mary and suffered on the cross and rose from the tomb.[83]

As Crockett points out, Radbertus employed a language and theology familiar to the patristic writers when talking about the Eucharist. But unlike the patristic writers, his theology is thoroughly Western, and is missing the ecclesial aspect of Christ's "Body." It is the bread and the wine which, at the consecration, become "really and substantially" the Body and Blood of Christ.

Interestingly, like Augustine, he spoke about the sacrament possessing both "figure" and "truth":

> If we look at the matter correctly, we can see that (the Eucharist) is simultaneously image and truth. What is experienced externally (in this sacrament) is an image or figure of truth; but what is rightly believed or understood internally about this sacrament is truth.[84]

Thus, while holding to the absolute change in the elements at the consecration, Radbertus nonetheless affirmed that if non-Christians (or even "unworthy" Christians) were to receive the Eucharist, they would receive only the symbol, the outward signs of bread and wine. But when a Christian communes, it is "truth" that is received as the very body and very blood of Christ.

For Radbertus, as for the patristic writers, it is the glorified and resurrected Body of Christ which is present in the elements, and it is by partaking of these elements that our salvation is effected. As Radbertus wrote, "Spiritually an organic part of our own body, the flesh of Christ is capable of transforming us so that Christ's substance exists in our flesh as evidently as he has taken our substance into his divinity."[85]

Radbertus' theology was well adapted to the times. With it, the church had a weapon against the extreme spiritualistic "heresy" of the Cathars, who were exerting a great deal of influence in the West. But although it may have deterred some from following the Cathars into "extreme error," the Realist emphasis also encouraged great fear and trembling in the common people. As Macy writes,

> The congregation...understood that the Lord of heaven and earth, the judge of all, stood before them in majesty during the Lord's Supper. To recklessly receive this, the Lord of lords, would bring about certain damnation. Commentaries on the mass from the Middle Ages stress again and again that one should only approach the Lord's table after purifying one's life. The custom grew up (and was made law in 1215) that Christians needed to receive the body and blood of the Lord only once, at Easter, after the proper preparation of the Lenten season.[86]

The people were already convinced of the "miracle" of the Mass. At the elevation of the host during the recitation of the Institutional narrative (where the consecration is believed to occur in the West), a bell was rung to call people's attention to it so that they might worship it. People rushed from one Mass to another to see as many elevations of the host as possible, believing that they were accumulating grace by so doing, since if a worshipper were to say the Lord's Prayer during the elevation, he or she could expect a hundred days off of their stay in Purgatory. Eventually, the consecrated host was displayed in a monstrance for the purpose of adoration and worship.

During the first half of the Middle Ages, the powers of the holy elements became more and more crude and "magical" in popular imagination. Stories about the consecrated host bleeding at the fracture were very popular, as well as the fear of chewing the host. Even in recent times, many people who were educated in Roman Catholic schools can remember being told to let the wafer dissolve rather than biting it so that they would not "hurt the baby Jesus." Thomas Brinton, Bishop of Rochester, preached the following in a sermon in the fourteenth century:

> If a man serves the Lord daily in honest watchings, in prayers, and especially in hearing Masses, so will the Lord have care of him, that nothing will be lacking to him for his livelihood. It is no wonder, then, that the doctors say that to those who hear Mass devoutly the following privileges are conceded: first, that they have all that is necessary to support life that day; secondly, that they are spared idle gossip and oaths; thirdly, that they do not lose the sight of their eyes; fourthly, sudden death does not befall them; fifthly, that while they are hearing Mass they do not grow older; sixthly, that all the steps they take going and coming to Mass are counted by the angels.[87]

In the eleventh century, the Realist thread was taken up by Lanfranc, who later became the Archbishop of Canterbury, who did away with Radbertus' distinction between "figure" and "truth," and spoke instead about the difference between "appearance" and "substance":

> We believe that through the ministry of the priest, the earthly substances on the Lord's table are sanctified by divine power in a manner that is unspeakable, incompre-

> hensible, marvelous; and that [these substances] are changed into the essence of the Lord's body, even though the appearences of earthly elements remain...[88]

At this point, there was no distinguishing those who ate with faith and those who did not. Anyone who consumed the consecrated elements was understood to have partaken of Christ's flesh and blood whether they believed it or not (albeit if they did not, they ate to their own damnation). Many scholars were outraged at the notion that a mouse might break into the sacristy and consume Christ, but as Guitmund of Bec countered, "Well, Jesus was in the tomb, which was just as bad."[89]

For Lanfranc, then (and as it was to be, for the whole of the Western church), the bread and wine actually become the flesh and blood of the risen Christ, but still *look like* bread and wine. For Guitmund, the consecrated elements were like clothes which Christ uses to cover his flesh and blood so that we may eat it without repulsion: "The substance of the things is changed, but the taste, the color and the other sensible accidents which previously existed subsist."[90]

Coined by Stephen of Beaugé, Bishop of Autun, the term "transubstantiation" was soon taken up by Pope Alexader III in his writings from 1140 to 1150. It was soon to catch on. At the Lateran Council of 1215 the word "transubstantiation" was first proposed as an official means of describing the change in the elements,[91] and although variously interpreted, it has been the Roman Catholic Church's term of choice ever since.

Many theologians, even those who advocated a Realist interpretation, were concerned that the literalism was going too far. It was a time when "signs and wonders" were practically ubiquitous, and the Eucharist was the most awesome and predictable wonder of all. Nor was this popular realism curbed by the centuries that followed in Roman Catholicism. Although Thomas Aquinas was an outspoken critic of the Realist tendencies of his day, the subtleties of his arguments evaded common people and scholars alike, and his explanations of "transubstantiation" were ironically to be used to support the very position he strove to amend (see the Real Presence thread, below). The acceptance of his philosophy as the official dogma of the Roman Catholic church served only to fan Realist fires and to perpetuate the proclivities of popular piety.

The Real Presence Thread

The magic of medieval "priestcraft" and the gross literalism that marked the popular understanding of the Eucharist created an intellectual crisis that incited fierce opposition—first sparking internal opposition in the subtle philosophies of Thomas Aquinas, but later full schism in the Reformation under Martin Luther. While the theological positions of these men (and the many other theorists in this thread) are far from agreement, their positions are the result of a reaction to the Realist Thread, and though formulated in vastly different ways, they share common ground—namely, that the Eucharist is "really and substantially" Christ's body and blood; however, Christ is not present in a physical manner, but in a mystical one. This distinction is difficult to grasp for many. Macy, in his wonderful book, *A Short History of the Lord's Supper*, provides an insightful explanation:

> I am not physically present to you, but [through this book] I certainly am present. I am directing the flow of the words and the presentation of the material... There is an offer here to share part of my life, my ideas, my life work. You can accept it by reading the book (or at least buying it), or reject it by heaving it across the room (or at least setting it down)... Now, would you say I was present in, under, or with the book..?
>
> Now the presence of the risen Lord is inestimably more real than my presence to you in reading this book, of course, but there is at least a useful analogy here. People (persons) can be present to us when they are not physically present, and actually can be absent to us when their bodies are present.... Presence...is a more complex issue than mere proximity.[92]

The first to really advocate the Real Presence position was Thomas Aquinas. Far from advocating a Realist perspective, Aquinas was disturbed by the inadequacy of neo-Platonism to address what Thomas felt to be the true and historic theology of the Eucharist. In the newly-rediscovered writings of Aristotle, Aquinas found a suitable vocabulary to bring the Eucharist back into a more orthodox context. To understand Aquinas, we must first say a few words about Aristotle.

In Aristotelian philosophy, as in Platonic, all things consist of two natures: the perceived thing itself (*res*) and the reality which lies behind it. In Plato's thought, the reality exists in a transcendental

World of Forms. This world is the only true world, and all things on earth are but shadows and signs that participate in and have their identity in the Forms. Aristotle, however, would have none of this fantastic "World of Forms." For him the perceived thing can be spoken of as the "accident," or "how the thing just happens to appear." The greater reality that lies behind it and provides its identity, however, is the thing's "substance," which resides not in some nebulous other-wordly plane, but in the mind. In Aristotelian thought, *substance* is "the essence of any particular thing, grasped by the mind alone. *Accidents* are sense data which change from individual to individual without changing the substance."[93]

As Aquinas struggled with how to present the Eucharist in an appropriate way, he explained transubstantiation in Aristotle's terminology rather than Plato's. As Aquinas writes,

> Since in this sacrament there is the true body of Christ and it does not begin to be there by a movement of locality; since moreover, as we have shown, the body of Christ is not there as in a place: we are really obliged to affirm that it begins to be there by the conversion of the substance of the bread into it ...And that is what is produced, by the divine virtue, in this sacrament. For the whole substance of the bread is converted into the whole substance of the body of Christ, and the whole substance of the wine into the whole substance of the blood of Christ. This conversion, therefore, is not of form but of substance. It does not figure among the various kinds of natural movements, but we can call it transubstantiation, which is its proper name.[94]

For Aquinas, transubstantiation was literally a change in substance (the metaphysical "essence" that is a thing's true reality) while the accidents of bread and wine remain as they were—the change in the elements is not something that can be detected by sense data, but could only be perceived by the eyes of faith. And since the substance of a thing is the domain of the mind (for that is where substance is comprehended), it is the mind that receives the substance. As the accidents of bread and wine are taken physically into the body, the substance of Christ's body is received intellectually and spiritually.

It was with this formulation that Aquinas addressed the gross literalism rampant in the church when he wrote, "Christ is taken under the species of bread and wine as spiritual refreshment, and not as common food and drink, in a horrible and cannibal manner."[95] But the church can hardly have expected the average layperson to understand this distinction (let alone most of the clergy). In fact, without a grounding in Aristotelianism, the careful distinction between substance and accident is meaningless. As John Wyclif would later remark, "The people and a thousand bishops understand neither accident nor subject."[96]

Not surprisingly, therefore, not everyone felt that Aquinas' formulation was adequate either philosophically or practically. Even those who held to a realist view found much to fault, not only in the Aristotelian spin of Aquinas' theology, but also in the effect the literalism was having on the church's life, which Aquinas' carefully articulated position totally failed to curb. One of the most outspoken critics was the Oxford theologian John Wyclif, who was condemned by his university in 1381. Wyclif was the first to publicly voice many concerns that would later be echoed by the Reformers. Wyclif mercilessly attacked the abuses of the clergy of his day, coming down especially hard on the friars.[97] He also rejected transubstantiation outright.

As Macy points out Wyclif was not only upset by the absurdity of transubstantiation, but he also felt its teaching led to gross impieties:

> First, it left people worshipping mere accidents hanging in the air, and not God. Second, even stupid and immoral priests were given the power to make God present daily on the altar. Holiness, not ordination, should be required for the presence of the Lord, and Wyclif suggested that worthy laity could also confect the Eucharist. Wyclif's attacks on transubstantiation, then, were not just philosophical. He felt that this teaching was an example of a church which used its teaching to deceive and fleece the people of God.[98]

Rejecting transubstantiation did not mean that Wyclif rejected the Real Presence of Christ in the Eucharist, just the Aristotelian formulation of it. Instead, he offered an explanation of his own which, while affirming the Real Presence, allowed the bread and wine to keep their former substance. He called his new formulation "Remanence," and taught that after the consecration the bread remains bread, but that the body of Christ is added to it. Thus, Wyclif could assert that in the consecrated host there remains the body of Christ, "truly and really.... Yet I dare not say that the body of

Christ is essentially, substantially, corporeally or identically that bread."[99]

This position was to be taken up and expanded by the first great reformer, Martin Luther, a Roman Catholic priest and theology professor who railed against the "Babylonian Exile of the Church." While Luther's early theology stressed a more patristic and ecclesial understanding, his later writings were more concerned with how the individual "receives" Christ in the Eucharist, and of course, in what way Christ is in fact "received."

For Luther, bringing Aristotle into the argument as Aquinas had done had simply made a messy situation worse. Rejecting all human explanations, Luther appealed to a non-rational approach, asserting that scripture and faith were sufficient to understand the Eucharist. Luther wrote,

> The authority of the word of God goes beyond the capacity of our mind. Thus, in order that the true body and true blood should be in the sacrament, the bread and wine have no need to have transubstantiation, and Christ contained under the accidents; but, while both (bread and wine; body and blood) remain the same, it would be true to say: "This bread is my body, this wine is my blood," and conversely. That is how I would construe the words of divine Scripture and, at the same time, maintain due reverence for them. I cannot bear their being forced by human quibbles, and twisted into other meanings.[100]

One cannot fault Luther for not having access to the historical documents modern scholars enjoy, but he might be surprised just how much "twisting" the Eucharist had already experienced! Though he could not have known it, his thread, while vitally important to the church's history and life, was just one of many historical and orthodox understandings of this sacred meal. For Luther, refuting the Realist thread and returning the Eucharist to a position of spiritual integrity was one of the most important tasks of the Reformation theologian.

Luther's own position came to be known as "consubstantiation," though he never used the term himself. As Luther explains,

> Although the body and the blood are two different natures, each in itself, and that, when they are separated from one another, the one is certainly not the other, when they are united and become a complete new entity they lose

> their difference, as far as this new unique being is concerned; and as they become and are one thing only; it is therefore unnecessary for one of them to disappear and be annihilated, but that the two, the bread and the body, should subsist, and because of the sacramental unity we say and rightly: "This is my body," indicating the body with the word "this." For it is now no longer simply bread from the oven, but bread-body or body-bread, that is to say bread which has become one entity only and one sacramental thing only with the body of Christ. It is the same too with the wine in the cup: "This is my blood" with the word "This," which indicates the wine. For it is now no longer simply wine from the cellar, but wine-blood, that is to say wine which has become with the blood of Christ one single sacramental entity. Whether the wine is still there or not, it is enough for me that the blood of Christ is there. Be it with the wine as God wills. And rather than not have anything there but wine, with the visionaries, I prefer to agree with the pope that there is only blood. Better still I said above that when the wine became Christ's blood, there is not simply wine, but wine-blood, so that I can show it and say "This is the blood of Christ."[101]

Luther did not find it necessary to explain away the reality of the bread in order to affirm the presence of Christ's body. For Luther, Christ's body was present "with" the bread. The reality of the Body of Christ did not negate the reality of the bread, but now co-existed with it. "Why should not Christ be able to include his body within the substance of bread," he asked, "as well as within the accidents?"[102] As Thurian explains, Luther's formulation,

> ...instances the mystery of the two natures, the human and the divine, which are one in the person of Christ. If we name the humanity of Christ, declaring: This is the Son of God; it is not necessary for his humanity to disappear or to be changed into divinity; on the contrary, the christological faith of the Church affirms the permanence of the humanity and the divinity in the unity of the person of Christ, who is at the same time God and man. Why could the same mystery not take place with the concomitance of the substance of the bread and that of the resurrected body of Christ?[103]

To further safeguard his interpretation from charges of Realism, Luther asserted that the Body and Blood of Christ were not "localized" in the bread and wine, because Christ's body is "ubiquitous," present in all places at all times: "Scripture teaches that God's right hand is not a place in which a body might be situated, as on a golden throne," he wrote, "but is God's almighty power, which at once cannot be in any place, and yet must be in every place."[104] This doctrine betrays Luther's debt to Meister Eckhart's panentheistic theology and provides a wonderful point of departure for a Lutheran mystical tradition that, unfortunately, has never really emerged.[105]

For Luther, philosophical arguments were pointless: it all came down to faith. Either you believe Jesus when he said "this is my body," or you don't. How Christ's body is present is not nearly so important as the belief that it is. Luther's insistence on the Real Presence in the Eucharist would lead him into a very painful and unsatisfactory clash with Zwingli and other reformers, which we shall examine in the Spiritualist thread, below.

Not all the reformers, however, shared Zwingli's Spiritualist tendancies. John Calvin sought to reconcile Luther and Zwingli, but ended up falling on the Real Presence side of the fence. Calvin's objection to Realism is that it places God at the disposal of mere mortals to do with what they will, which Calvin considered a logical absurdity. As Crockett explains, Calvin believed that

> God is never at our disposal. We are always at God's disposal. This is the deepest theological motivation for [Calvin's] rejection of any understanding of the Eucharistic presence that would tie it too closely to the elements. Calvin affirms the Real Presence, but he wants to preserve the freedom of God in relation to the material signs. In doing so, he is not opposing either sacramental objectivity or sacramental realism. He does not make the Eucharistic presence dependent on the faith of the recipient, nor does he regard the sacraments as empty signs. The sacraments are true signs through which God really gives grace to those who receive them in faith, but the sacraments do not contain grace and they are not causes for grace in their own right.[106]

We might well ask at this point, if the sacraments "do not contain grace and they are not causes for grace in their own right," how is it that the Eucharist is even a sacrament in Calvin's view? His answer is typically Reformation-oriented: grace comes through faith, not through the sacrament. The sacrament is not a means of *affecting* union with Christ for Calvin, but a means of *expressing* a union that is already present. In this Calvin supports an ecclesial understanding of Christ's presence. "Union with Christ means being grafted into Christ's body, the Church. For Calvin, the Eucharist is always an act of the Church, the community of believers. The Eucharist unites one with Christ by uniting the members of Christ's body with one another and with Christ as their head."[107] Thus, when the Eucharist is celebrated, Christ is really and substantially present, not in the elements themselves, but in the celebration, and made effectual by the faith of the gathered believers.[108]

As Calvin himself writes,

> For the Lord so communicates his body to us there [in the Eucharist] that he is made completely one with us and we with him. Now, since he has only one body, of which he makes us all partakers, it is necessary that all of us also be made one body by such participation. The bread shown in the sacrament represents this unity...I prefer to explain it in Paul's words: "The cup of blessing which we bless is a communicating of the blood of Christ; and the bread of blessing which we break is a participation in the body of Christ... Therefore...we..are all one body, for we partake of one bread.[109]

Thus, for Calvin, the "mode" of Christ's presence is one of personal and relational presence, not the kind of presence enjoyed by a natural object. As Crockett writes, "Christ is present in the Supper not as an object on the altar, but as the Lord of the Church for the purpose of nourishing his people and uniting them to himself."[110] What keeps Calvin firmly in the Real Presence thread is not his rejection of the actual, physical presence of Christ in the Eucharist, but his insistence that the elements of bread and wine are more than "mere" symbols. Calvin strongly affirmed the participation of the "signs" of bread and wine in the reality that they signify.

Unlike Luther and Aquinas, Calvin rejected a wholesale identification of the elements with the Body and Blood of Christ; unlike Zwingli and the Free Churchers (see below) he rejected an absolute distinction between the elements and Christ. The Eucharist is, for Calvin, a case of "unity in distinction," which restores for him the patristic writers' understanding of the participation between symbol and reality. As Crockett writes, "...otherwise, the Eucharistic presence is made to depend entirely upon our faith (Zwinglians), or placed at our disposal (Rome), or bound to the elements (Rome and the Lutherans), thus threatening the freedom of God."[111]

For Calvin it is through the agency of the Holy Spirit that the Eucharist is made effective. He writes,

> The cup and also the bread must be sanctified...in order that the wine may be a figure of the blood of our Lord Jesus Christ and the bread of his body, in order to show that we have truly fed upon him, and being as it were grafted into him may have a common life, and that by virtue of the Holy Spirit may be united to him, in order that the death and passion that he has undergone may belong to us and that that sacrifice, by which we are reconciled to God, may be attributed and imputed to us now as if we had offered it ourselves in person.[112]

Although the churches that followed Calvin's teachings decided (against Calvin's own objections) to celebrate the Eucharist infrequently, Calvin remained insistent on its central place in Christian worship, and on its efficacy as sacrament for those who believe.

The final proponents of the Real Presence thread were part of the most important—and most ill-defined—movements of church history: the English Reformation. From its inception, the English Reformation has been eager to affirm the Real Presence of Christ in the Eucharist, but reticent to discuss the mode or manner of this presence.

Thomas Cranmer, the compiler of the first *Book of Common Prayer* and the architect of Anglican theology, set the precedent for Anglican ambiguity early in the Church of England's history. There is a great deal of debate about Cranmer's actual theology of the Eucharist. This is due to the fact that, although an excellent theologian, he was an even better politician, and we see a definite evolution of his theology as time passed and differing circumstances arose. Under Henry VIII, he was as adamant as his king about transubstantiation, but after Henry's death, his views swung from Lutheran to Zwinglian perspectives. In the prayer book, however, Cranmer set down what was to become typical of the Anglican approach and opted for a liturgy that could be construed in a number of ways.

For the most part, however, Cranmer cautiously followed Calvin in his ecclesial understanding of Christ's presence. For Cranmer,

Christ is present in the celebration by virtue of the believers' true participation, not in the elements themselves. Thus, while he maintained that "it is my constant faith and belief that we receive Christ in the sacrament verily and truly,"[113] he was fairly agnostic about exactly how that presence occurs. As Bridge and Phypers explain, "the Real Presence was indeed real; it was to be known by faith, and its mode was not a subject for conjecture."[114]

Cranmer himself wrote,

> Really, carnally and corporally Christ is only in heaven, from whence he shall come to judge the quick and the dead. And since a body can be in only one place at a time, the bread and wine remain bread and wine, before, during and after the Eucharist. Yet when the elements are received and eaten by believers, then Christ is truly present to their spiritual health and protection.
>
> Thus our Savior Christ, knowing us to be in this world, as it were, but babes and weaklings in faith, hath ordained sensible signs and tokens, whereby to allure and draw us to more strength and more constant faith in him. So that the eating and drinking of this sacramental bread and wine is, as it were, a showing of Christ before our eyes, a smelling of him with our noses, a feeling and groping of him with our hands, and an eating, chewing, digesting and feeding upon him to our spiritual health and protection.[115]

Thomas Hooker, under Elizabeth's reign, was one of Anglicanism's greatest scholars, and it was he who picked up Cranmer's ideas and molded them into a coherent and guiding theology. For Hooker, as for Cranmer, the Eucharist is a "real partaking of the body and blood of Christ...rather than a doctrine of the real presence of Christ in the Eucharist, although...he by no means denies the latter."[116] As Crockett explains,

> In placing the emphasis in his theology on the real partaking of the body and blood of Christ in the Eucharist rather than on the real presence, Hooker acknowledged, like Cranmer, that the primary purpose for which the Eucharist was instituted is the nourishment of Christian believers. The Eucharistic gifts are primarily spiritual food and drink. This early Anglican tradition sought to shift the axis of Eucharistic theology away from its medieval center, where the primary question was the manner of the Eucharistic presence in relation to the elements, and to

> reorient it around the act of sacramental communion. In this way, it sought to relate the presence of Christ in the Eucharist in a more integral way to the sacramental acts of eating and drinking.[117]

Thus, while professing the belief that Christ is "really present" in the *act* of communion, Hooker nonetheless refuses to deny a relationship between Christ and the bread and the wine, and maintains a typically Anglican agnosticism in regards to the presence of Christ in the elements themselves. As Hooker himself wrote,

> Let it therefore be sufficient for me presenting myself at the Lord's table to know what there I receive from him, without searching or inquiring of the manner how Christ performeth his promise; ...what these elements are in themselves it skilleth not, it is enough that to me which take them they are the body and blood of Christ...[118]

Hooker felt that the real meaning of the Eucharist was the union of Christ with the believer (hence the proper Anglican name for the Eucharist has always been "Holy Communion"), and any speculation as to the mode of that presence ought not be given undue attention. For him, that the presence is there is attested to by scripture and the patristic writers, and is a primary tenet of orthodox faith. Exactly *how* the presence is there is open to a broad range of theological opinion on which the Church of England declines to rule.[119]

The Anglican tradition of the Real Presence would have far-reaching influence as various schisms from the Church of England maintained much of its Eucharistic theology. The Methodist reformers sought to return the Eucharist to its central place, embracing the Real Presence interpretation of their Mother church, with a peculiar twist: in John Wesley's theology, the bread and wine do not become the Body and Blood of Christ, but instead are signs of Life and Power, changed by the Holy Spirit into "channels of God's love, to renew and fill their hearts."[120] One of Charles Wesley's hymns states this position eloquently:

> Come, Holy Ghost, Thine influence shed,
> And realise the sign;
> Thy life infuse into the bread,
> Thy power into the wine.
>
> Effectual let the tokens prove
> And made, by heavenly art,

> Fit channels to convey Thy love
> To every faithful heart.[121]

The Wesleys ultimately failed in persuading their congregations to celebrate a weekly Eucharist. Even had they been successful, when their movement spread rapidly in the American West there were too few preachers on the frontier for the widely disparate churches of the Methodist expansion to have weekly Eucharists.

The Puritans (later the Congregationalists), which separated from the Church of England, did not oppose the theology of the Eucharist as taught by the latter, but only the performance of the rite. The Puritans favored having the option to pray spontaneously, using as much or as little formal liturgy as the congregation felt at ease with. However, the ecclesial and agnostic attitudes of the "Real Presence" theology found an abiding home in many "free church" traditions as well.

The Spiritualist Thread

The Realist and "Real Presence" threads not only opposed each other, but they found opposition in yet another thread: the Spiritualist. Whereas many of the threads of the early church were complementary in nature, in the Western church we see theologies arising in responsive opposition. Mostly in reaction to the Realist thread, the Spiritualists would be accused by the "Real Presence" faction of overcorrection in their zeal to amend the gross literalism sweeping the church.

For the Spiritualists, Christ's presence in the Eucharist is only figurative. Most of its proponents would concur that the bread and the wine remain as they are; only our understanding of them has changed. The Spiritualists embraced a Platonism divorced from its native presuppositions about the relationship between indicator and indicated.

In the eleventh century, where the Real Presence Thread first begins to assert itself, people were already understanding the concept of symbolism in a way that resonates with us in modernity: "If something is 'real,' it must be sensed; if it is 'merely' spiritual, it is not real."[122] In subsequent centuries, this "deflated" symbology leads to a gradual devaluing of the Eucharist, until, in the worship practices of many "free church" Spiritualists, celebration of the Eucharist is a sporadic and often anemic observance.

The first to formulate a Spiritualist theology of the Eucharist was a monk under the supervision of Radbertus, Ratramnus of Corbie, who opposed his abbot's theology publicly and with some degree of notoriety (Emperor Charles the Bald consulted Ratramnus on the matter of Eucharistic theology rather than his abbot). Ratramnus' objection to Radbertus' theology was a simple one: a person cannot be in two places at one time. Even God obeys God's own laws. Therefore, since the resurrected body of Christ was "ascended into heaven and seated at the right hand of the Father" as the Creed states, Christ cannot also be physically present on the altar. Instead, the bread and wine are "mere figures" of Christ's body given to us for our celebration of his life and death, and for our spiritual nourishment.

In answer to questions from Charles the Bald in the 10th century—whether Christians received the Eucharist in truth or in mystery, and whether that presence was the same body born of Mary—Ratramnus wrote:

> This is confessed most plainly by saying that in the sacrament of the body and blood of the Lord, whatever exterior thing is consumed is adapted to refection by the body. The mind, however, invisibly feeds on the Word of God, Who is the invisible bread invisibly existing in that sacrament, by the vivifying participation of faith.[123]

Ratramnus felt it was silly to suggest that "bones and blood" were present "under" the signs of the elements. It is only in a spiritual sense that Christ is present: present to our imaginations in the rite.

One might assume that Ratramnus was excommunicated or at least silenced by his abbot for publicly opposing his theology, especially to the emperor. Fortunately for Ratramnus, Christian love seems to have prevailed in what could have been a very touchy situation indeed. There is no record of any friction between the two men over the affair, and amazingly, abbot and monk seem to have coexisted in the same monastery and communed at the same altar without incident.

Berengar of Tours (1088) was not so fortunate. Following Ratramnus, Berengar opposed the Realist Thread and was subsequently forced to recant his position twice. Berengar believed that the spiritual and physical, while equally real, were irreconcilably distinct entities. He found the notion of Jesus' physical body and blood being present in the Eucharist simply absurd, and he often employed a quick wit and a biting tone to make his point. As Macy explains,

> To believe that the Lord was physically present in the Eucharist would mean that "little bits" of Christ's flesh would daily be subjected to the indignity of eating and digestion. It would mean that the body of Jesus would be subject to cannibalism, to digestion, to desecration by rot, fire, and animals. If the body of the Lord appeared every day in every liturgy all over the world, then surely every day the body of the Lord would grow bigger and bigger, and finally there would be a mountain of Jesus' body.[123]

In some ways, Berengar might just as easily have fallen into the "Real Presence" camp, except for his absolute insistence on the distinction between physical and spiritual reality. Berengar would have strenuously objected to an undefined "mystical" presence of Christ in the bread and wine. Christ's presence had nothing to do with the bread and the wine; they were but signs, "place-holders" with no spiritual efficacy inherent in themselves.

Berengar was twice taken to task for his teaching. The first time was at the Synod of Rome in 1059, at which he was forced to sign a statement reading:

> The bread and wine which are laid on the altar are after consecration not only a sacrament but also the true body and blood of our Lord Jesus Christ, and they are physically taken up and broken in the hands of the priest and crushed by the teeth of the faithful, not only sacramentally but in truth.[124]

The signing of this did not stop Berengar from turning around and continuing to teach his own interpretation. Consequently (and hardly surprisingly) he was once again called on the carpet for his offenses at the Synod of Rome twenty years later in 1079, where he was forced to sign another statement:

> The bread and wine which are placed on the altar...are changed substantially into the true and proper vivifying body and blood of Jesus Christ our Lord and after the consecration there are the true body of Christ which was born of the virgin...and the true blood of Christ which flowed from his side, not however through sign and in the power of the sacrament, but in their real nature and true substance.[125]

The Aristotelian nature of the second statement resembles and foreshadows Aquinas' theology. This interpretation might have set a little easier with Berengar than the first document, but it was still far from satisfactory.

Another early Spiritualist was Hugh of St. Victor. For Hugh, the Eucharist (as well as other sacraments) were tools used by God to draw us into deeper relationship with the Divine. Hugh believed that the sacraments—the bread and the wine—are used by God to communicate the "real (albeit spiritual) presence" of Christ, culminating in the believer's union with God. As Hugh writes,

> Your heart says to you: What becomes of the body of Christ after it has been taken and eaten? I hear you. Do you seek the bodily presence of Christ? Seek it in heaven. Here Christ is sitting at the right hand of the Father. He wishes to be with you at those times when and where it is necessary. He showed himself to you at the time of His bodily presence in order that He might draw you to his spiritual presence. This is why He came to you in bodily form and showed Himself to you during the time of His bodily presence in order that through this presence you might find His spiritual presence, which is not taken away. Thus He came into the world at a certain time by assuming flesh, and by means of this bodily presence lived with humans, in order to rouse them to seek after and then discover His spiritual presence. After having completed this mission, He left in His bodily presence, but remained in His spiritual presence.... So too, in His sign He comes to you in a temporal way, and in it is with you in a bodily way, in order that through this bodily presence, He might urge you on to seek His spiritual presence, and aid you in finding it.[126]

The result of Hugh's theology was that it was union with God that was important, and the Eucharist was just one of many tools used by God. Thus, if a person chose not to receive communion, God would just as willingly use other means to effect a spiritual union with that person. This led to the medieval practice of "spiritual reception," in which "certain ritual actions or prayers which took the place of the eating of the bread and wine were understood as being just as effective for the believer's salvation as long as the person performing the action was leading a life of faith and charity."[127] Thus there arose an ironic situation in popular piety that Hugh could neither have foreseen nor, probably, prevented: people who were too terrified of receiving Christ's physical presence in the Eucharist would happily settle for the less-scary "spiritual communion" of merely observing at the mass without communication.[128]

The implication of this for future generations is clear: salvation is the result of a personal, individual, and interior communion with God; it is not the communitarian soteriology embraced by the early church. Until this point, one was saved by being in the "ark of the church;" if you are in the boat you are saved; if you are outside the boat you are lost. Hugh's theology, however, paved the way for an increasingly individualistic notion of salvation that was to find deep resonances in the Spiritualist reformers and the evangelical tradition in general. This individual approach to salvation and the devaluation of the Eucharist in corporate worship were the legacy left to the West by Hugh's formulations.

The Spiritualist thread was to find its greatest proponents much later in the theology of Zwingli and the Swiss reformers. This position was the cause of much pain between members of the German and Swiss reformations. Rejecting Luther's insistence upon the Real Presence, Zwingli and his followers asserted what later theologians would wryly refer to as a doctrine of "Real Absence," a belief that Christ is not present in the elements in any way save a very nominal symbolism.

Zwingli embraced a radical dualism almost reminiscent of the Gnostic heresies of the first few centuries of the church's history. Flesh is flesh, and spirit is spirit, and "never the twain shall meet" might suffice to sum up Zwingli's philosophy. Thus, the Eucharistic elements could in no way contain the Body or Blood of Christ. Christians, in Zwingli's teaching, should not concern themselves with matters of the flesh, but only with the spirit. Zwingli himself describes this distinction in a letter to Matthew Alber:

> For it is forever true: what is born of flesh is flesh, and on the other hand, what is born of spirit is spirit. Christ therefore, means here a spiritual eating, but of what nature? Such that we are to say that Christ is eaten here physically? Are to eat spiritually and to eat physically one and the same thing, then? Even the logician knows that is absurd. If it is spiritual eating why do you call it physical? If it is physical, what else can it do but comfort the body? Christ means,

> therefore, that unless we eat his flesh, that is, unless we believe that he underwent death and poured out his blood for us, we shall not attain life. Again, that if we eat his flesh, that is, believe he died for us, and drink his blood, that is firmly believe that his blood was poured out for us, then Christ is in us and we in him. But is Christ in anybody physically? By no means. Why, then, are we speaking about eating the body? His body is eaten when it is believed that it was slain for us. It is faith, therefore, not eating about which Christ is speaking here.[129]

Clearly Zwingli makes some logical leaps in the above passage that could easily be challenged. As Bridge and Phypers comment, "It is almost as if Jesus had commanded, "*believe* this..." or "*understand* this...: or "*say* this..." rather than "*do* this in remembrance of me."[130]

This very issue was to be the sticking point in the many attempts made by their followers to reconcile Luther and Zwingli in their lifetimes. One historic "summit" began with Luther writing, "This is my body" in Latin on the table top, and pointing to it as his only answer to Zwingli's objections. The meeting ended with Zwingli in tears, and the two men deeply grievous of the gulf that remained between their two branches of the Reformation.

For both reformers, faith was primary over all other concerns. But whereas Zwingli felt that this primacy was threatened by a doctrine of Real Presence, Luther disagreed. Zwingli's focus on the spiritual eclipses any possibility of corporeal participation or mystery in the Eucharist. Faith is a matter of the spirit only, and is the only operative or efficacious aspect of the observance. Any reliance upon the tokens themselves as being in any way "effective" for the believer's life was threatening to Zwingli, promoting idolatry and papism. As Crockett notes,

> Historically...Zwingli represents the point at which the symbolical and spiritualistic traditions in Eucharistic thought threaten to become antirealist and even antisacramental. This does not mean that for Zwingli the Eucharist is unimportant. It means that the tension is now broken between two strains in the Eucharistic tradition, which up to this point had belonged together. It was in this way that the Zurich reformer sought to safeguard the Reformation principle of justification by faith alone. No visible sign can

> bring salvation. Only Christ brings salvation. Is Christ's flesh of no avail, then, asks Zwingli? "I answer," he says, "that Christ's flesh avails a great deal. It avails through his death, not through our eating." It is faith, and faith alone that embraces salvation.[131]

Zwingli's doctrine is not without a note of Realism, however. It is not a realism with respect to the elements, but to the assembled believers. Thus, Zwingli revives the ancient ecclesial aspect of the Eucharist. Christ's body is really and truly present, but in the church, the people, not the bread and wine. Zwingli writes,

> They who here eat and drink are one body, one bread; that is, all those who come together to proclaim Christ's death and eat the symbolical bread, declare themselves to be Christ's body, that is, members of his church; and as this church holds one faith and eats one symbolical bread, so it is one bread and one body.[132]

This doctrine is based on Paul's testimony in his first letter to the Corinthians, in which he writes, "Because there is one bread, we who are many are one body, for we all partake of the one bread" (1 Cor. 10:17).

Zwingli's formulation would prove to have more influence on Reformed Christianity. One Baptist pastor, John Smyth, wrote in 1610,

> The outward baptism and supper do not confer and convey grace...but as the word is preached, they serve only to support and stir up repentance and faith...The outward supper (which only baptized persons must partake) presents and figures that spiritual supper...in the communion of the Spirit."[133]

Although common ground would be found in Calvin's formulations, the left wing of the Reformation (such as the Anabaptists) and its grandchild, evangelicalism, owes much of its Eucharistic understanding to Zwingli's insistence on the primacy of spirit over the flesh and of faith over observance.

Even Zwingli's radical division between the carnal and the celestial was not enough for some of the Reformation's left wing, however. Many still regarded the Spiritualist interpretation to be too much like sacramentalism for comfort.

Memorial & Communitarian Threads

In an effort to retain the practice of the Lord's Supper because Jesus had commanded it, many Christians decided that nothing more was meant by the observance than a simple remembrance. The bread and wine (or, more likely in evangelical churches, grape juice) were simply mnemonic devices, "object lessons," to help us remember Jesus. As Baptist preacher Dr. Alexander MacLaren of Manchester proclaimed in 1884, "All our theories about the meaning and value of this Communion Service must be found within the four corners of that word ["memorial"... it is] a memorial rite, and as far as I know, nothing more whatsoever."[134]

As Tripp notes, "the content of the rite suggests a very simplistic but perennially popular version of the Memorialist view of the Eucharist: we do just this, because our Lord told us to; and as we do it, we think of him."[135] Consequently, many evangelicals are very unclear as to why they celebrate the Lord's Supper. For many of them it is done merely because Jesus said to. The command seems odd, and often remains unexplained, but it is followed, albeit in some churches exceedingly infrequently.

Fortunately, not all evangelical observances are so anemic. When genuinely and devotionally practiced, the memorial view can evoke a deep reverence, and a true "communion" with Christ in the experience of many evangelical Christians. There is good reason for this. In some ways, the Memorial Thread is a return to the most primitive of Eucharistic threads, the *Brachot*, where Thanksgiving was given for God's salvific acts. Likewise, in the Lord's Supper, Reformed believers celebrate Jesus' life and death.

There are, however, striking differences between the two threads. In the *Brachot* thread, the emphasis is on praise and thanksgiving, while in the Memorialist celebrations, self-examination and grave reverence are encouraged. Also, the *Brachot* blessing is a communal act; participants kept their heads held high, and shared in a feeling of the joy that comes with being a community of faith. The Memorialist celebrations tend more towards the deeply interior experience. As popular Baptist writer William Barcley writes, "We remember to realize again what our blessed Lord has done and suffered for us" that we may reappropriate its many benefits, and we are remembering "someone who is gloriously alive. And therefore we remember Jesus Christ in the sacrament in order to encounter Jesus Christ."[136]

While communion is being served, each believer is "alone with the Lord," and is encouraged to meditate upon Christ's great sacrifice, and that "Christ would still have suffered on the cross if it was only for you alone."[137]

The first to articulate the Memorialist thread was the pre-Reformation leader Peter Waldo. After his sudden conversion around 1175, this French merchant gave himself over to a life of poverty and ministry. Waldo not only translated the Bible into the vernacular (people have been burned for far less), but he taught his followers to receive communion in both kinds, bread *and* wine (only the bread was taken in the Roman church at the time). Furthermore, he taught that the rite was "merely a remembrance of the Lord's body given for them, and at the same time...[he gave] a strong exhortation to yield themselves to be broken and poured out for [Christ's] sake."[138]

Though not very popular in Waldo's day, the Memorialist Thread was to dominate the more radical Reformed Churches, coming to America by way of the Anabaptists and English Baptists. These, together with a Zwinglian Spiritualism, constitute the basic Eucharistic theology of the majority of Baptist, Pentecostal, and other evangelical denominations.

As we have seen, the Church of England has never lacked for dissenters. There have always been plenty of people, laypersons and clergy alike, who felt that the compromise of the *Via Media* failed to go far enough in either one direction (Catholicism) or another (Reformation). John Nelson Darby was one such clergyman in the Church of England who reacted strongly against the "popery" of the Oxford movement, and left the national church to found what was to become the Plymouth Brethren. Completely rejecting any conception of clergy, Brethren embraced an ultra-Calvinist doctrine of election, and revived the Communitarian aspects of the early *Brachot* thread. As Darby writes:

> The Communion Service is the outward symbol and instrument of Unity amongst God's people...I believe that the bread remains absolutely bread, and the wine, wine—that physically there is no change whatever in the elements...The Lord's Supper is a solemn declaration to God

> that you regard all those who come to his table as being one with you and one with God.[139]

Not surprisingly, the Plymouth Brethren practised a "closed communion," permitting only those accepted as being among the "elect" to commune. Many other churches (such as some Baptists) do the same.

The Moravians, who are the Czechoslovakian descendants of the Hussites, have for over 250 years been celebrating a very interesting communion service that attempts to resurrect the early church's *Agape* Meal in terms of its simplicity and its communitarian character. What makes this service so novel is that it takes place only once a year during the Christmas season and is celebrated with coffee and cakes! Some Unitarian Universalist churches have borrowed the rite, which has proved to be enormously popular in those congregations that celebrate it.[140]

Not surprisingly, it is the Unitarians and Universalists who have historically been most active in liturgical re-visioning. They have always had to ask the difficult question: "What does the Eucharist mean to *us*?" Unitarian Universalist history is full of experimenters, dissenters, and those who took the middle road of occasionally celebrating a rite very close to the English Prayer Book Eucharist.

One such innovator was Mrs. Judith Stevens of Gloucester, who in 1782 wrote a Universalist Catechism in which she insisted that Communion be an "open" celebration, welcoming any to the table who would eat. In her catechism, she describes the Eucharist as a strongly communitarian rite, drawing on the *Didache*'s Eucharistic Prayer for her imagery:

> As the bread which he broke was a gathering together of the many grains constituting one lump in which all distinctions were lost, and of which he says this is my body; lo, in him are collected the scattered individuals of humanity, forming a compleat man, and constituting the comprehensive character of our Lord... The many grapes pressed together, constituting one wine, hold up to us the oneness of the soul of Jesus with the spirits of the human race.[141]

Universalists and Unitarians have always felt a profound ambivalence towards the Eucharist, their celebrations ranging from the weekly and highly liturgical services of King's Chapel in Boston, to the curious but popular "flower communions," to no communion at all.

The Liturgical Movement and Ecumenism

Most of the reformers sought only to balance Eucharistic practice with the proclamation of the Word, not to supplant it. Calvin, Luther, Wesley, and many others insisted that weekly communion was the ideal for the local church, but even in their own lifetimes, their advice in this regard was ignored, even hotly rejected, even by their "own" churches. What they most feared, that the Eucharist would be devalued and consequently fall into disuse, was of course precisely what happened in many communities.

Many evangelical churches now celebrate the "Lord's Supper" only on a quarterly basis, and in denominations such as the Quakers, the Salvation Army, Unitarian Universalist, and New Thought churches (such as the Unity School of Christianity), the practice has been either discontinued altogether or spiritualized to the point that no elements are actually even used in the "celebration."

By the end of the nineteenth century, each of the myriad denominations were firmly entrenched in their own peculiar theologies and practices. As John Owen pointed out, "If liturgy was designed to promote unity, it had done exactly the opposite; if it is designed to preserve the true faith, it is odd that it has to be so often altered; and if it comes from God himself, it is puzzling to see men before our eyes devising it and haggling over it as they go along.... For my part, I know not anything that ever obtained a practice and observation amongst Christians, whose springs are more dark and obscure than those of liturgies."[142]

As chaos theory has taught us, systems usually reach a state of ultimate dissolution only to see order begin to reassert itself. This can certainly be said of the Eucharistic celebration. Order began its "reassertion" in the twentieth century with what has come to be called "The Liturgical Movement." This movement, unprecedented in the long history of the church's bitter struggles, unselfconsciously took on a life of its own and has succeeded more than any one could have hoped, in the ecumenical convergence of Eucharistic celebration.

This convergence was possible because of two independent but complementary occurances: the ecumenical impulse and the development of textual criticism. With the recent discovery of many previously unknown documents from the first centuries of the early church and the application of literary critical methods, Christians the world over began to explore the Eucharist as the early church had celebrated it.

The rediscovered *Brachot* thread provides the basis for the modern *anamnesis*, the blessing of God for the good gifts of Creation and Redemption. The Divinization thread influenced the rediscovery of the *epiclesis*, the invocation of the Holy Spirit upon the celebration, as well as the Eschatalogical Thread, which often re-emerges in many modern *epicleses* and Post-Communion prayers.

The Liturgical Movement—a true grass-roots, diffuse "growing together" of scholarly consensus across denominational boundaries rather than any sort of organized "movement"—thus uncovered the vast multifaceted traditions of Christianity's most central rite. Amazingly, this scholarship has brought theologians as diverse as Roman Catholics and American Baptists to construct Eucharistic Prayers that are nearly identical in form if not in content.

Protestants began to forget exactly why they were separated from each other; they began to welcome one another to the Lord's table indiscriminately. Even the churches of the Anglican communion open their communions to "all baptised Christians." Some Christians would go even further, saying that Jesus would not turn away anyone from his table, regardless of their lifestyle or beliefs.

As Colin Buchanan has said,

> It is as if the Holy Spirit has been preparing the Churches, through the work of their liturgists, for just such a celebration...what matters is what God works by the power of the Holy Spirit through the sacramental signs, not our attempts to define what we should do or say when we celebrate the Lord's Supper.... We do not, I believe, have to wait until we can discern what are "valid orders" in those who preside over Eucharistic celebrations. What we have to obey is the prompting of the Holy Spirit and the orderliness which he reveals...That is why the *epiclesis* has been rediscovered by Christians of different Churches in such a vital way. It cuts across our denominational barriers as a sword-like word from God, and it reflects profoundly our increasing faith; by the Spirit God really is fulfilling his promises.[143]

Though the ecumenical impulse was already burning brightly in the mid-twentieth century, the Liturgical Movement fanned the flames, making it clear to the world's churches that they had far more in common than their forebears would have admitted. As Procter-Smith writes,

> Although ecumenicity has not been a primary goal of the liturgical movement, it has certainly been a happy result. The recovery of liturgical norms based on scholarship has become increasingly ecumenical and derives from a period of the church's life that predates many of the controversies that have divided us. Thus the recovery of liturgical norms has made sharing of liturgical resources inevitable.[144]

The ecumenical impulse led to national and world-wide councils of church leaders from most Christian denominations, meeting regularly to explore issues of unity, liturgy, and Christian responsibility in a world filled with pain and injustice. Church leaders eagerly lent their support, and both the National and World Councils of Churches have since been potent tools not only for unity, but also as a barometer of Christian consensus.[145]

Although relative to the rest of the church's history, the ecumenical convergence seems like a lightning-fast development, it has actually been painfully slow for those in the thick of it.

Church leaders, excited by the possibilities for greater union, have often moved faster than the inertia of the people in the pews has allowed. The United Church of Christ merger (joining the Congregationalists and the Evangelical and Reformed Churches), to cite but one example, was not a happy one for everyone involved, and while most of the members of the two denominations went ahead with the union, many Congregationalist churches felt that they were being "bullied" by their representatives into an agreement that many felt compromised the denomination's most cherished tenet: the sovereignty of the local church in governing its own affairs. Thus ecumenicity, though a good thing in itself, is not valuable when it proceeds in an unjust or insensitive manner.

The late Archbishop of Canturbury, Lord Coggan, expressed the Anglicans' impatience for unity by calling for "immediate intercommunion between Roman Catholics and Anglicans."[146] This has yet to happen, even though many Roman Catholics have taken matters into their own hands, and, ignoring the "rules" of the magisterium, commune regularly with their "separated brethren."[147] But as Bridge and Phypers point out, all is not lost with regard to Roman Catholic ecumenicity:

> Unless it is going to be claimed that the leadership of the Roman Catholic Church is engaged in a gigantic plot to hoodwink Protestants (a kind of worldwide ecclesiastical Watergate) then it must be acknowledged that their thinking is undergoing very considerable change.[148]

Certainly the greatest barrier to Roman Catholic and Protestant intercommunion is the issue of validity. Although Roman Catholics do not dispute the obvious workings of the Holy Spirit in the ministries of other denominations, the question of validity continues to complicate the situation. As Bridge and Phypers describe,

> To many Protestants, the whole thing...is a matter of taste and custom and aesthetics. They wish to use appropriate and fitting words at the Eucharist, and they probably notice whether the few actions involved are suitable, but it is little more than that. There is no "right place" for the Lord's Prayer to be included, no great significance in the timing of the Offertory, no anxious ascertaining that the required actions are performed when the words of institution are repeated. For their minds simply do not work that way, and their faith is not committed fundamentally to that kind of issue. But to the Catholic mind, these things are crucial. Certain phrases employed by certain people make the whole thing valid. If those factors are not present, it is invalid.[149]

The question of what makes a Eucharist valid is the single greatest stumbling block to intercommunion. In time, however, we may see even this resolved. There is reason to hope in the theological shifts of Vatican II, especially the affirmation that liturgy is the work of the whole congregation, and the rediscovery of the Catholic church itself as the "People of God" rather than simply the hierarchy. As the people gradually reclaim their power, they will begin to decide for themselves—as Protestants have been doing for centuries—what constitutes a valid Eucharist.

In retrospect, even though it has its shadow side (such as presumptuous mergings and an eagerness to agree that denies the hard path of history trod by various traditions), the Ecumenical Movement has been one of great hope and great optimism in the churches of the world. Through their participation with one another in the various National and World councils they have found that there is much more that unites than divides us, and have been able to be free of the cultural and historical blinders that often separated our predecessors. Our churches have learned that they can learn again, especially from each other, and the convergence of our liturgical rites is a powerful testimony to our progress, even as we cry for their further reformation.

But in what way must we now be reformed? In this section we have seen how each new crisis nudged the church into a renewed and reformed understanding of what the Eucharist is and how it should be celebrated. What is the crisis we currently face? What pressure is building that will once again shift how and what we are fed by God in our sacred meal? I believe the crisis is one of power. In Part Two we will explore the issues of power that now confront our churches, and see how our current liturgies exacerbate the problems.

PART TWO

The Need For Change

The Crisis of the Contemporary Church: Power

The chief crisis facing today's church is the issue of power—specifically, the phenomenon of "power-over," manifesting in the church's liturgies, theology, and administration. In a culture that is increasingly individualistic and diverse, old ways of defining order are seen by many as suspect, if not sinful in and of themselves.

In Judaic, patristic, and later medieval thought, the universe was a celestial hierarchy with God as the Emperor/King at the top of the pyramid, with angels and humankind—"His" subjects—beneath, and with the earth and its creatures at the bottom. This hierarchy was mirrored in domestic life as well. As Paul writes: "Christ is the head of every man, and the husband is the head of his wife, and God is the head of Christ."[1]

This perception of "power over" as a divinely inspired model has almost always been the norm in Christian thought. Why is this? It is because we tend to interpret our faith in terms which are philosophically relevant to us. Political philosophy has favored a hierarchical model for most of the church's history. But now that in our own time the dominant model for politics has shifted to a more democratic philosophy of shared power and responsibility, we see that the church still has a long way to go in internalizing this shift. People who have equal voice in choosing their national and local representatives often do not understand why their spiritual leaders are not likewise appointed. The position of bishop as an administrative rather than an exclusively pastoral position continues to induce a cognitive dissonance that must be addressed if the church is to emerge from this crisis as a potent and life-giving force in the world.

The "power-over" paradigm has begun to crumble in every sphere. Oppressed peoples are demanding economic justice, women are claiming their own right to shared power, politically we are shamed by our own imperialist tendancies, and the lie of our dominance over the earth has been exposed by the ecological crisis, which insists that we abandon our illusions of omnipotence and begin to live in community with the earth. One woman I interviewed for this book—an Anglican solitary—saw the crisis facing the church today not in negative terms, but as "the opening of the church. The tearing down of the walls. The release of the spiritual prisoners. The tossing away of the security blanket of complacency." This is a hopeful vision of opportunity emerging from tragedy, professing that even the church "as we know it" is dying and being resurrected or reborn.

The Anglican solitary above continues, saying, "To be 'reborn,' one steps on a spiritual path. The Eucharist should be open to all, without any criteria other than that they are spiritual seekers." Fortunately, we are well-provided for on this "spiritual path" by our scriptures, particularly the justice imperative so prominent in the Gospel. Jesus' assertion that "many who are first will be last, and the last will be first"[2] reveals that God has never been terribly pleased with the traditional stratification of spiritual and political communities. Nor is Jesus unique in this, for he is but echoing what Isaiah said centuries before: "Every valley shall be lifted up, and every mountain and hill be made low; the uneven ground shall become level, and the rough places a plain."[3]

In many ways Jesus' ministry was a continuation of the Hebraic prophetic tradition exemplified by Isaiah and Ezekiel, who "formulated [their] vision of liberation in the context of socioeconomic oppression of the poor by the wealthy and of the small colonized nation by the great empires of antiquity."[4] Jesus' genius was that he expanded the idea of God's advocacy of the economically impoverished to include an imperative for justice for those who were oppressed or excluded for any reason. Rosemary Radford Ruether points out,

> The writers of the New Testament recognized other areas in which social relations needed transformation. Under the impact of Jesus' deepening of prophetic criticism, the Jesus movement began to glimpse the possibility of transforming the relationships of race (ethnicity), slavery, and sexism.... Paul...anticipated this in the new relations of the baptized in the messianic community, where Jew and Greek, male and female, slaves and free would become brothers and sisters and work together in preaching and teaching.[5]

For Christians, the prophetic tradition in both the Hebrew scriptures and Jesus' ministry comprise a critique of power and social structures that polarize and promote the dominance of one group over another, whether for reasons of race, gender, profession, or political inclination. Jesus welcomes both the political outcast (the tax collector), and the social outcast (the prostitute) to his table, and receives a cup of water from the ethnic outcast (the Samaritan woman). This was all considered terrible heresy in Jesus' time.

Religious structures continue to operate in exclusive ways, even—and most poignantly—those institutions that trace their origins to Jesus' simple mealtime gatherings. The church seems not to have understood the message Jesus tried so hard to impart in his followers. We have at various times excluded Jews and peoples of other faith traditions from our tables of fellowship, even murdering them in the name of Christ. We have dominated and enslaved native peoples in the same name. And in this name many denominations continue to exclude women and sexual minorities from positions of leadership.

One woman I interviewed—an Episcopal priest—told me, "We still spend most of our energy on ways to keep out the 'wrong' people. We do very little to strive for justice for society's outcasts, like the mentally ill who populate so many of our prisons and streets. Instead, we scapegoat them, so we don't have to deal with the reality of our own sin. The church needs to quit looking at its own navel...and start looking out into the field of mission."

Another woman (a layperson) I interviewed concurred:

> For me, the largest problem Christians face is intolerance and self-righteousness. Most, I think, interpret Jesus' message as one of exclusion. Only those who make a direct commitment to Christ are considered to be saved. I believe

> this is contrary to Christ's true message of inclusion and love of all Creation. To me, spreading hatred and ill will in the name of Christ is blasphemy. Closing off your community so that it remains free of contamination from non-believers is equally opposed to Christ's message of inclusion. It doesn't just increase division in an already unhappy world. I believe that these actions also inhibit the spirit of the perpetrator and keep him or her from truly opening to Christ.

The Spectre of Patriarchy

How did this twisting of Jesus' original message of radical inclusivity come about? Feminist scholarship has in general held patriarchy responsible for the church's ills—and society's ills as a whole. In 1923 feminist philosopher Charlotte Perkins Gilman published her book *His Religion and Hers*, examining the role of gender in our perceptions of religious and political systems.

Gilman's book identifies two fundamentally opposing religious orientations held by women and men, respectively. She sees the male as being the hunter, whose pivotal transcendent experience is the taking of life, at the risk of his own. For men, "religion becomes centered on the 'blood mystery' of death and how to escape it."[6] In contrast, she describes the female, whose pivotal religious experience is giving birth, as being more concerned with nurturing life here on earth.

As she writes,

> To the death-based religion, the main question is, "What is going to happen to me after I am dead?"—a posthumous egoism.
>
> To the birth-based religion, the main question is, "What is to be done for the child who is born?"—an immediate altruism.
>
> . . . The death-based religions have led to a limitless individualism, a demand for the eternal extension of personality . . . The birth-based religion is necessarily and essentially altruistic, a forgetting of oneself for the good of the child, and tends to develop naturally into love and labor for the widening range of family, state and world.[7]

Ever since Gilman's prophetic book, feminist thinkers and theologians have been critiquing the facets of "male-dominated religion" that are perceived as perpetuating the very injustices the church has always claimed to abhor. And while these thinkers are not themselves immune to the very polarizing and demonizing tendencies they are critiquing, their voices are invaluable to the whole of the church, not because their critiques should be uncritically embraced, but because their voices bring a long overdue corrective to the many theological issues the church continues to face.

Even though women have made up at least half of the church's population throughout its history, their voices have rarely been heard, and their experiences have seldom been permitted to critique or guide it.[8] But women are finding their voice, and it is time for the men in the church to recognize how we have silenced that voice, to repent, and to learn to live in collaborative community with women, not as their superiors or spiritual betters, but as equals, seeking out consensus and truly striving to hear the experiences of women, ethnic minorities, and the outcast in our communities.

We must do this because it is difficult for men, the inheritors of privilege, to understand the pain and experience of those affected by our "reign." It is too easy to dismiss dissenting voices that we do not want to hear, and it is almost impossible for us to really understand how our actions have impacted those who have been wounded by us. As Procter-Smith writes:

> Defining patriarchy...is like a fish trying to define water. It is...so much the natural environment in which we all live that it is almost impossible for us to see it. Yet if patriarchy is the water in which we live, then the water is toxic, especially for women and for many men who are non-white, non-Western, or non-wealthy.[9]

Men of privilege need to have the humility to admit that perhaps our perceptions are not the most accurate, and to listen to the testimony of those whose sight may well be keener. We risk great loss if we don't.

Little has been written on the negative impact of patriarchy upon men, but surely this point must also be considered. What violence does it do to men to always be expected to have the answers, to always be strong, to always lead? How wounding is it to be artificially inflated by society, to bear the burden of expectations that go beyond what can reasonably be expected? Such projections are often exhausting when we try to live up to them, let alone discouraging when we cannot.Yet such projections, having been internalized by men, make the possibility of sharing power, responsibility, and status even more difficult to consider.

We are indebted to feminist theologians for bringing so many important points to light, but the truth is that the liberation called for is for everyone, for no one is liberated until everyone knows liberation. Ruether points out three typical reactions to institutional corruption, none of which are exclusive to the experiences of women or oppressed people. However, all three of them can be clearly seen in the writings of various feminist and liberation writers of the past thirty years.

The first reaction is a fairly common one: new insights bring subtle shifts in our understanding and redirect the course of the institution. The second, more radical reaction, is to see that the institution has become corrupt, but that the original revelation is still valid. (This was the approach of the Reformation, which sought to reclaim primitive Christianity while stripping away the accretion of centuries of man-made tradition.) The primary revelation is still authoritative and simply needs to be uncovered and reclaimed. The third and most radical reaction is to reject the institution altogether.[10]

Most of those who are writing feminist or liberation critiques favor the second approach, and there are a number of possible ways to view it. Mary Hilkert identifies three: the revisionist, the sublimationist and the liberationist positions:

> The revisionist holds that the patriarchal framework of the Jewish and Christian traditions is a historical fact but is not theologically necessary. The male supremacist, androcentric, and sexist elements of the Bible are not intrinsic to its message but can be sifted from it by means of exegetical methods and analysis of cultural context.
>
> The sublimationist option is based on the "otherness" of the feminine as witnessed in the imagery and symbolism of culture. Either the feminine is seen as innately superior to the masculine, or the life-giving and nurturing qualities of woman are considered to be of such a different order that any crossing of sex roles runs counter to nature itself. In this option the typically feminine characteristics of Jesus and the Spirit are emphasized.
>
> The liberationist alternative proposes that the central message of the Bible is human salvation as liberation, either as found in the prophetic tradition (freed from its patriarchal contexts) or in those texts that transcend androcen-

trism and patriarchy and point to the conversion and transformation of society today and in the future.[11]

All three of these views have yielded exciting scholarship that is challenging the church and calling us to justice. Most importantly, writers from these perspectives are holding up new mirrors to the church. What we see in these mirrors is often ugly, and we are wise to be grateful for the gift of honest and open-hearted assessment.

This is not to say that these writers are doing their formidable work for the benefit of enlightening privileged men. Nor are the women writing strictly for other women, or liberation theologians for oppressed peoples. These critiques are being written to call the church back to the vibrancy of its origins: to the creation of a community where men and women, oppressed and powerful, rich and poor, homosexual and heterosexual, conservative and liberal, can sit at a common table as equals and break bread as a family.

Dualism and Ambiguity

The idea that there is a fundamental distinction between how women and men experience the world is not new. From Charlotte Perkins Gilman to the sublimationist writers mentioned above, many writers have asserted as much. Unfortunately, as Susan A. Ross points out, catalogs of "these distinctive [female] elements...look suspiciously like stereotypically feminine qualities attributed to women by men."[12]

What is needed, says Ross, is not some catalog of what women are like so that men can understand, but "the concern to know and value women's experiences and not to model expectations for women on male experience alone; and second, a recognition of the *ambiguity* of women's experience."[13]

The ambiguity of women's experience is precisely one of the most important points in this discussion. Ross asserts that women have an acute awareness for ambiguity that evolved because they have for centuries been both included in and excluded from the category "men" (depending on the context). Because they have been both included in society as "domestic architects" and yet excluded from political positions of power, "women have developed a dual consciousness, an awareness of 'twoness'—in short, a sense of radical ambiguity that does not lend itself easily to strategies of separation and isolation."[14]

By contrast, and perhaps because of centuries of conditioning, or some innate psychological distinction, the masculine drive towards stratification, objectification, categorization, and atomistic examination of the "parts" of reality in isolation have often seemed alien to women's own experience of the world. But because "the world" continues to operate based upon patriarchal assumptions, women who have chosen to break out of the traditional feminine role of homemaker have still had to "play or pay" according to the rules set by men.

What if men were to listen to the universe as described from a woman's experience? What might such a universe look like?

For one thing, ambiguity may be hailed as an asset to "seeing" the world as it really is. The real world is not pigeon-holed into neat black and white categories, but is an evolving, complicated web that does not lend itself to simplistic and isolationist categorization. A recurring theme in many feminist theologies is the critique of dualism, the forming of arbitrary distinctions which, as many writers assert, has led to the demonization of, among other things, the dark, the female, the unknown, the body, and the earth; while exalting the light, the masculine, the empirically verifiable, the spiritual, and the transcendent.

The danger of dualistic thinking is that for every "good guy" there must be a "bad guy," and thus the arbitrary exaltation of one set above another. Similarly, people have too often needed someone or something to demonize in order to allow their own self-perceived goodness to truly shine. As singer Bruce Cockburn has put it, it is often difficult for some people to love themselves without insisting that someone else holds a lower card than they.[15] This oppositional formulation of all things in the universe has predictably led to unquantifiable terrors. As Ross writes,

> Dualisms such as nature/history, body/spirit, female/male are oppositional—one side is seen over and against the other—as well as hierarchical—one side must control the other. Violence against women, children and nature, that is, the animal world and the fragile ecosystem that supports all life on the planet, can result when one side rejects the other as evil. A Catholic feminist perspective bases its critique of these dualistic conceptions on a retrieval of the Incarnation, seeing God's taking on the condition of humanity as God's own self-expression. Sacramentality grows out of human embodiment and its

> connection to the natural world, not in contrast to it. Feminist theology thus argues for a closer connection between nature and history body and soul.[16]

Thus, for Ross, the Incarnation itself is God's answer to dualism—that the natural world is just as capable of hosting God as heaven, that the flesh is just as important to God as the spirit. To be able to hold the Whole in one's gaze and to see all as God did upon creating it[17] is one of the most valuable gifts the world could be given. In fact, it is in this realization that feminist theologians have made some of the most far-reaching and important advances in sacramental theology. J.D. Crichton writes,

> A human being is not just a reasoning mind, much less a mass of emotion. We are body-soul creatures or, as it has been said, "man [sic] is not a spirit lodged in a body, he is a being in which the body is consubstantially united to the spirit." A human being is a unity; you can indeed mentally distinguish in us body and soul, but when we act, we act in the wholeness of our personality. We lay hold of the faith and the whole of our being, assisted by revelation and institutions like the family and the Church. When in worship, we respond to God in faith, in praise and thanksgiving, as well as with love, we do so with our whole being and feel the need to express our worship, our out-going from self to God, in words and song and gesture.[18]

Ever since the church embraced Platonism—beginning as far back as Paul—it has taught that "what the flesh desires is opposed to the Spirit, and what the Spirit desires is opposed to the flesh" (Gal.5:17). We are instructed by the Apostle to "live by the Spirit...and do not gratify the desires of the flesh" (Gal. 5:16), since, according to Platonism, there is another, more real world that is our true home, and next to which this world of flesh and blood is of little account. If this sounds dangerously like Gnosticism, it is. And ever since Augustine, the gross extremes of Manichaeism have also been appropriated by the church, denying, in some scholars opinion, the very heart of Jewish spirituality and Christian sacramentality. Gary Macy writes,

> In the message of Jesus...it is the earthly and the everyday that is supposed to be celebrated. If the body, and the everyday is not important, then why did Jesus become a human being, why did he take on the everyday problems of

> people, feeding them, curing them, encouraging them? It seems that the bodily and the everyday are not only real, but involved intimately in our salvation. This is what the incarnation is supposed to mean.[19]

While for centuries men have been concerned with "important things" such as philosophy and salvation, women in general have never lost touch with the Zen touchstone of true spirituality: chop wood, carry water. Or, in more Gospel terms, mending, cleaning, feeding, clothing, befriending, and creating. Ross writes,

> What some psychologists label as the greater permeability of women's ego boundaries, and what some ethicists have labeled as the inability of women to make clear moral distinctions, have been understood to handicap women. But women's sense of ambiguity, reluctance to make separations, and tendency to identify with the other are closer to the heart of Christian sacramentality than the strict separations that have become pervasive in much sacramental theology and practice. Such a sense of interconnection and an appreciation of the often conflicting realities that coexist in such interconnection is characteristic of much of contemporary feminist theory in psychology, literary theory, history, and ethics.[20]

The danger in pinpointing a "feminist" theology is that we risk yet another dualistic attitude, this time dividing masculine and feminine ways of seeing the world; we may end up demonizing one or the other. In fact, I believe that neither of these two "ways"—the transcendent nor the immanent—are absolute. One is not more correct than the other, but instead both need to be acknowledged as equally valid and complementary ways of viewing reality. If every story has at least two sides to it, human experience has no less. The solution is not that the traditional "masculine" drive for order, particularity and transcendence is evil, only that it has run rampant, unchecked by a traditionally "feminine" affinity for ambiguity, diffusion, and immanence.

A balanced view reveals to us that while the "masculine" view is necessary to attain and maintain order, in isolation order comes at the expense of justice. Feminist theology (at its best) seeks to reclaim the justice at the very heart of tradition. Ruether explains,

> Feminist theology is not assserting unprecedented ideas; rather it is rediscovering the prophetic context and content

> of Biblical faith itself when it defines the prophetic-liberating tradition as norm. On one level, this means that feminist theology, along with other liberation theologies, strips off the ideological mystification that has developed in the traditions of Biblical interpretation and that has concealed the liberating content. The prophetic advocacy of the poor and the oppressed and the denunciation of unjust social hierarchies and their religious justifications leap in to clear focus as one assumes a stance of social justice rather than of collaboration with unjust powers. The entire Biblical message becomes radically transformed in meaning and purpose when the full implications of the Church's social advocacy for the oppressed are grasped today.[21]

Thus, the things women are saying to us from their experience are not alien pronouncements; they are in fact neglected elements that were an essential part of the Judaic and Christian revelations. These elements are needed desperately by the church if it is going to regain and maintain relevance and integrity. The elevation of one idea, one class, one people, or one sex over another is addressed and condemned by the Gospels, the Prophets and even the fables of Jonah and Ruth. Women's voices call us to renounce the sin of hierarchical dualism in the church, and to return to true community, becoming a "discipleship of equals."[22]

Perhaps the greatest gift of feminist theology is the establishment of a pragmatic critical approach to both scripture and tradition.[23] Feminist women, by rightfully and scripturally calling us to repentance, also give us the critical tools to evaluate our faith. That which is redemptive is not that which divides, stratifies, alienates, or objectifies. We have a responsibility as church and as community to critically examine the canon of faith that we have received. This is no heresy or dangerous innovation. As Ruether explains,

> On the basis of an early Christian principle of ethical interiority, much of Hebrew ritual law was set aside as no longer normative, despite these texts' continued appearance in the canon of the Old Testament used by the Christian Church. Texts in both testaments justifying slavery and hostility to religious and racial outsiders fall below most Christians' ethical sensibilities today. Thus all theologies, regardless of their claims that the Bible is totally the work of inspiration, in fact never consider all parts of the Bible

> equally authoritative; rather they use texts according to implicit or explicit assumptions of Biblical faith.[24]

Christians would do well to engage in the Jewish discipline of *midrash*, the continual reevaluation and interpretation of scripture and tradition as it relates to given circumstances and one's present culture. When we begin to include women and other oppressed peoples in our "midrash" we find fundamentalism to be almost impossible, as feminist thinking rejects absolutism and embraces the experience of all peoples, daring to hold conflicting views, feelings, and revelation in tension.

It is with this embracing of human experience, ambiguity and a new-found humility that we turn to some of the most painful aspects of our Christian heritage.

Power-over in the Church's liturgy

Exclusive language. Since the beginning of the feminist renewal in the church, the issue of how God is imaged and addressed has been paramount. While attitudes and orientations tend to be philosophical and abstract, the use of exclusively masculine images and language in reference to divinity is a concrete and immediate concern, and many denominations have struggled mightily with issues of "inclusive language," while many others have dismissed out of hand any need for revision.

Procter-Smith provides a simple critique:

> ...exclusively or dominantly male language about God grants authority to men in a patriarchal culture and religion. This is particularly true when titles ascribed to God duplicate those also given exclusively to men, such as father, king, or master. Such titles operate in a dual manner. That is, they suggest not only that God is like a father or king, or master, but also that fathers, kings, and masters are somehow like God.[25]

Or, in Mary Daly's pithy formulation: "Where God is male, the male is God."[26] It is hardly surprising that denominations that are not even open to dialogue on this matter (such as the Roman Catholic, Orthodox, and many fundamentalist evangelical churches) are ruled exclusively by men. Yet even in churches that claim to be open to women's experience (such as many Lutheran and Anglican bodies), while inclusive language has gotten much lip-service, masculine imagery and language have not yet been significantly challenged. As we shall see, this half-hearted dialogue has caused much pain for women who choose to remain in these traditions. Karen Bloomquist says, "To continue to use exclusively male references to God while we claim to be opposed to patriarchy is to reinforce [a] schizoid situation ... The hostile reactions that female references to God continue to arouse in many church-related and secular audiences are indicative of the deep symbolic and emotional hold that patriarchy still has on most people."[27]

One Episcopal priest, a woman, told me, "Occasionally I get really alienated by all the male language... I feel constrained to use the established liturgy, so [I] sometimes feel enraged about it. Language needs to be more inclusive. As long as we are excluding women linguistically, we are teaching our people to exclude."

In opting not to hear and take seriously the feelings of our fellow pilgrims in faith, and even more, in not having the willingness to reevaluate and change, we compromise the very radicalness of the first-century Gospel. The early Christians were liberated by Christianity precisely because of its universality. Where in Christ there is "no longer Jew or Greek, there is no longer slave or free, there is no longer male and female" (Gal. 3:28), the limitations of religion and culture were transcended, and the radical notion of a discipleship of equals was possible.[28]

This is truly Good News where it is lived out, and as Procter-Smith notes, theological language has traditionally stressed the Gospel's universality, transcending race, social status and gender by pointing to "supposed universal categories of experience." Unfortunately, as Procter-Smith adds, these allegedly "universal categories," are, in fact

> ...based on the experience of white western men, [and] have been challenged by theologians representing third world perspectives—Black perspectives, Hispanic perspectives, Asian perspectives—as well as women's perspectives from the same varieties of cultures and traditions. Emancipatory language cannot claim universal human experience as its basis without denying the diversity of human experience as well as the social and political realities that divide us.[29]

Thus, by presuming that the European-American male experience has been normative for the entire human community, we have succeeded in straightjacketing God by our perceptions. God has been "installed" as a white male hierarch, significantly compromising the Gospel's impetus towards universality and making real justice impossible. And so long as we continue to idealize a deity who archetypally embodies these attributes, the sins of patriarchy are not likely to even begin to be addressed.[30]

The irony of maintaining this traditional imaging of God is that European-American men are not even representative of the majority of church goers, who statistically are more likely to be women (or even women of color) than to be white males. As Nancy A. Hardesty notes,

> For at least a century Christians, male and female, have been observing that the ratio of women to men in most church services is two to one. Sociologists and quantitative historians researching the exact figures are finding that observation accurate. Thus the use of male language excludes roughly two-thirds of any given congregation from the most meaningful participation.[31]

That this results in a great deal of frustration and anger is hardly surprising. Episcopal priest Pauli Murray believes that declaring to a congregation of both women and men that we worship the God of Abraham, Isaac, and Jacob is equivalent to speaking of the "God of white people" to a Black congregation.[32]

I have had first-hand experience with how this language affects women. Worshipping as I often do in more traditional parishes, I myself have more than once watched a woman leave the service in tears, only to find out later that instead of being moved and inspired, she had found the language and imagery of the liturgy so disturbing and painful that she simply had to get out. Hardesty says of her own experience, "Instead of joining in the intercession, one begins to count the times the pastor uses 'Father' in a prayer. One begins to lose the points of sermons while fuming over statements like 'Christ died for all men' and 'God in Christ became man.' The pain and anger become excruciating."[33]

The tragedy is that many men in authority within the church are not willing to even hear, let alone sympathize, with the feelings of women. Predictably, when one's needs are discounted and ignored, the urgency of the need mounts exponentially. Hardesty continues:

> Rage mounts until one boils over or blows up. All of the pain and wrath pour out on whoever happens to be present. Rather than understanding the problem, the recipient of the anger usually just concludes that the assailant is crazy. This experience has led some to conclude that inclusive language is just an issue with the lunatic fringe of the women's movement. Actually it is an issue with every person, man or woman, whose consciousness has been raised concerning justice and equity for all people. One either walks out and never returns, as so many have, or one numbs out, becoming deaf to most of the message.[34]

As one woman I interviewed recalls, "After visiting X parish, I went to speak to the pastor after the sermon. I noted that the model of the universe that he had preached about left no room for femininity in divinity. I asked him if he was aware that this was the logical outcome of his sermon. He listened to me for a couple of minutes, and then dismissed me saying, 'Well, you can't have everything.'" The rector was correct, the woman could not have everything, but what she *should* have had was the opportunity to be truly heard and appropriately responded to, even if the priest did not agree with her. Understandably, this woman is no longer attending X parish.

This pastor, and many, many others, have a hard time understanding women's feelings of exclusion. Frequently I have heard traditionalist colleagues complain that "man" in English literature is *of course* understood to be inclusive of women, yet if that were so, women would not have to engage in conscious or unconscious "translation" just to get through a service. Hardesty writes,

> In the far past there may have been a time when the word man meant both male and female, but it has been clear for some time now that I as a female cannot properly designate myself as a "man." It does not take a diagram on the door to tell me that a room labeled "Men" is not meant for me. The term is no longer generic in ordinary usage. For religious leaders to suggest that one should continue to read it and hear it as generic in religious contexts is similar to arguing that services should continue to be conducted in Greek or Latin or German even when not a soul in the congregation understands the language.[35]

Masculine language in liturgy renders women invisible, which, as Procter-Smith points out, has philosophical and moral implications:

> The philosophical implications suggest that women are at best insignificant, at worst secondary and derivative from the normal human being, the man. Thus it is implied that women are abnormal or not fully human. The moral implications of the invisibility of women lie in the ability of language to create what it names. Invisible women have no voice, make no claims for themselves, possess no rights, exercise no moral agency. And the use of androcentric language makes the truth of whatever is said suspect, since women are in fact not visible.[36]

Not only does masculine language exclude women from visibility in the liturgy, but holding the masculine as normative for humanity often involves a demonizing of the feminine, and an implied denial even of women's creation in the image of God. Ruether writes,

> The naming of males as norms of authentic humanity has caused women to be scapegoated for sin and marginalized in both original and redeemed humanity. This distorts and contradicts the theological paradigm of imago dei/Christ. Defined as male humanity against or above women, as ruling-class humanity above servant classes, the imago dei/Christ paradigm becomes an instrument of sin rather than a disclosure of the divine and an instrument of grace.[37]

The report on "Language About God" presented to the Presbyterian Church affirms that "language about God commonly used only a decade ago has now become for many an impediment of communication, community, and to faith itself."[38] It is encouraging that such a statement should be presented to a major denomination. It may, unfortunately, take a long period of time for men and women of conscience "voting with their feet" to make the leaders of the churches take notice. Perhaps it will only be that this notice will be taken when such "voting" affects the finances of the institution. It is sadder that such exclusion may in fact bar people from conversion. If the Gospel is for, by, and about men, educated and aware young women are not likely to put up with simultaneously being both church members and perpetual outsiders. That young women are turning to Goddess spirituality in droves is telling: if the Gospel is for men, women must go elsewhere.

The Trinity. This issue becomes even more complicated when we turn to the doctrine of the Trinity. The most self-apparent observation about the Trinity is that all the "persons" in this allegedly perfect community are male! Brian Wren refers to the Trinity as "an all-male one-parent family with a whoosh of vapor."[39] This is in itself extremely problematic (couldn't at least one of the persons be female?), but the Trinity also excludes women by the example of its very structure.

Classical Trinitarian theology images God the Father at the apex of the Godhead, with the Son and Spirit subordinate under "Him," revealing a hierarchy even within the Godhead. Though the subordinance of the Son was formally condemned as heresy in the early church,[40] it is clear that the Trinity functions this way in the popular imagination and in Paul's epistles. LaCugna explores the implications of this arrangement for women:

> First, trinitarian theology has been seen to compromise the feminist concern for the equality of women and men, primarily because the relationship among the divine persons has been seen as hierarchical. This arrangement has been used to reinforce a "complementarity" theory of the true nature of male and female. According to this theology, femaleness and maleness are radically different ways of being human. Man is the head over the woman; man fully images God while woman images God by virtue of her relationship to man. Women's being is derived from man's. Further, sexual differentiation between women and men is interpreted to mean that it is God's will that men serve in public leadership roles, while women are created for domestic roles. These roles are not interchangeable. Although women and men are equal with respect to their God-given dignity, it belongs to natural law and to the order of creation that women be subordinate to men. Although the theology of complementarity belongs properly to theological anthropology, it emerges...because appeal is often made to the doctrine of the Trinity to support the subordination of women to men.[41]

Thus the doctrine of the Trinity sends two messages to women: (1) You have no part in God, and (2) your subordination is divinely mandated.

Pychologists have made us increasingly aware of the price that verbal abuse exacts from its victims, how our self-image or image in relation to our community or environment can be negatively impacted by the messages we are given about ourselves. Yet the use of non-inclusive language is rarely given serious consideration on the same basis. This is ironic and tragic, since there is not a more fundamental message about who we are as people and what our place is in the universe than how we think and talk about God. There is not a more logical place to begin affirming the Gospel for everyone than in the language of healing and love that Christ modeled. Janet Schaffran says, "An unwillingness on the part of church people to use inclusive language is especially difficult to understand because of all the times and places to use words responsibly and sensitively, common prayer and public worship would seem to merit a priority of care and attention."[42]

As we have seen, images of God that are exclusively male and exclusively hierarchical have caused a great deal of pain and distress, especially to women. Whether or not the reader agrees with the assertions of these distressed people is irrelevant; our assent or lack of it will not change lived experience, or the fact that there are real people who have been really hurt. It is our responsibility to really listen, and finally, to really act.

The first step is to hear, not just by reading this book, but by hearing the voices of those around us who are hurt by the very thing that seems most life-giving to others—our image of God. Yet it is precisely the "image" of God that is the problem, not God's self. The Hebrew scriptures give ample warning against precisely this kind of idolatry, urging the children of Jacob and Rebecca to eschew the anthropomorphisms of the dieties of surrounding nations. This resulted in a rich diversity of metaphors for God, none of which were elevated to the level of literal objectivity. This left God free to respond to the Jews as a person, in authentic and diverse ways; as both "Lord of Hosts" and as the protective "she-bear." In this way Israel sought to avoid the idolatry of their neighbors. The church has not been so wise.

As Hardesty points out, "Yawheh, the most High God, is not some white Anglo-Saxon Protestant male American tribal diety... [Yet] we persist in speaking of God in male terms despite the second commandment's prohibition of making images and likenesses of the Diety (Ex 20:4) and God's express statement in Hosea 11:9:

'I am God and not man ['*ish*, male], the Holy One in your midst'."[43]

For most women, neutering God is not on the agenda. What is important is reclaiming the diversity of God-images inherited from our Jewish forebears. Hardesty says, "Our language should reflect the richness of our biblical heritage and theological beliefs,"[44] and the fact that it doesnt is not only unfortunate for women and oppressed peoples, but for all people who, unbeknownst to many of them, are straightjacketed into a liturgy and a language that is imaginationally impoverished. The elevation of the Trinity (or any other single metaphor) as the monolithic image of divinity in Christianity courts idolatry, and whether we are willing to admit it or not, we all pay a price in serving such an impoverished deity.

We tend to forget that the Trinity is not, in fact, a biblical image, but inferred by the early church from the New Testament. The Trinity, if allowed to take its place beside the many images for God that are actually biblical, can teach us useful things about God: that God is relational, that God is in fact a community. Fine as these teachings are, there are many other images that are actually biblical that have just as much to teach us if we are ready to listen.

Besides being non-biblical, the Trinity is also not the last word on who God *is* for Christians. For as long as our world continues to change, God will continue to change in our imaginations, our cultural perceptions, and in the way salvation meets us on our many journeys.[45] Episcopal Bishop John Shelby Spong speaks about the scripture in his fine book *Rescuing the Bible from Fundamentalism*, yet much of what he says is also applicable to liturgy:

> Both the sacred scriptures and the creeds of the Christian church can point to but they can never finally capture eternal truth. The attempt to make either Bible or tradition "infallible" is an attempt to shore up ecclesiastical power and control. It is never an attempt to preserve truth. Indeed, those who would freeze truth in any words, concepts, or creed will guarantee a time warp that will finally doom that truth to extinction. Only truth that is freed from its captivity to time and words and allowed to float in the sea of relativity will survive the ravages of subjectivity.[46]

Thus there is a need for "fluidity" and ambiguity in our understanding of God and in our God-language—including such time-honored ideas such as the Trinity—as our understandings of God and of ourselves as a human community evolve, and especially as women reveal the damage done by millennia of male myopia.

Liturgical Tradition. Women been absented not only from our conception of God, but from the history of tradition as well. As many feminist theologians have pointed out, historical tradition has been so dominated by men that women have little they can point to within the canon of that tradition that they can truly own. The pain of this realization is clearly evident in this quote from Procter-Smith:

> Women suffer from amnesia. We lack a sense of tradition, especially where our traditions are concerned, for our association with the liturgy has historically been built on limitations. Insofar as we have any sense of liturgical tradition, it is a tradition of restrictions: these things we may not do, these things we may not touch, these places we may not enter, these roles we may not take, these words we may not speak. This negative tradition gives us no sense of participation in the liturgy, no sense that the liturgy is our work. The full, active, and fruitful participation of women in the liturgy demands a construction of tradition in which the lacuna is filled, in which the memory of women is recovered.[46]

This is not to say that women have no tradition, but that their tradition has not been permitted to influence or in any substantive way speak to the Christian tradition.

Procter-Smith continues, stating the logical conclusion of the situation for women:

> Because women have been excluded from the traditioning process, the movement is suspicious of arguments based on "tradition." Due to this liturgical lacuna, the feminist liturgical movement has had open to it two possible paths: to reject tradition altogether and create liturgies *de novo* and *ad hoc*, or to reject patriarchal traditions but reconstruct a feminist religion outside of existing traditions, as the Goddess movement has done. Feminist ecumenism, then, cannot rest on "tradition" as understood by the liturgical movement. Its source must be women's experience, which is more ancient than any religion.[47]

For many women, the search for a tradition that reflects them has necessitated leaving the church, or at least, participation in more than simply Christian communities. The emerging Goddess tradition has gained popularity specifically because it is primarily drawn from contemporary women's experience, and because God is imaged as female.

Much to the dismay of some, Goddess attitudes, prayers, and ritual elements are finding their way into the everyday practice of feminist Christians. Even within the more liberal mainline churches such as the United Methodist and Presbyterian (USA) churches, for instance, a huge furor erupted over the Re-Imaging Conference in 1993 when prayers to "Sophia" (a biblical name for the pre-incarnate Christ) were used. But Procter-Smith explains why the appropriation of these elements has been important to many women:

> The primary basis for borrowing Goddess-worship practices is that they answer a deeply felt need. To women raised within and identified with traditional Christianity or Judaism, the experience of praying to and encountering a female deity generates a profound shift in perspective. This perspectival shift not only involves a change in one's understanding of and relationship with God, but also one's sense of self, one's relationship with others, one's interpretation of reality in general. For women who are unable to find a female face of God in their own traditions, or for whom such a face has yet to be presented to them with sufficient power, the Goddess tradition, as reconstructed by contemporary feminists generates positive changes. Among the positive changes some Christian women report upon experiencing Goddess-worship are a new love and appreciation for their own bodies; stronger sense of identity with other women, even those with ideological or theological differences; greater confidence in their own perceptions and intellectual abilities; and a sense of power as something that comes from within themselves rather than granted to them by others.[48]

It is tragic that the Christian tradition has found so little place for the experience of women that women have had to seek outside the boundaries of their spiritual homes in order to be fed.

What would happen if we allowed women's experience to begin to inform the Christian tradition? The immediate effect of women's voices finally being heard in our churches is the move toward inclusive language, which we have just considered. But even this most initial and immediate of changes has far-reaching effects. Hardesty points out that "on a human level, an effort to use more inclusive language makes us aware not only of our sexism, but also of our racism, elitism, nationalism, classism, ageism, homophobia, and all other prejudices."[49] Once a wall comes down, all the other walls behind it are revealed, and must also be toppled. Once the child announces that "the emperor has no clothes," no amount of scrambling, arguing, or appealing to "tradition" will bring our illusions back.

The fear of some of those interviewed who opposed the ordination of women was that once women achieved a position of influence, Christianity would become unrecognizable. This may be so, but it depends upon what elements of institutional Christianity one deems intrinsic to "the church." If one's conception of the church is bounded by an ecclesiastical hierarchy ruled by males and preaching a Gospel of spiritual and cultural colonialism, then yes, indeed, Christianity may be unrecognizable in fifty years' time. But if through these influences the church rediscovers the Gospel imperative for justice, equality, community, and universality that Jesus taught and died for, the church will become more truly itself, more recognizable as the Community of God in our midst.

The church has always struggled between the poles of Jesus' radical teachings and the believers' own cultural inertia. The early church argued bitterly over whether the Gospel was for the Jews alone, or for the Gentiles as well. The Book of Acts vividly portrays Peter's traumatic wrestling with this very issue in his encounter with Cornelius the soldier (Acts 10). Paul was the great advocate for a universalist Christianity, battling James, Jesus' own brother, and the other leaders in Jerusalem to have Gentiles admitted as full members of Christ's body without having to make themselves subject to Jewish ceremonial law. And though Paul proclaimed this universality, extending it to women and slaves (Gal. 3:28), he was not convinced enough of this to actually put it into practice, as evidenced by his other writings.[50]

Yet in advocating that the Gospel was for all peoples, Paul was not appealing to the past, but pointing to a future made possible by the Gospel itself. At the heart of many very early church Eucharists was the eschatological (end-of-time) hope that what God has begun in them, God will bring to fulfillment in the whole of the world. *This places the locus of authority not upon what has been, but on what is possible through a renewed vision given by Jesus.* As Ruether writes,

> We appropriate the past not to remain in its limits, but to point to new futures. In applying the prophetic principle to the critique of sexism and the liberation of women, we deepen our understanding of social sin and its religious justifications and expand the vision of messianic expectation. By applying prophetic faith to sexism we reveal in new fullness its revolutionary meaning.[51]

If we are to be the church Jesus calls us to be, our relationships and our language must reflect the universality of his teachings and the eschatological hope that his vision might be made manifest. The purpose of inclusive language is not to enforce some malevolent feminist agenda on the church, but just the opposite, to finally proclaim for all people "a fuller vision, a deeper understanding of the One we love and to offer to others a relationship with the God who will heal their wounds, satisfy their longings, and make us all whole persons."[52] If the Gospel is truly for the healing and liberation of all peoples, then, as Hardesty writes, "All of our language must be inclusive. It must reflect the fact that all human beings—male and female, black and white, yellow, brown, and red, rich and poor, gay and straight, old and young, educated and illiterate, healthy and infirm—all are made in God's image, loved by God, and candidates for salvation."[53]

The commonly heard objection that introducing inclusive language will rob the liturgy of its beauty and its power says more about the commentator's lack of faith in contemporary poetic ability than it does about the appropriateness of inclusive language. It also reveals a laziness in our churches and a lack of true concern for the Gospel. Hardesty writes,

> If making changes in the way we speak of God seems too difficult and not worth the bother, we need to remember that we are speaking of the One we say we worship and we are influencing our own souls and the souls of others. If God is the One to whom our lives are ultimately committed, then we should be willing to endure a bit of bother! Indeed we should enjoy the exercise of thinking more deeply and creatively about our God, of expressing more eloquently and persuasively what we feel and believe about the One we love and worship.[54]

Convenience or lack of poetic esteem are not sufficient reasons to ignore this most important of issues. There are few considerations about our common worship that are more important; in fact the need for beautiful and appropriate language should challenge and provoke us as justice-makers and artists to new heights of creativity.

The development of liturgies and lectionaries that employ inclusive language should be a profoundly exciting venture for the church's next generation of liturgists. In the process of writing and revising liturgies for the worshipping community of which I am a member, the Festival of the Holy Names, each of us in the community has been gifted with an expanded vision of the Gospel, and found our faith challenged and renewed by our struggle to be church for one another. It has given us a profound sense of how radical and exciting Jesus' message really was, and many of us who were wondering whether there is really a place in Chrisianity for us have come to feel that our path is more authentically Christian than we could have ever imagined.

Power-Over in the Church's Theology

While the use of inclusive language is certainly one of the most visible struggles in the church, it is by no means the only one. The abuse of "power-over" and the projection of this abuse even onto God has resulted in some theological twists that we shall be sorting out for some time to come. For though the marginalization of women in our communities is a grave sin, so too is the perpetuation of sins such as our domination of the earth and our dualistic demonization of the world and the body.

Our liturgies still place heaven over the earth in importance, ("Keep [your child] unspotted from the world")[55] honor spirit over matter, and proclaim the abject depravity of human beings in relation to God ("We are not worthy so much as to gather up the crumbs under thy table"),[56] while our lections still proclaim our "dominion over the earth."[57]

As we have become more psychologically savvy, people have begun to see through some of the power abuses involved. Or, at the very least, they feel uneasy about the dynamic even if they can't exactly put their finger on the reason why. These abuses of power are not only reflected in the words of our public worship, but even in our most basic understanding of what Christianity is all about, our theology. As Juan Oliver writes,

> Even after all the Episcopal churches in the country switch to nonsexist language, they will still be emptying out. Let me explain. There are increasing numbers of people with good spiritual intentions who cannot handle commonplace Christian concepts like: Creation, Fall, Sin, Forgiveness, Salvation, Atonement, Grace (except as graciousness in the sense of polite kindness) and so on. It is not that they disagree with these concepts. It is much worse. The concepts are at best meaningless, and at worst they imply an understanding of God which is utterly uninteresting and undesirable to these people, an understanding of God and how God acts that they find deeply suspect, an understanding of God invested in concepts of law, obedience, power and rebellion. They are suspicious of this God. They find such a God undesirable. And what good can an undesirable God be?[58]

Thus, the issue goes far beyond language. It asks the most basic questions of the personality of God and the mechanics of salvation. It demands a critical examination of them as well.

One of the chief culprits in this case of questionable theology is the doctrine of the atonement that has prevailed in the West. Although a very different schema evolved in the Eastern church,[59] in the West it is the Anselmian formulation of the atonement that has won the day. According to St. Anselm (1033-1109 C.E.), it is impossible for God to simply "forgive" sins, for, as he writes,

> "To remit sin in this manner is nothing else than not to punish: and since it is not right to cancel sin without compensation or punishment if it be not punished, then it is passed by undischarged. It is not fitting for God to pass over anything in his kingdom undischarged."[60]

Thus, his formula requires compensation. As Harrison and Heyward briefly summarize,

> The Christian drama of salvation has been staged historically as a transaction between an almighty God and a powerless humanity. As the lower relational entity, humanity has been cast as a "fallen" partner, able to be "saved" or "redeemed" into right relation only insofar as human beings know ourselves to be unworthy of anything but punishment from God. Into our unworthy lives comes Jesus, the Christ, to bear our sins and to submit, on our behalf, to the

> Father God's will. Thus, standing in for us (as only the elder obedient Son is worthy to do in this patriarchal schema), Jesus is humiliated and killed, becoming thereby a perfect sacrifice to the Father. As the classical portrait of the punitive character of this divine-human interaction, Anselm of Canterbury's doctrine of the atonement...probably represents the sadomasochism of Christian teaching at its most transparent.[61]

The contradiction of this sacrificial view of atonement would be much clearer if we weren't culturally conditioned to accept it as "default reality." The question to ask about this "penal" theory of atonement is: how can a God, who in Jesus told us that we were never to exact vengeance, and that we were to forgive each other perpetually without retribution, demand of us behavior that God "himself" is unwilling or unable to perform? If God's sense of honor has been so offended by human sin that God cannot stand to be in relationship with us, why can God not simply forgive as we are instructed to do, rather than mandating that some "innocent and spotless victim" bear the brunt of "his" reservoir of wrath? The ability of humans to freely forgive when God will not or cannot logically casts humanity as God's moral superior. With this realization we have reached a level of absurdity that cannot be accommodated!

Johnson notes that "today, such a view is virtually inseparable from an underlying image of God as an angry, bloodthirsty, violent, and sadistic father, reflecting the very worst kind of...behavior."[62]

If we are content with an image of God as a monster, then we should be content with Anselm's formulation. But for most folks, monsters, no matter how big, powerful, familiar, or articulate, are not worthy of our worship. Yet all of our most powerful and "worthy" ideas such as grace, redemption, and atonement are bound up in this punitive paradigm. While Christianity pays lip service to a good and gracious God, making it seem, as Rita Nakashima Brock writes,

> ...as if God accepts all persons whole without the demand that they be good and free of sin, such acceptance is contingent upon the abuse of the one perfect child. The experience of grace is lodged here, I believe, in a sense of relief at being relieved of punishment for one's inevitable failings and not in a clear sense of personal worth gained from an awareness of the unconditional nature of love. The

> shadow of the punitive father must always lurk behind the atonement. He haunts images of forgiving grace.[63]

We have lived for centuries as children in a dysfunctional family, making excuses for, and bearing the guilt of, our relationship with our abusive "Father." Psychologists tell us that a child is abused when it must watch a sibling being abused. This is true for every Christian who has contemplated the wrathful abuse of Jesus by his "Father." How is it possible to give our most intimate selves over to the divine child abuser? How can the punitive "Father" of Christianity be redemptive of the pain and betrayal many have suffered at the hands of abusive earthly parents? How can people whose human fathers beat and abused them find comfort in a Heavenly Father whose power and abuse are magnified to archetypal proportions?

Such questions not only reveal how we image and relate to God, but they also raise other questions about our experiences as humans. How could Jesus' tragic suffering—not at the hands of humans, but according to Western theology, literally at the hands of God—be redemptive for us? The Anselmian formulation has taught us a number of ideas that need be explored further, ideas about the redemptive nature of suffering and the very meaning of justice. According to Sheila A. Redmond,

> The value placed on suffering in the Christian context has at least three important aspects. First, since the Christian god is just and merciful, if one has suffered, one has sinned. Suffering is part of the punishment meted out to those who disobey. Second, suffering and repentance teach humility and are the way back to forgiveness from this Christian god. Third, martyrdom, which is an extreme form of suffering, holds a special place of honor within the Christian tradition.[64]

It is the opinion of a number of feminist and liberation scholars that the glorification of Jesus' suffering—to the extent that it is worshipped as much as any action can be—is a glorification of suffering in general. The recent film *The Passion of the Christ* is an example of just such glorification. As Brown and Parker put it, "To sanction the suffering and death of Jesus, even when calling it unjust, so that God can be active in the world, only serves to perpetute the acceptance of the very suffering against which one is struggling."[65] On this same subject feminist theologian Carter Heyward has written,

> Any theology which is promulgated on an assumption that followers of Jesus, Christians, must welcome pain and death as a sign of faith is constructed upon a faulty hermeneutic of what Jesus was doing and of why he died. This theological masochism is completely devoid of passion. This notion of welcoming, or submitting oneself gladly to, injustice flies in the face of Jesus' own refusal to make concession to unjust relation.[66]

Thus the real question for us is this: what is the effect of this glorification of suffering on the daily lives of Christians? According to feminist and liberation theologians, the toll has been great, especially when, in most strands of Christian practice, we have been exhorted to follow Jesus' example, to accept suffering and oppression willingly, even gladly, even "for our own good" or for the good of those we love. We have, in fact, been told a number of stories of how suffering is a good and right thing for the edification of a Christian's life. Brown and Parker write,

> Suffering is sanctioned as an experience that frees others, perhaps even God. The imitator of Christ, which every faithful person is exhorted to be, can find herself choosing to endure suffering because she has become convinced that through her pain another whom she lives with escapes pain. The disciple's role is to suffer in the place of others, as Jesus suffered for us all. But this glorification of suffering as salvific, held before us daily in the image of Jesus hanging from the cross, encourages women who are being abused to be more concerned about their victimizer than about themselves. Children who are abused are forced most keenly to face the conflict between the claims of a parent who professes love and the inner self, which protests violation.[67]

Messages such as these have far-reaching implications for intimate relations of all kinds. Brown and Parker continue,

> When a theology identifies love with suffering, what resources will its culture offer to such a child? And when parents have an image of a God righteously demanding the total obedience of "his" son—even obedience to death—what will prevent the parent from engaging in divinely sanctioned child abuse? The image of God the father demanding and carrying out the suffering and death of his own son has sustained a culture of abuse and led to the

> abandonment of victims of abuse and oppression. Until this image is shattered it will be almost impossible to create a just society.[68]

Thus, while the image of God the "Father" (or even God as "Parent" or "Mother" in inclusive liturgies) has indeed been comforting for many, it will be a problematic image so long as there is parental abuse in the world.

In addition, the image of Jesus as the suffering servant has been particularly destructive for women. Suffering in silence, caring for and giving their lives for the men and the institutions around them, women not only identify with the unjust sacrifice of Christ on the cross, but are compelled to repeat it with their own flesh and blood on the Golgotha of their own professional and family lives. Heyward writes,

> ...in carrying the sins of the male half of the world on their shoulders, women are discovering that they have allowed men to escape from the responsibility of bearing their own burdens and coming to terms with their own sin and guilt... Thus the suffering servant role model, a product of the patriarchal consciousness, has *functioned to perpetuate that very dichotomy and alienation between human beings that the tradition claims to overcome.* In accepting that particular interpretation of the Christ even as normative for their lives, women have participated in their own crucifixion. As feminists, we must exorcise that image from our midst in order to discover the roots of that true reconciliation which can only come about between equals (Emphasis mine).[69]

Thus, for many Christians, a theology of crucifixion and suffering is the very antithesis of the Gospel. It is not healing or liberating, but instead alienating and destructive.

There is a great irony in Christianity: we are told that Christ "died once for all" and that the crucifixion spelled the end of the power of suffering and death for believers, and yet we are compelled both subtly and explicitly to go forth and repeat that great act of sacrifice ourselves, as if God were not quite satisfied, as if just a little more suffering—ours—would be enough to redeem the world, or at least those we love and care about

In fact, however, for women, it is literally impossible to succeed, revealing this model to be a dead end. For women trained by our culture to be servants and victims, the "suffering servant" model offers little hope. Mary Daly writes,

> The qualities that Christianity idealizes, especially for women, are also those of a victim: sacrificial love, passive acceptance of suffering, humility, meekness, etc. Since these are the qualities idealized in Jesus "who died for our sins," his functioning as a model reinforces the scapegoat syndrome for women. Given the victimized situation of the female in sexist society, these "virtues" are hardly the qualities that women should be encouraged to have. Moreover, since women cannot be "good" enough to measure up to this ideal, and since all are by sexual definition alien from the male savior, this is an impossible model. Thus doomed to failure even in emulating the Victim, women are plunged more deeply into victimization.[70]

The pervasiveness of the "suffering servant" model is apparent when we realize that women have been given *no other model* within which to live out their faith. The highest woman in the Christian "pantheon" is Mary. Although she becomes "the mother of God," she does so only by becoming God's handmaiden (Lk. 1:46-55).

When many women come to this realization, it is difficult to continue in the church. Until they can see an alternative to the "suffering servant" model, there is no place for them. As Brown and Parker describe,

> The only legitimate reason for women to remain in the church will be if the church were to condemn as anathema the glorification of suffering. Only if the church is the place where cycles of abuse are named, condemned, and broken can it be a haven of blessing and a place of peace for women. That the church is such a place is not clearly evident. Whether Christianity in essence frees or imprisons is the issue that must be considered.[71]

All of which is not to say that there is no value in sacrifice. There are few parents who have not "gone without" for the good of their children. The tales of many battlefield veterans are filled with noble stories of one soldier giving his life for his comrades. And this selfless giving of ourselves is indeed part of what makes us both human and blessed.

We are far from being blessed, however, when such extraordinary measures are forced upon us as a way of daily living. Sacrifice must be chosen, the will to give neither mundane nor insincere. It is not something for which one can be groomed, and it is certainly not a redemptive "way of life." For those who have been taught that it is their place to suffer and sacrifice, it is only human—indeed it is inevitable—that resentment results more often than redemption. As Ruth Duck writes,

> Self-giving without self-nurture can lead to sin. Personal needs are rarely suppressed entirely; they emerge in disguised and perhaps destructive ways. Those who sacrifice themselves for others may be "helpful" in ways that subvert others' growth. A life-style of self-sacrifice without self-nurture creates tired, distracted people who may lack good judgment about ethics or make mistakes that endanger human lives. Further, when self-sacrifice is expected of some social groups and not others, injustice and abuse are supported.[72]

Such a situation can lead to the sins of not honoring oneself, not properly caring for oneself, and looking to others for a sense of one's own worth or identity. And while the suffering God carries great weight in our imaginations, the suffering human servant does not inspire us to awe, since it is a servant's lot in life to suffer. As Procter-Smith says, "the idea of sacrifice carries no transformative message for those, like women, who are expected to be sacrificial by nature."[73] Thus we have for centuries thrust upon women an inhuman yoke in the name of the one who promises a yoke that is "easy and light" (Matt. 11:30), robbing them of the gift of their own volition to offer legitimate or meaningful personal sacrifices, and also of the possibility that their sufferings might be redemptive for someone, anyone, if not for themselves.

All of this was for what Hardesty called above a "faulty hermeneutic of the crucifixion."[74] We in the West have put much emphasis on the sacrificial death of Christ as the pivotal moment of redemption. Thus the consecration in the Eucharist occurs during the institutional narrative, which is interpreted as a metaphor for Jesus' impending death. Early Christians did not share this assumption, nor do the Eastern Orthodox today. As we shall see in the following section, the Eastern church views the crucifixion as almost incidental in comparison with the Resurrection. In the East the transformative moment in the Eucharist occurs at the *epiclesis*, the prayer for the descent of Holy Spirit upon the elements, symbolizing the eventual "divinization" afforded all creation by virtue of Christ's resurrection. Since for early and Eastern Christians, the Resurrection, rather than the crucifixion, is the pivotal point in redemption history, what, we may ask, is an appropriate view of the crucifixion that does not glorify suffering, and yet can appreciate Jesus' intentions?

Harrison and Heyward offer one perspective:

> God did not send Jesus to the cross as a test of his faith, as punishment for his sin, or to build his character. The Romans crucified Jesus and made him a victim of overt and deadly anti-Semitic violence. It was a devastating experience for Jesus' followers who watched him murdered. They were overwhelmed by fear, despair, and meaninglessness. They left the scene of the crucifixion feeling abandoned and betrayed by God. *The resurrection and subsequent events were the surprising realization that in the midst of profound suffering, God is present and new life is possible.*
>
> *This retrospective realization in no way justified the suffering: it transformed it.* It presented the possibility of new life coming forth from the pain of suffering. Sometimes Jesus' crucifixion is misinterpreted as being the model for suffering: since Jesus went to the cross, persons should bear their own crosses of irrational violence (for example, rape) without complaint. But Jesus' crucifixion does not sanctify suffering. It remains a witness to the horror of violence done to another and an identification with the suffering that people experience. It is not a model of how suffering should be borne but a witness to God's desire that no one should have to suffer such violence again. The resurrection, the realization that the Christ was present to the disciples and is present to us, transformed but never justified the suffering and death experience. The people were set free from the pain of that experience to realize the newness of life among them despite the suffering (Emphasis mine).[75]

Thus it is not the purpose of the cross to inspire us to re-enact that archetypal sacrifice in the little mystery plays of our lives, but to so horrify us that we will do all in our power to prevent such horror from ever befalling another human being. *The cross should be for us a symbol of the beginning of the end of suffering, not the beginning of a movement of suffering.*

If the cross is not the central moment of salvation history, it is also not a model given to us to imitate. Instead it serves as testimony that there is great injustice and inequity to be faced and overcome. The central moment should be for us, as it was to the early Christians, the Resurrection, which, far from encouraging us to seek out ever greater opportunities to suffer, offers hope that God will not abandon us in what suffering we cannot avoid when we choose to enter fully into life. As Brown and Parker say,

> It is true that fullness of life cannot be experienced without openness to all truth, all reality; fullness of life involves feeling the pain of the world. But it is not true that being open to all of life is the equivalent of choosing to suffer. Nor is it right to see the death of Jesus as a symbol for the life-giving power of receptivity to reality.
>
> It is not acceptance of suffering that gives life. The question, morever, is not, Am I willing to suffer? but, Do I desire fully to live? This distinction is subtle and, to some, specious, but in the end it makes a great difference in how people interpret and respond to suffering. If you believe that acceptance of suffering gives life, then your resources for confronting perpetrators of violence and abuse will be numbed."[76]

Thus, the cross inspires us to face the realities of our lives with courage, embracing both the joys and the challenges. It tells us that conviction can come with consequences. But the resurrection gives us hope that if we dare to enter fully into life, to fight for the dignity of others, to speak truth to those who have power over us, to stand and fall for the community that God is striving to create in our midst, that all will not be lost. Beverly Wildung Harrison writes that,

> ...those who love justice, and have their passion shaped toward right relation, act not because they are enamored of sacrifice. Rather, they are moved by a love strong enough to sustain their action for the right relation, even unto death... Jesus' paradigmatic role in the story of our salvation rests not in his willingness to sacrifice himself, but in his passionate love of right relations and his refusal to cease to embody the power-of-relation in the face of that which would thwart it. It was his refusal to desist from radical love, not a preoccupation with sacrifice, which makes his work irreplaceable.[77]

A further important aspect of the cross is what it tells us about God in Christ. Without glorifying suffering in the least, the crucifixion reveals that the Incarnation was not a sham: God was not "playing along" at this humanity thing. In Jesus' death, the entire cycle of human life was revealed to and felt by the Creator.

The crucifixion also provides us with a "snapshot" of what is true for all time: that even though we spat on him, cursed him, violated him in the most ghastly ways, God in Jesus did not abandon us, but remained faithful to the end. The crucifix is an icon of this truth, that no matter how we hate, torture, abuse and despoil each other, this planet, the whole of Creation (and therefore the Creator), God does not abandon us. Instead, as Jesus did on the Cross, God endures our betrayal, remaining in compassionate union with us, continuing to call us to repentance and transformation.

This is the God of Process Theology, whom Alfred North Whitehead termed "the fellow sufferer who understands." In this paradigm there is nothing glorious about Christ's death. It is tragedy pure and simple. But in it we see truth: that the God who feels what we feel does not abandon us to our lot, but as with the children of Israel, God walks with us through the Red Sea; as with Shadrach, Meshach, and Abednego, God is with us in the fiery furnace, not rescuing us by magic, but suffering as we suffer.

But because the Process God is also endlessly creative and perpetually creating, there is also the promise of transformation and resurrection. Fortune writes,

> Transformation is the alternative to endurance and passivity. It is grounded in the conviction of hope and empowered by a passion for justice in the face of injustice. It is the faith that the way things are is not the way things have to be. It is a trust in the righteous anger in the face of evil which pushes people to action. Transformation is the means by which, refusing to accept injustice and refusing to assist its victims to endure suffering any longer, people act. We celebrate small victories, we chip away at oppressive attitudes cast in concrete, we say no in unexpected places, we speak boldly of things deemed secret and unmentionable, we stand with those who are trapped in victimization to support their journeys to safety and healing, and we break the cycle of violence we may have known in our lives. By

> refusing to endure evil and by seeking to transform suffering, we are about God's work of making justice and healing brokenness.[78]

Thus, Jesus calls us not to mirror his suffering, but to proclaim his Gospel: to take a stand for right relationships regardless of the consequences. Ruether tells us, "Jesus as liberator calls for a renunciation, a dissolution, of the web of status relationships by which societies have defined privilege and deprivation."[79]

An appropriate imitation of Christ for all those who suffer from oppression is not to suffer in silence, but to speak up and act. Rosa Parks is an imitator of Christ, not because she suffered for taking her stand (or keeping her seat, in her case), but because she had the courage to believe in her own dignity and fought for it in spite of the conflict that resulted. Nelson Mandela is an imitator of Christ, not because he suffered in prison, but because he held out for peace and justice, and led a nation to resurrection. In each case it is not the suffering that is redemptive, but the courage to pursue justice in the face of pain and evil.

Believers who accept the doctrine of the substitutionary atonement usually emphasize personal, individual salvation. One lay person I interviewed identified the primary issue facing the church today as "the relation between global justice and personal salvation." This insight needs to be explored. The Bible, in fact, knows nothing of individual salvation; its story is the history of two peoples: the Jews and the early Christians. For both, God acts on behalf of the community. Sin is regarded in terms of its effect on the community, and God's redemptive activity has always been for the salvation of the Jews and the church as a people.

In the Protestant West, however, the notion of collective salvation has been downplayed and the importance of individualized salvation and personal, individual relationship to God is preeminent, reaching its extreme form in fundamentalist Evangelical thought. This individualizing has been harmful not only for women and oppressed people who have been told that the salvation of their immortal souls is dependant upon toeing the patriarchal line, but also destructive for the self-concept of the church as being "one people." This has resulted in the extreme fragmentation into many sects and denominations, some of whom disdain all other Christians, let alone non-Christians.

Not surprisingly, the individualizing of salvation has resulted also in the individualizing of sin. When this happens, according to Ruether,

> ...Sin is recognized only in the individual acts, not structural systems. One is called to examine one's sinfulness in terms of abuses of oneself and personal unkindnesss to one's neighbor, but not in terms of the vast collective structures of war, racism, poverty, and, least of all, the oppression of women. In more sophisticated circles, Reinhold Niebuhr's division between "moral man" and "immoral society" is used to declare that altrusim and love is possible, if at all, only on the interpersonal level. Collective groups, especially large ones, like nation-states, can only pursue an ethic of self-interest.[80]

In our focus on personal sin, we have completely ignored both the majority of sins "committed," as well as the gravest. As we keep our attention turned exclusively toward personal morality, social morality is completely ignored. This privatization is not limited to the Evangelical tradition. Within the Catholic tradition, much emphasis has been placed on private, sexual sin. Catholic moral theology, in fact, seems obsessed with it. This emphasis, according to Ross, "keeps the stress on Christian living within the home and not in the wider society."[81]

Not surprisingly, when our attention is kept firmly on ourselves, our awareness of others suffers. The most disastrous effect of the privatization of sin and salvation is the myopic disregard for Creation. Systems theorists and deep ecologists are now forcefully speaking the truths that seemed self-evident to native peoples: we are not separate from this earth. The hierarchical conception of the universe put forth by the apostle Paul with God the Father as King, Christ as Prince and so on down the hierarchy to women at the bottom of the list, ignores those even lower on the ladder: children, animals and finally the earth (1 Cor. 11:3). Ever since the Manichean heresy entered the church (largely through Augustine), the Gnostic notion that the Creation and the body are corrupt and evil, existing only to tempt "men's" minds from "things above," has been prevalent, especially in the Western church. Thus, for centuries the earth has been seen as something given to us as property, to govern as we will, without consideration for its own holiness and dignity.

This attitude of disdain for Creation has taken a new and apocalyptic form recently, growing out of contemporary Evangelical eschatology. Many Evangelicals take the position that since Jesus is going to come back any moment now, and it is "all going to burn" anyway, we should not waste any energy worrying about the earth, especially when there are "individual" human souls to save.

The problem with this line of thought is that every generation of Christians has believed the *parousia*[82] was at hand. What if Jesus were to delay another 2,000 years? What kind of earth will our grandchildren's grandchildren inherit? How will they live while they are about the work of saving the souls of their own generation?

For Christians who are not Evangelicals, this picture looks even worse. The Evangelical doctrine of the "rapture," when all the Christians are caught up into heaven and the earth is literally left to go to hell, is not a doctrine of the historical church and has only been around for 200 years. For non-Evangelicals, Christ's coming is thought of in a much more metaphorical manner, which has prevented most of the church from falling into the same "it's all going to burn anyway" mentality. For most mainline or "liberal" Christians the Second Coming will be realized when the Community of God is manifest on earth, when the church succeeds, not in "saving souls" from some alleged debt of sin to God, but in preaching the Good News of Jesus: the liberation of all from fear, oppression, and desperate poverty.

This "all" includes the earth. So long as we set ourselves above it as its ruler in a divinely ordained chain of command, we will continue to exploit and abuse it. But many Christians are discovering, as Walter Rauschenbusch says, that "our universe is not a despotic monarchy with God above the starry canopy and ourselves down here; it is a spiritual commonwealth with God in the midst of us."[83] Ruether writes,

> An ecological-feminist theology of nature must rethink the whole Western theological tradition of hierarchical chain of being and chain of command. This theology must question the hierarchy of human over nonhuman nature as a relationship of ontological and moral value. It must challenge the right of the human to treat the nonhuman as private property and material wealth to be exploited. It must unmask the structures of social domination, male over

> female, owner over worker, that mediate this domination of nonhuman nature. Finally, it must question the model of hierarchy that starts with non-material spirit (God) as the source of the chain of being and continues down to non-spiritual "matter" as the bottom of the chain of being and the most inferior, valueless, and dominated point in the chain of commmand.[84]

The gift of intelligence does not give us the right to exploit those without intelligence—that is, intelligence as we understand it. Rather, it is our responsibility to care for the defenseless and to protect those without voice.

A theology of corporate salvation thus includes not only the peoples of the earth, but the earth itself. Just as the early church taught that we are saved as a people or not at all, the insights of our century have made it clear that we will be saved as a planet or not at all. So long as we continue to see ourselves as "rulers of the earth," we shall continue in our corporate sin. For if the earth has no future, we have no future. If mother earth who is being crucified is not resurrected, then all the Eucharistic feasts of the Divinity thread[85] that have ever been celebrated will have been for naught. If, as the early church taught, the whole of creation has been redeemed in Christ and is in the process of resurrection, we should start preaching—and living this truth.

Christology and the Abdication of Power

Related to the question of Christ's suffering being redemptive is the very question of who Jesus was and what his intentions were. If Christ's death was not itself redemptive or even unique in the pains of the world, what is the role of Jesus as Christ? How can Jesus—a male—be Christ for women? And, perhaps most importantly, who is Jesus for us in the twenty-first century?

Whether Jesus was in some way a unique incarnation of God has been the subject of much debate in our time. The arguments have been fierce, because the possibility that Jesus' Incarnation was *not* unique threatens the power of the institutional church. As a result, the church's teachings about Jesus have paid lip service to the Incarnation, while in fact being frighteningly Docetic: Jesus' humanness has frequently been glossed over in our adoration of his status as the second person of the Trinity. Thus, the earthiness, indeed, the humanity of Jesus' real ministry has likewise been glossed over in the interest of a "sacramental" preoccupation with transcendence.

This is ironic; the inseparability of the divine and the earthly is precisely what sacramentality is all about. This is the meaning of the doctrine of the Incarnation. Jesus does not embody God because he "came down from heaven" visiting upon the earth God's glory, but because God's glory is so pervasive in the Creation that God can be embodied in it as it is.

Turning theology on its ear like that was one of Jesus' own peculiar charms. We tend to forget that he was executed as a heretic because he had some radical ideas that did not sit well with the religious authorities who pretended to wield the power of salvation over the masses. The poor and the ignorant had no hope of salvation in Jesus' time because salvation came through knowing the Law and keeping it. The "faithful" of Jesus' time were those who were wealthy enough to have the leisure time to educate themselves in the Law. Only the rich had the means to live in the state of grace that God "required." Yet Jesus ridiculed the religious leaders of his day, called those obsessed with the Law "a brood of vipers," and to the horror of all, shared the holy Sabbath table with outcasts and sinners. What was his intention?

It is hard for us to understand the radicalness of some of Jesus' actions, because we are not privy to the cultural assumptions and expectations of his day. The story of Jesus drinking water at the well with the Samaritan woman sounds quaint, yet it is essentially the same kind of scandal that many pre-civil rights Alabamans would have felt if a white man—especially a priest or minister who had the responsibility to uphold the God-given order—had disregarded cultural taboo and ate a meal with a black woman in a section of a diner designated for "Negroes Only."

Feminist theologians are divided on the import of Jesus' maleness. While some gloss over it, stating, as Aldredge-Clanton does, that "the maleness of the earthly Jesus, just like his Jewishness, has no ontological significance,"[86] others feel that only as a male could Jesus have taught what he did with such power and integrity in his time and culture.[87] And only a male could abdicate the power-over authority that was a male's birthright in first century Israel. A woman in Jesus' time could have preached about surrendering power-over, but only someone with that power in the first place can actually surrender it. Thus for many feminists, it is "...both historically significant and theologically important for a feminist interpretation that Jesus was historically seen as a male."[88]

This surrendering and abdication of power is Jesus' primary mode of action, going back even, according to St. Paul, to the Incarnation event itself:

> Let the same mind be in you that was in Christ Jesus, who, though he was in the form of God, did not regard equality with God as something to be exploited, but emptied himself, taking the form of a slave, being born in human likeness. And being found in human form, he humbled himself and became obedient to the point of death—even death on a cross (Phillipians 2:5-8).

Continuing throughout his life and ministry, Jesus repeatedly rejects the social privileges and prejudices enforced in his culture, and considers even the lowliest persons his equal. The *Tao Te Ching* says prophetically that "only one who assumes the shame of a people is worthy to redeem them" (Poem 16). Jesus' redemption of the tax collectors, widows and orphans, prostitutes, and other "sinners" occurs not in paying some cosmic debt on the cross to the Monster God, but by identifying himself with these outcasts as his friends and his spiritual community.

The relief felt by the myriads of outcasts that followed Jesus is hard for us to imagine. Here is a rabbi and religious authority, who breaks as many laws as they do (and on purpose!), and who treats them as people with dignity and purpose. Suddenly, those who have been told since birth that they are pariahs in the sight of God are being invited to the table of God's blessing as if they owed no debt to God for their—or their ancestors'—sin. As Albert Nolan writes,

> By accepting them as friends and equals Jesus had taken away their shame, humiliation and guilt. By showing them that they mattered to him as people he gave them a sense of dignity and released them from their captivity. The physical contact that he must have had with them when reclining at table and that he obviously never dreamed of disallowing (Lk 7:38-39) must have made them feel clean and acceptable.
>
> Moreover, because Jesus was looked upon as a man of God and a prophet, they would have interpreted his gesture of friendship as God's approval of them. They were

> now acceptable to God. Their sinfulness, ignorance and uncleanness had been overlooked and were no longer being held against them.[90]

In his life and ministry, Jesus abdicates his social standing, his reputation amongst the religious leaders, and eventually his life, all for the privilege of sharing his bread with sinners. *That* is redemption.

Jesus dies in the same spirit. The old evangelical hymn states, "He could have called ten thousand angels to destroy the world and set him free...,"[91] yet even in death he abdicates his power and privilege and dies as any mortal does.

If, as stated above, the *imitatio dei* for oppressed peoples is in courageously standing for the truth, heedless of the cost, the *imitatio dei* for those who are privileged and in authority is the voluntary abdication of privilege and authority, sharing in the redeeming work of Christ by assuming equality with every person regardless of their gender, social station, or perceived morality. The radicalness of Jesus' demand that the disciples be "servants of one another" lies in its direction at those who do not see themselves as servants, but as free "men," which the disciples certainly were. As Ruether writes,

> Central to Jesus' message is a radical criticism of...ideological deformation of religion. The first will be last and the last first. The poor will be filled with good things, the mighty put down from their thrones. The prostitutes and the tax collectors will go into the Kingdom of God ahead of the Scribes and Pharisees. This language in the Gospels belongs to the tradition that criticizes existing power systems and places God on the side of the oppressed. But Jesus criticized the temptation to see this simply as a reversed system of domination and privilege. Rather he pressed beyond the critique of the present order to a more radical vision, a revolutionary transformative process that will bring all to a new mode of relationship.[92]

Try to imagine the force of this teaching in the lives of the early followers of Jesus. They were being told that not only were they forgiven and accepted by God, but that they were truly free: slaves were not subject to their masters, women were not subject to men, and "sinners" were not subject to religious "authorities." Thus Jesus can say of himself in the Temple: "The Spirit is upon me, because God has anointed me to bring good news to the poor. God has sent me to proclaim release to the captives and recovery of sight to the blind, to let the oppressed go free, to proclaim the year of the God's favor" (Lk. 4:18-19).

This is the cornerstone of Christology. Jesus does not teach these things because he is the anointed one—just the opposite: Jesus is the anointed one because he teaches these things! Furthermore, Jesus could say, "Your sins are forgiven you," not because he was himself forgiving any sins, but because he was stating the simple truth: that God holds nothing against us, never has, and never will. *We are forgiven.* Likewise we are the Body of Christ when we proclaim the same message, and not the other way around.

Power-Over in the Church's Government

This has profound implications for what it means to be "church." Jesus tells the disciples in no uncertain terms what will distinguish them from the religious authorities of his day:

> But Jesus called them to him and said, "You know that the rulers of the Gentiles lord it over them, and their great ones are tyrants over them. It will not be so among you; but whoever wishes to be great among you must be your servant, and whoever wishes to be first among you must be your slave" (Matt. 20:25-27).

Lao Tzu said, "the Sage puts himself last and finds himself in the foremost place" (Poem 31). Likewise, Jesus leads by not leading: the true master lives as a servant. Only in this way is true ministry possible. Unfortunately, the church has a short memory. Jesus' ideal of "servants not lords" was not to survive two centuries after his death, and we still use the term "Lord" today, long after it has lost any secular meaning, especially in the United States. Since the imperialization of Christianity under Constantine, all of the abuses and pharisaical attitudes which Jesus railed against during his earthly ministry became institutional in the church which hailed him as Lord.

This power-over wielded by the clergy has been a tragic source of pain for many Christians. When I asked one man about the most painful aspects of the Eucharist for him, he replied, "Seeing the Eucharist and its corollaries used to dominate and oppress; seeing it used to drive a fellow parishioner mad and eventually to suicide." One woman I interviewed had very similar feelings. She said,

> Some priests...seem to believe that the Eucharist is a magic trick that only they are licensed to perform. Their "audience" should be passive and give them great affirmation for their tricks. To them, they are the sole mediators of Grace. They treat their parishoners as beneath them... The rigid hierarchy of the Catholic Church, with its righteous and self-affirming attitudes...has more invested in preserving and extending its power than in promoting the healthy faith of Church members. They seem like parents who make a huge and equal issue over a child wilfully stealing and accidentally breaking a glass. It is all about power—and making the people powerless... When I experience the Eucharist at their hands, I find little of the holy and am left feeling sad that they miss the wonder...

The worst abuse of this sort in contemporary times is the withholding of communion from secular leaders because of their voting record, as in the recent furor over John Kerry. This is clearly the use of a sacrament as an instrument of political coercion.

The pain of this struggle was of much concern to Jesus and to many Christians throughout the ages. Not until the Reformation was the monolithic imperial "version" of the Gospel successfully challenged. Even then, the attempts to democratize the various churches of the Reformation met with only limited success. The English and German Reformations left the episcopal authority intact, while others complained that even in the Genevan Reformation, "presbyter is but priest writ large." The most successful Christian attempts to throw off the episcopal hierarchy were made by the Anabaptists and the English Puritans, or Congregationalists. For both movements the church is understood to be the local community of believers, a discipleship of equals. This local community is the *church in this place* and is united to the universal body of Christ by the agency of the Holy Spirit, not episcopal succession.

In both of these movements each local congregation is sovereign unto itself, electing its clergy from among its own numbers and sharing equally the responsibility for administration, worship, and spiritual education. The episcopal churches have been slow to acknowledge the wisdom and the true Gospel fidelity of these movements, and they deserve our respect and attention, for these "humble churches" have much to teach us.

An unfortunate side effect of these churches' "jettisoning of the episcopacy" was the attendant rejection of a large portion of our Christian heritage as well. The Reformation churches have always struggled with what to keep and what to be rid of, and are sometimes accused of "throwing out the baby with the bathwater." Finding a balance between what should be cherished and what needs rethinking in Christian tradition is as difficult a concern for us today as it was for Martin Luther or Thomas Cranmer.

The liturgical movement has been helpful on this score. While cherishing the Western liturgical tradition as a vital link to our apostolic heritage and as an expression of our unity, the movement has nonetheless rightfully addressed issues of power as well. As Procter-Smith reports,

> The liturgical movement's concern with clericalism has focused...on redefining the minister's role as servant to the worshipping community, and has attempted to curtail abuses such as gratuitous concelebrations, the multiplication of unnecessary clergy in roles of leadership, and the clerical usurpation of the people's liturgical actions such as the prayers of the people and the kiss of peace. The use of the image of the servant as a corrective to clericalism is useful only from the perspective of those who already have authority to exercise, and need help in redefining that power.[93]

Communities that start from scratch have the advantage of not having to justify existing roles. The Festival of the Holy Names—an alternative Christian community in Berkeley, California, where much of the field work for this book was done—is just such a community. Comprised mostly of Christians from liturgical traditions (Episcopal, Roman Catholic, and Lutheran) with a Baptist and an occasional Unitarian Universalist joining in, the Festival proclaimed the "royal priesthood of all peoples" (1 Pet. 2:9), and had no designated clergy. This had been a vital part of the Festival's identity as a liberation community.

At the Festival, which met on Sunday nights, members took turns presiding at the Eucharist. There were two presiders for every Festival, usually a man and a woman, or two women. An occasional "presider's workshop" helped prepare the shyer members for the task. This sharing of presiding responsibilities was significant for the celebrators at the Festival, as the majority of them were clergy, seminarians and active laity who served at parishes in their own denominations on Sunday mornings. They welcomed a space where administrative power was exercised only by consensus, and where issues of authority and leadership could be explored and questioned without fear or the need to justify previous positions. This kind of community not surprisingly caused some distress to casual observers. Ruether writes,

> Many people assume that if "just anyone" presides at the Eucharist or baptism, it will be done in a sloppy or uninformed way that will erode the seriousness of the symbol. But this is not so if the members of the community are really becoming skilled and empowered to minister. European basic communities accomplish this by dividing the larger community into smaller study groups that reflect on Scripture and study theology and tradition together. These small reflection groups then become the base for the development of preaching and Eucharist. Each week a different reflection group takes responsibility for preparing the homily out of their discussion, and the whole community then enters into dialogue. The reflection group also shapes the songs and symbolic expressions of the Eucharist to reflect the theme of the week's reflection.[94]

This kind of structure frees—and trains—the community to do true ministry. Instead of the old model of ministry where the clergy hand down the bread from heaven, in this new model "ministry means exercising power in a new way, as a means of liberating one another. Service to others does not deplete the person who ministers, but rather causes her (or him) to become more liberated. Ministry overcomes competitive one-up, one-down relationships and generates relations of mutual empowerment."[95]

This model is genuinely Christian, as it abdicates all hierarchical power relationships and proclaims the discipleship of equals modeled by Jesus in his ministry.[96]

Freed from the administrative tyranny that perpetually tries to remake the church in its own image and in its own self-interest, Festival participants were at liberty to explore such all-important questions as "how do we make church *for us*?" in a way few have ever experienced before.

Feminist and liberation theologians have been exploring for some time what changes are required to form authentic—and authentically Christian—communities. In nearly every critique, the dismantling of clericalism and the embracing of power-with, or *co-agency,* is one of the most important. If, as we have been discussing, the primary crisis of the contemporary church is one of power, then the primary corrective must be the recovery of shared agency.

Instead of church being a show put on for an "audience," a one-way communication system (that some would argue is no communication at all), agency demands "the right and responsibility of those most deeply affected to bring their own views, experiences, and even shortcomings to the table. It is a community of ethical agents that will begin to formulate a meaningful, erotic theology."[97] As one layperson I interviewed said, "Celebrants who do not truly celebrate 'with' the people should not be doing it."

At the Festival, this need is addressed at a monthly planning meeting, where anyone—even someone who has attended only once—is welcome to come and share equal voice and equal vote in all Festival affairs. Once the planning meeting has started, there are no forbidden subjects as all struggle towards consensus. In this way, "rather than [being] viewed as something one has to the exclusion or diminishment of another, power and authority are exercised in community in a way that empowers and authorizes others."[98]

The Italian Basic Christian Community Movement has described what it calls "reappropriation theology," which reclaims clerical power for the people. Ruether describes the movement:

> Clericalism has expropriated the people's collective participation in ministry, word, and sacrament. Reappropriation theology reflects on and facilitates the taking back of ministry, word, and sacrament by the people. Reappropriation of the sacraments means that not only the exercise but also the interpretation of the sacraments arises from the community's collective experience of its life in grace. The baptism of each individual involves all members of the community, who midwife each other's rebirth from alienated to authentic life. Penance means forgiving one another, it is not the disciplinary tool of any elite. Eucharist is not an objectified piece of bread or cup of wine that is magically transformed into the body and blood of Christ. Rather, it is the people, the *ecclesia*, who are being transformed into the body of the new humanity, infused with the blood of new life. The symbols stand in the midst of and represent that communal reality.[99]

For the Italian Base Communities, as for the Festival, the people have assumed the right and responsibility to create community for each other, to celebrate and administer the sacraments as servants and priests of one another, and also to decide what the sacraments mean to *them* as a community.

In the estimation of many theologians such as Schüssler Fiorenza, this sort of egalitarian model is a return to early church practice, recalling that the early church was "countercultural, radically egalitarian, and inclusive."[100] Fiorenza holds that her "egalitarian model for the reconstruction of early Christianity accounts for both the traditions of women's leadership in the church and for the process of the church's practical adaptation to and theological legitimation of the patriarchy of its Greco-Roman cultural setting."[101]

This raises the issue of women's ordination, which is of paramount importance to our discussion. In churches whose structures necessitate clergy (the majority, of course), this egalitarian model is not so easily implemented. Given that, however, the re-visioning of the role of the clergy as "servant" mentioned above in connection with the liturgical movement is certainly progress.

Another useful image is that of "healer." Brock writes,

> In healing the function of the healer is not to gain power but to share it. In the sharing process, woundedness reveals the sacred. Between healer and sufferer, an inequality of power exists that denies the afflicted the capacity to become whole. Hence, the flow of power between the healer and afflicted represents the balancing of power inequalities and the emergence of wholeness.[102]

Thus the healer is one who *shares his or her power* in order to empower—and heal—others. This model needs to be taught in seminaries, for, just as in domestic situations, people who have been wounded by the church are more likely to perpetuate abusive situations rather than to correct them.[103] Instead, the minister-as-healer assists those who have forgotten or been denied their worth to rediscover it in empowering and redemptive ways. As Brock says, "remembrance of ourselves requires a loving person who helps us search, who is not afraid of the painfulness of the search, and who can mirror back our deeply rediscovered selves."[104] In this way a re-visioned clergy can play a vital and necessary role, a role performed today in our society only by professional psychologists.

The subject of clergy is of course a painful one for women, who, until this century, have been denied leadership roles in our churches, and have been relegated to "supportive" roles and ministries. This arrangement is of the familiar "man is the head over women, as Christ is head over the church" variety, which unfortunately finds support in the Pauline epistles.[105]

Although in some Protestant denominations women pastors are becoming commonplace, we must remember that not all communions have made such progress. When well over half of the world's Christians still cannot witness a woman at the altar of Christ, the struggle is not by any means won. With the recent exception of the Church of England and many member churches of the Anglican Communion, none of the historical Catholic churches ordain women. Within the tiny Old Catholic Communion of Utrecht a split has recently occured over this very issue. The German Old Catholics ordained their first women priests in the summer of 1996, without the consent of the Archbishop of Utrecht. One bishop of the Old Catholic diaspora writes passionately,

> A week from Sunday, Pentecost Sunday, the first women "priests" shall be ordained and forced down the throats of Traditional Old Catholics everywhere, begging a question from me, an American Old Catholic bishop: What does this mean for our movement? How does it unify the same? Am I to become a pagan now, at the risk of being labeled a male sexist pig, should I refuse to unite myself to such an action? Will I be forced to leave the Old Catholic Movement, as I was forced to leave the Anglican Church because of this brazen heresy? Am I to preach Artemis, Athenia, and Isis, instead of the Historic Father, handed down to me by way of the Apostles? What about the vows I took to the Church and to God, to remain faithful to the historic teachings? Are they to count for nothing, now that "He" is to be destroyed? If I maintain my orthodox position, have I permanently excluded myself from membership in the international counsel of Old Catholic bishops?

The Polish National Catholic Church, the largest Old Catholic group in the United States, did indeed sever its communion with Utrecht over the European Church's ordination of women.

Even within the American Lutheran churches there is no consensus. While the more liberal Evangelical Lutheran Church in America

(ELCA) has ordained women since 1970, they are the only Lutheran body in the U.S. to do so. This is ironic, since, as Ross points out, "In his stress on the priesthood of all believers, Luther unwittingly paved the way for the ordination of women to the ministry by describing all people, women as well as men, as priests to one another."[106]

The pain that this exclusion has caused women is difficult to communicate. Perhaps among men, only black men and the men of other oppressed peoples could begin to glimpse the psychological damage done to women as a result of this exclusion, especially as women have increasingly discovered their personhood, identity, and worth in the latter half of our century.

While there is certainly a long way to go before the church embraces the equality necessary to become the Community of God, the tide is turning. This pain is not just women's pain: it is the birth pain of the church as a whole. When St. Paul wrote, "If one member suffers, all suffer together; if one member is honored, all rejoice together," (1 Cor. 12:26) he could not have been addressing any other issue more appropriately. As long as some are not free, none of us is free. As long as the church insists that "some are more equal than others" there is no equality. But change is happening, and more change is coming. And with it, as the Old Catholic observer mentioned above feared, the face of the church is becoming unrecognizable. Women are bringing their long-silenced perspectives to bear upon the church's liturgy, administration, and theology of ministry. Transformation is beginning.

Women's experience also has much to teach us regarding the nature of the sacraments, especially the Eucharist. Yet the Eucharist itself is a painful issue for many women. Ross writes,

> The theology of the Eucharist is, in many ways, inseparable from the issue of ordination. Religious communities of women as well as groups of lay women have come increasingly to find the Eucharist a source of pain and anger as much as a source of grace and unity. Groups of women must "import" a priest, often unknown to the community, to ensure the "validity" of the Eucharist. That the sacrament of unity is a symbol of sexual inequality causes many to question its centrality in their own spiritual lives.[107]

One Roman Catholic nun I spoke to confessed that she would only be practicing Native American spirituality until women are ordained in her church. Until then, she would not only refuse the Eucharist, but she would not set foot in a church building.

Many women are not waiting for their communions to change, and are simply taking the Eucharist into their own hands, meeting in small groups to break bread and share wine together. Such groups as WomenChurch are emerging as either independent communities or as cell groups supplemental to (mostly Roman Catholic) parishes. People are taking responsibility for their own lives and the direction of their worship communities and are demanding that they be places of equality and justice *now.*

Many women feel that the Eucharist has been a tool used by male hierarchs to remind women of their "place." Such motivation could illustrate what some feminist theologians consider to be styles of power-management peculiar to our sexual cultures: men are taught that power is a precious commodity to be hoarded, but women, not traditionally leaders in our culture, have made do with what power they could share. These cultural tendencies make for very different leadership styles in our churches.[108]

The fact that women's experience is now informing the church's life on every level in those communions where women are being granted full membership is reason for rejoicing, for it is because of this that the church is becoming more like the Community of God; it is becoming more authentically itself. Those who object to women's ordination often employ some variation of the argument that only males may be priests because Jesus only chose males to be his disciples. The speciousness of this argument is clear when one recalls that although Jesus also only called Jews as his disciples, a Pole presumes to sit on the throne of Peter.

These issues of power-over, in liturgy, theology, and ministry are not surprisingly interrelated. Aldredge-Clanton reports that,

> ...in a study of 174 men and women in six mainline denominations, 91% of those who imaged God as both male and female believed that women and men should serve equally in leadership positions in the church. Only 69% of those who imaged God as exclusively male believed the church should practice equality in ministry.[109]

Thus many of those who insist that God is male will continue to insist that a male represent God at the altar. But as we have seen God "is not a man (male)," and many women and men are fed up with what Ruether calls "linguistic and Eucharistic" famine in our churches, calling for us to "incarnate the community of faith in the liberation of humanity from patriarchy in words and deed, in new words, new prayers, new symbols, and new praxis."[110]

This new orientation is rooted in the radical inclusivity preached by Jesus. In age after age, the Spirit has worked through the church to bring salvation to all peoples, but there is also the tendency for humans to take the most radical of doctrines and twist them to their own advantage. Then the cry for reformation is heard, and new wine is poured again. Women and men of conscience the world over, after taking a hard look at what the church has become, are returning to the radical inclusivity of Jesus' teachings, to the building of the Community of God in our midst. New wineskins must be made to contain this wine.

In this section we have examined many issues that I believe contribute significantly to the crises faced by the Christian church today. Such issues as power-over in the church's liturgy (exemplified in gender-exclusive and militaristic language), power-over in the church's theology (most notably in the cult of suffering into which Western Christianity evolved), and power-over in the church's government (hoarded power and the devaluing of women and laypeople in general) can no longer be ignored if the church wants to remain an entity relevant to today's culture. Addressing such issues is imperative because it is the clear call of the Gospel of peace that we do so.

Feminist and liberation theologians have presented us with the same gift Jesus brought to the scribes and the Pharisees: the mirror of truth. They have asked the most difficult questions of our age:

- Is the Community of God possible in churches where individual sin and salvation are emphasized and structural and societal sin and salvation are ignored?
- Is the Community of God possible in churches where the experience of "the other" (women, the young, the poor, the "sinners," the earth) is ignored or disparaged?

- Is the Community of God possible in a church dependent on the financial support of the rich and powerful?
- Is the Community of God possible when "tradition" is held more dear than the tender souls being told to "shut up or get out?"

Mary's *magnificat* rejoices in God's overthrowing of the powerful on behalf of the weak, as she consents to give birth to God in a radically new way:

> My soul magnifies you, Adonai,
> and my spirit rejoices in God my Savior,
> for you have looked with favor
> on the lowliness of your servant.
> Surely, from now on all generations
> will call me blessed;
> for the Mighty One has done great things for me,
> and holy is your name.
> Your mercy is for those who reverence you
> from generation to generation.
> You have shown strength with your arm;
> you have scattered the proud
> in the thoughts of their hearts.
> You have brought down the powerful
> from their thrones, and lifted up the lowly;
> you have filled the hungry with good things,
> and sent the rich away empty.
> You have helped your servant Israel,
> in remembrance of your mercy,
> according to the promise you made to our ancestors,
> to Abraham and Sarah
> and to their descendants forever.[111]

Meister Eckhart said "What good does it do if Mary gave birth to Christ 1500 years ago, if I do not give birth to him today?"[112] Incarnation is the work of the church, being the hands and feet of Jesus on earth, embracing the outcast and repudiating the systems of political and religious oppression. The decisions we make will decide whether we begin to usher in God's Community or whether Jesus is crucified yet again. Building the Community of God has always been the rightful task of the church.

As we have seen in Part One, "getting on with it" in no way betrays our history. Indeed, it makes us greater participants in the unfolding tapestry of the life of the church. For when we call for change or reform in our liturgies, we are merely asking for what Christians in every age have received from God: a tradition flexible enough to fit our needs in our own time. Our liturgies and even our theological understanding of the Eucharistic feast have changed with every crisis the church has faced. We are not heretics for demanding that the Eucharist be meaningful for us; we are simply faithful Christians.

In Part Three we will examine the many concerns involved in reforming our liturgical rites, the Eucharist most especially. We will look at issues of language and theology in current liturgies, and propose solutions derived from the long history of tradition, as well as creative leaps being made by small, self-empowered communities who gather to break bread with each other in Jesus' name. While I doubt that we shall come to any conclusions that will be acceptable to everyone, we will at least succeed in "thinking outside the box" and hopefully provide a way ahead in many areas.

PART THREE

Some Ways Ahead

Dreaming the Liturgy

Having seen in Section One that the Eucharist *can* change without betraying the Christian tradition, and in Section Two that it *must* change, we may now turn our attention to what sorts of changes are necessary. This last section is a bit of a guided meditation; we shall ask ourselves, what would a Eucharistic liturgy look like that was:

- Not hierarchical, dividing the presider from the congregation?
- Not sexist, but imaging and addressing God in a way that is affirmative of the experience of all gathered?
- Not endorsing of dangerous, hierarchical dualisms: man over woman, humanity over the earth, Europeans over Native peoples, spirit over matter, etc.?
- Not exploitative of others' cultures?
- Not dependent upon the opinions and strategies of the rich and powerful?
- Not a glorification of morbid sacrifice and self-immolation?
- Not controlled by others who have no contact with the life of the community?

Twin Dangers

As anyone who has wrestled with writing liberated and inclusive liturgies can testify, balancing one's reformed vision with the traditional form is quite a tightrope walk: we can err by going too far in either direction. If our vision is too radical, we are in danger of losing our connection to Christianity. Conversly, we can also err on the side of conservatism, which likewise distorts and obscures the Good News. McMichael writes,

> The nature of the Eucharistic prayer as theological exposition is distorted when it is viewed as a series of propositional truths or dogmas. This approach tends toward overly sensitive (paranoid?) assessments of the relative orthodoxy of a given prayer based upon some prior definitive schema of what the prayer should say and how it is to say it. The Eucharistic prayer is to have every word "right" and in the "right" order or somehow God will not do what God is supposed to do in the prayer. This approach becomes a linguistic straightjacket which confines the activity of the Spirit to our well-honed objectives. Ultimately, this type of striving for orthodox purity leads not to doxology but to the creation of an idol of our own theological and liturgical technique.[1]

This insistence on correct form (rather than, perhaps, correct spirit) was frequently commented upon in my interviews. One pastor told me that his negative experiences most often were centered

> ...on those occasions when concern for ritual or "right" rubrics have overshadowed the meaning of the service. There needs to be more intention in the form and practice of the Eucharist to lift up to consciousness and enact ritually the unity in diversity, the transcendent power of the Spirit symbolized in the people gathered to share bread and wine. Less focus on "doing it right" and more on including more of the community, both in leadership and in participation.

One woman I talked to spoke with great humor about what the traditionalist's God must say when "he" enters a Eucharist where the "proper" rubrics are being ignored: "What? No stole? I am *outta* here!"

The logical conclusion of the traditionalist adherence to form over spirit is that the Last Supper was not a true Passover, because Jesus remythologized it. Indeed, even among most of the conservative people interviewed, the "spirit" of the communion is of primary importance. The problem is that among traditionalists, it is felt that only by adherence to the proper rubrics is this spirit possible. Others sharply disagree.

As we have seen, Christians in different eras, in different situations, and of different cultures have all celebrated the Eucharist in myriad ways that have all been deemed "orthodox." What is the unitive element in these celebrations? Form? No, the form has varied greatly. Some Eucharistic Prayers contain an institutional narrative, and some do not; some contain an *epiclesis*, though it is missing from others. Language? Certainly not; the Eucharist has been celebrated in every tongue that has a Christian people. Then what is the common thread? Those interviewed, and much contemporary scholarship, point to *the simple truth that the Eucharist is where we meet Jesus, and where we covenant together to be Jesus for each other.*

One man I interviewed told me,

> No matter where the Eucharist takes place, whether with my friends of Metropolitan Community Church where the elements are often consecrated by a lay person, in a convent chapel in Switzerland, where the liturgy has been in a language I do not understand, or at our own chapel here at the Bishop's Close in the Diocese of Oregon, with our Bishop as celebrant, Jesus is always there in a real and unmistakable way. And I have come to realize that try as hard as I may through my theology, christology, liturgical rites and traditions, God breaks out of any "box" into which I try to force God, and comes and stands before me in a very real way, at times when I most need it.
>
> Each time I come to the Eucharistic table I bring those I love most, as well as my battered and bruised will and soul and my shattered dreams, and Jesus joins me there, and I know that He knows my anxiety and feels my pain, and there is renewed strength to continue on the journey, fed and refreshed by God's real presence.
>
> For me, Eucharist is not about bread and wine, wafers and grape juice, or any prescribed words or motions, it is about being nourished by the presence of God.[2]

John Spong echoes this when he writes that

> ...there is a consistency to the experience of God in every age. The inconsistency, indeed the fallacy, is in the words used to articulate the experience, for words are both limited and dated. Literalized words always distort experience, and if these words are frozen so firmly they cannot change with the times, then finally literal words will render inaccessible in another time the meaning they once conveyed.[3]

The insights of Bishop Spong and the "church hopper" go a long way in helping us determine the nature of a true Eucharist. The true Eucharist places function over form; it is pragmatic. It is also intensely mystical.

This begs the question: if the language and ritual of a Eucharist are rubric-perfect, and yet the Eucharist hinders rather than creates this "function" of making Jesus present, is it a true Eucharist? Although this is a question I leave for the reader to ponder, most people will agree that such a situation, though perhaps not "invalid," is certainly not optimal. As Bishop Spong writes, "If Christ is to be real for us, we must find words through which that reality can be articulated. This is not to suggest that our words will endure forever. Like the words of every age, our words will in time prove to be limited by our age, our ability to apprehend reality, and our time-oriented language."[4]

The goal is not to create a "timeless" liturgy. Such would be ill-conceived and ill fitted to most people's needs. Thomas Cranmer did not set out to create a definitive liturgy for all time, but a prayer book perfectly suited to sixteenth century England. One shudders to think what a contemporarily constructed "timeless" liturgy might look like. I would certainly have my doubts about using it!

One traditionalist priest, when contemplating "changing" the liturgy, responded heatedly, saying:

> This is the central problem with the changing of *any* Sacrament. After all it was Our Blessed Lord who founded them, and *not* the Church.... These, among others, are the reasons why I, too, can not go along with the changing of the foundations of the Sacraments. The feminists did not found them. The Church did not found them. Our Lord Jesus Christ is their founder. Where do we get the idea that we have a right to change what was founded by God, the Second Person of the Most Blessed Trinity? To me these quotes smack of paganism, and not Christianity, much less traditional Catholic Christianity! The Historic Councils of the Universal Church and the Church Fathers answered the question long ago.
>
> Each attempt to become "relevant" leads us to a new dilution or substitution.

This opinion, which is pervasive even among progressives who secretly fear that "changing" the liturgy might be wrong, is sadly in opposition to both history and tradition. That Jesus may have instituted the Eucharist in a moment of inspiration during a ritual meal with his close friends is not at issue, but the idea that Jesus handed down some timeless and canonical form that must be adhered to at all costs is, as we have seen by our examination of church history in Part One, simply erroneous.

The early Church fathers are in agreement. St. Gregory (c. 390 CE), in one of his writings against the Arians, refers to the ideas and the language we use to describe God as being like the tent that Abraham and Sarah used in their journey from Ur to the Promised Land:

> Like that tent...our ways of talking and thinking about God are equipment for pilgrims. They are not what we arrive at, but things that we need and use on the way. Tents are no doubt very important; it is crucial that the poles and cords be strong, and the skins...sound. No one wants a tent that will blow down at the first hint of a breeze, or one that leaks water in every springtime rain. But for all that, when the journey is over, the tents will be dispensed with. They will get us there, but they cannot contain "the glory that shall be revealed.[5]

This story is remarkably like a parable told by the Buddha:

> A man walking along a highroad sees a great river, its near bank dangerous and frightening, its far bank safe. He collects sticks and foliage, makes a raft, paddles across the river, and reaches the other shore. Now suppose that, after he reaches the other shore, he takes the raft and puts it on his head and walks with it on his head wherever he goes. Would he be using the raft in an appropriate way? No; a reasonable man will realize that the raft has been very useful to him in crossing the river and arriving safely to the other shore, but that once he has arrived, it is proper to leave the raft behind and walk on without it. This is using the raft appropriately.
>
> In the same way, all truths should be used to cross over; they should not be held on to once you have arrived. You should let go of even the most profound insight or the most wholesome teaching; all the more so, unwholesome teachings.[6]

When the rains are over, the tents will be discarded. When the river is crossed, we no longer need the raft. The liturgies of the past were God's gifts to the people of the place and time that developed and used them. But they are not necessarily useful in the same way to us. Although he is writing about theology, Spong speaks equally well to liturgy when he writes,

> So much of Christian theology today is not unlike the armor of the past that the elders wanted to place upon David as he journeyed to engage the realities of his world. This is not to denigrate that armor or that theology, for it may have served well in another era where it was appropriate to the circumstances that existed at that time. But that does not mean that it is appropriate to us in our time.[7]

How do we know what is appropriate for us? Although she is writing specifically about feminist concerns, Elisabeth Schüssler Fiorenza has made some suggestions for biblical hermeneutics that might be helpful for us in our approach to liturgy as well. She identifies four stages in evaluating a text: (1) the hermeneutics of suspicion, (2) the hermeneutics of proclamation, (3) the hermeneutics of remembrance, and (4) the hermeneutics of creative actualization. As Procter-Smith explains:

> A hermeneutics of suspicion recognizes the androcentric and patriarchal character of the biblical text... A hermeneutics of proclamation recognizes that the Bible is still a part of a living tradition, not only a historical document, and recognizes women's participation in the tradition. A hermeneutics of remembrance "moves history." And a hermeneutics of creative actualization extends the remembrance of women's biblical history into the present by means of creative participation in the continuation of the biblical story of liberation.[8]

In our study thus far, we have certainly embraced the hermeneutics of suspicion. We recognize that the liturgy—and the Christian tradition in general—is of a grossly androcentric (and anthropocentric) character. We have also given nod to the hermeneutics of proclamation, recognizing that while women have been denied power in respect to church government and ritual practice, they have never been absent from the church's life and worship. Women everywhere are beginning to embrace the hermeneutics of remembrance as they mine the tradition for the experience, stories, and traditions of women within their faith. Mariam Therese Winter's outstanding feminist lectionary cycle (*WomanWisdom*, *WomanWitness*, and *WomanWord)* is a fine example of women celebrating the forgotten and often misinterpreted women of the Hebrew and Christian scriptures. Even the "evil" women of the tradition (such as Jezabel) are held to the light for reinspection and perhaps a bit more compassion. But all of this introspection is for naught if it does not lead women and men to take creative action to correct the sins of the past. And it is through the process of these first three hermeneutics that we may evaluate and decide what is an appropriate way ahead to the hermeneutics of creative action. And according to Fiorenza, the move to creative action is the right and proper course.

Our challenge is to create ritual for ourselves as twenty-first century Christians. We need, as Procter-Smith point outs, to take a hard, critical look at our current liturgies and to decide: "is it true for us?"[9] We need to revisit the Jesus story in the Synoptics, to decide what Jesus is saying to us today, and then to embody it in our liturgies in a way that is relevant, worshipful, and just.

But this brings us to our second danger: going too far. As McMichael writes,

> The second way that we can distort the mutual relationship between the church's faith and the Eucharistic prayer is to create prayers that strive to articulate our current (trendy?) theological and ideological preoccupations. Prayers written in this way turn out to be nothing more than euchological mood rings by which we express our narrowly conscribed theological agenda. In other words, this distortion does not create Eucharistic prayers that spring from the great tradition of the church and the faith of the church taken as a whole. The result is theme prayers that repetitively drive home the point that is so important to drive home. This same charge can be leveled at theologically driven prayers such as Prayer I of Rite One [in the American 1979 *Book of Common Prayer*], the theme being Eucharistic sacrifice and the nature of the atonement.[10]

Like the traditionalist priest quoted above, who railed against any re-visioning as smacking "of paganism, and not Christianity, much less traditional Catholic Christianity!" many are concerned that in our attempts to run pell-mell into political correctness, we will leave the Gospel behind.

But as we have seen, the pejorative term "political correctness" is itself an apt synonym for the Gospel itself as taught by Jesus. In fact, the foundation for a feminist re-visioning of Christian liturgy is itself the Gospels and the rest of the biblical record when viewed by Fiorenza's hermeneutics.

For in these same Gospels, Jesus did not esteem tradition as something to be protected for its own sake, or to be regarded uncritically. When his disciples were caught shelling wheat as they walked through a field on the Sabbath, they were roundly attacked by the Pharisees as being in violation of tradition. Yet Jesus replied, "The sabbath was made for humankind, and not humankind for the sabbath."[11] By Jesus' own example, we are not to serve tradition; it is either in the service of the cure of souls, or it is useless or even harmful. We have to ask of tradition: "What will foster the full humanity of all women, men, and children as well as the well-being of all of creation?"[12]

Yet the danger of going too far remains. As Hilkert writes, "For Christians, fidelity to the apostolic tradition remains a touchstone of authenticity.... Even more basic than the question of how one remains faithful to the apostolic tradition in our age, culture, and social location, however, is the thorny question of what constitutes the apostolic tradition."[13]

Ironically, tradition provides us with a model with which to evaluate how we define and live out our faith.[14] While the Roman Church values scripture and tradition as having equal weight, the reformers went in two different directions. The Continental reformers took a minimalist approach, crying "*sola scriptura,*" while the English Reformers eventually came to regard Scripture, Tradition, and Reason as having equal weight. To this, Anglican clergyman John Wesley added a fourth factor to this equation: personal experience. I propose we apply the tradition of the "Wesleyan Quadrilateral" as found in Methodism as a ready framework within which to examine, critique and live Christianity.

Though most Christians (especially if they are not Methodists) have not heard of the Wesleyan Quadrilateral, many of them have intuitively applied the same criterion. As Ruether writes,

> The ordinary believers now have increasingly complex formulas of faith, customs, rituals, and writings proposed to them as the basis for appropriating the original revelatory

> paradigm as personal redeeming experience. These individuals, in their local communities of faith, are always engaged in making their own selection from the patterns of received tradition that fit or make sense in their lives. There is always an interaction between the patterns of faith proposed by teachers to individuals and the individuals' own appropriation of these patterns as interpretations of experience. But these differences remain unarticulated, held within the dominant consensus about what the revelatory pattern "means."[15]

But people are questioning consensus. Feminist critiques of the sacrificial theory of the atonement and the dualistic nature of the universe are causing people to reevaluate early Christian sources to try to discover a more "authentic" tradition, to re-examine the meaning of the incarnation, and to re-vision their liturgies to reflect their spiritual processes.

When I asked one woman what the chief issues are that are facing the church, she said "Accepting modernism: sexuality, science, and social changes (especially relating to women, gays [lesbians, bisexual, transgendered persons], and patriarchy). Reinterpreting the faith so that it is not ludicrous in a technological, urban, postmodern society."

Clearly in the estimation of many Christians, the church's teachings are in danger of seeming sorely outdated. But because Christians believe that there is something truly sacred and revealed in our tradition, it is also easy to believe that the fault lies not with the revelation itself, but with how it has been interpreted and handed down. In light of this perception, we err if we cling to conservatism in pursuit of "theological safety." Jesus does not call us to safety. We also err if we "throw the baby" of Christian tradition "out with the bathwater." A *via media* must be found that can intelligently and faithfully reinterpret the apostolic faith for a postmodern world that embraces not only scripture and tradition, but reason and lived experience as well.

Making the Word Flesh

While the liturgical movement sought after a primitive, prototypical Eucharistic prayer, one that would be the "correct" model for us as inheritors of the apostolic faith, it is the opinion of many

Christians that "correctness" is irrelevant. What is most important is not finding or developing the "perfect" Eucharistic liturgy, but the ongoing experimentation of individual communities to discover what sort of Eucharistic feast is nourishing for them as a local body. As one man I interviewed put it, renewing liturgy,

> ...requires building a sense of community in order to be more communal at Eucharist. But the Eucharist is also itself constitutive of community. This makes a kind of feedback loop. How we do this in concrete ritual and ceremonial terms is something a few among us are working out for ourselves. We need to let a thousand flowers bloom and then find the ways that really do work. To letting those flowers bloom there is great resistance. The resistance also contributes to the process.

There is indeed a great deal of resistance to allowing people's creativity to flow freely. But it is precisely the commitment to this process that can give life and purpose to a community. Since common prayer shapes and informs the life of the whole community, the constituent elements of their prayer need to be carefully, critically, and continually re-evaluated. The community must, first of all, be willing to experiment, to "think outside of the box," to make "holy fools" of themselves in the midst of their journey together. As Jay Rochell writes,

> There must be a conviction on the part of the community—or at least a percentage of it—that liturgical experimentation is not a gimmick. If...contemporary worship patterns are gimmicks, then all worship is a gimmick. Who has established the lines of judgment that read: anything new and original in worship is a gimmick; anything old and familiar is not? Why is it not possible to reverse the decision and conclude that the old thing is a gimmick whereas the novelty and originality are the reality? After all, what is a gimmick but a tool of deception, whereby reality is hidden for a while? A gimmick is a trick, and tricks have no place in real life. The older patterns of worship may be tricks for those who can't possibly relate to them. Those who protest new worship forms as gimmicks have made three decisions: (a) only the old and traditional has value; (b) we have made our own judgment about the criteria of a worship experience; and (c) there is no need for worship to relate to life in a meaningful way. To these, we need to answer: then the

> entire worship life of the church is automatically called into question, because truly to be worship it must relate to life![16]

There is also a tendency for a community to seek after a "definitive" liturgy that defines them and must therefore be set in stone. But liturgy is an ongoing "work of the people." As one editor of a book of experimental liturgies wrote, "These liturgies are not finished products, but just steps along an unending path."[17] At the Festival of the Holy Names we have a planning meeting once a month at which any word, idea, or even punctuation mark in our ever-developing prayer book may be challenged by anyone who cares to show up. The objection is discussed, and a revision is worked out and voted upon. (The Festival spends a lot on printing!)

This brings us to a second point of importance. Just as important as the willingness to experiment is the commitment to stick with the process of revising these liturgies. As Procter-Smith relates,

> Writers reflecting on a given liturgy remark that the process of creating it was at least as important as the liturgical event itself. This experience is particularly intense if the liturgies were created out of a group process. The mixture of joy and pain [in these processes] is echoed throughout the published commentaries on the liturgies, with the process most often described as "struggle." The process serves as a kind of conscientization as planners attempt to express in word and ritual act the complex experience of being Christian and feminist.[18]

I can personally attest to this struggle from my experience with the Festival. My wife and I, both founding members, wrestled with our early liturgies so much it brought us to the brink of divorce! What this process revealed to both of us is how much power our prayers have for us, how important the issues that we have been discussing (in Part Two) really are, and how very difficult it is to write a prayer that speaks for a diverse group of individuals. As Gail Ramshaw-Schmidt has written, this is no small task, for "one must know the gospel, the tradition, and the contemporary situation, and must hold them together in liturgical language."[19]

Creating a just liturgy is not simply a question of "inclusive language." Inclusivity goes far beyond gender. The Festival had to wrestle with all the various power-over issues inherent in the liturgy: God as monarch, the bi-level model of the universe (God is "up there"), the valuing of matter over spirit and other dualisms, sacrificial theology, the person of Jesus, the role of the clergy, and much, much more. In addition, we had to craft the prayers that were emerging in language that was beautiful and appropriate for corporate worship—and as any first-year seminarian knows, liturgical poetry has rules and a logic all its own.

For the liturgical Christians in our midst (Roman Catholics, Anglicans, and Lutherans), deviating too much from the liturgical form was uncomfortable and, in fact, simply unacceptable. For the Free-Churchers in our midst, empty ritual in any form was non-negotiable. Thus we were primed to walk an important tightrope, seeking to honor and preserve our Western liturgical heritage, while at the same time demanding relevance of these rites with every line, idea, and punctuation mark. This pushed all of our boundaries: as laity, as clergypersons, as budding theologians, as poets, and as Christians. For some of us, myself included, creating the Festival has been one of the most difficult and rewarding experiences of our history of "church."

In this tightrope walk we discovered the "twin dangers" mentioned above. The liturgical among us had to let go of the "divinization" of the form of the prayers, while the "free church" folks in our number learned the value of these forms. McMichael describes this tightrope walk:

> Implicit in any approach to the Eucharistic prayer and the proclamation of the church's faith is an understanding of the relationship between revelation and experience, or between the great tradition (tradition taken as a whole) and the contemporary situation of the church with its attendant questions and concerns. That is, the first distortion would emphasize a given and definitive, even formulaic, revelation at the expense of current dynamics of the church's life. The second distortion would emphasize present experience and issues of the day as the source of revelation in isolation from the tradition and contemporaneity, or revelation and experience. We are never to consider these present realities of the church's life as irreconcilable polarities, but as ever-present dimensions of the ongoing transformation of the church into the fullness of Christ. Eucharistic prayers are always to be traditional and contemporary, faithfully proclaiming God's revelation and reflecting the church's experience of the Spirit.[20]

The experience of the Festival has been so valuable that most of us believe that all worshipping communities should be actively engaged in creating liturgies for themselves. This forces the complacent pew-warmer and the power-comfortable clergy to both wrestle with the difficult questions of what it means to be Christian in the twenty-first century, and what it means to be church for each other. If this were to happen on a large scale, it would have a number of important effects.

First, it would accelerate the process of change within the church. As Procter-Smith writes,

> Far from being committed to preserving the status quo or being a conservative force, as liturgy is sometimes called, it is in the nature of liturgy to call forth change, since God calls forth change. If liturgy has seemed to be, or has actually become, a force preserving the state of things as they are (or even as they might once have been), it is due to our human resistance to change and not to the nature of Christian liturgy itself.[21]

Even if we truly listened to the words of our "old" liturgy, conversion in our worship life would occur. New liturgies would speed this process exponentially.

The second effect is the explosion of diversity that would erupt in liturgical celebration. Our worship would become more polyphonic, more personal, more human, and oddly, more universal. This is as it should be, for as Ellen K. Wondra writes, worship "should have the character of a rich symphony whose harmonies are produced by complex arrangements of individual elements and movements and whose discords serve to increase the abundance of the whole."[22]

Such abundance can be difficult, as we in the Festival can attest, but the result is intimacy and community. Thus the third effect of such hard work would be renewal, as each community learns for themselves what it means to be Jesus to one another, and gropes towards the authentic meaning of "being church." As LaCugna writes, "Fidelity to the Christian tradition does not rule out openness to experience, to a new situation or new needs, but rather demands it. The church is not the sole proprietor of truth. The Holy Spirit speaks through many voices, many reformist movements, which teach the church and call it back to its apostolic charisms and to the message of the reign of God."[23]

Christianity is a religion that continually calls its people to conversion. Unlike some sects that believe conversion is a one-time occurrence, the apostolic faith is one that confronts us anew every morning, and in every moment of our lives, calling us to repentance, giving us grace, and spurring us to new lives and new behaviors. The Gospel seeks to transform all human structures by the continual urgings and longings of God the Spirit: liturgy no less than any other human institution.

People in many denominations—especially in those communions which have historically been suspicious of "set prayers"—are rediscovering liturgy as a powerful force in their spiritual lives. A Baptist professor and friend once half-joked that there were as many Baptists who secretly use the Episcopal *Book of Common Prayer* for their private devotions as there are communing Episcopalians! Slowly, this clandestine use is "spilling over" into corporate life, with the result that even Baptists are beginning to publish prayer books as a "guide" to corporate celebrations by clergy.[24]

Two happy results of this renewal are the return of ritual to the Protestant vocabulary and the great proliferation of creative liturgies by people beginning to explore what liturgy means for them and their local communities. One scholar has noted that there have been more Eucharistic prayers written in the twentieth century than in all the rest of the church's history combined. As Procter-Smith writes, the Liturgical Movement has resulted in

> ...a fresh awareness of ritual as a basic human activity rather than a mark of neurosis or superstition. Attentiveness to movement and gesture; to space and its arrangement; to the use of elements such as bread, wine, and water, which are capable of bearing the full theological weight placed on them; and to the rhythm of a liturgy is now part of the liturgical renewal process in all traditions and denominations.[25]

The intensive scholarship inspired by the movement has surprised many: there seems to be great consensus on so many aspects of liturgical life, especially in regards to the Eucharist. The subsequent theological consensus of both Catholics and Protestants appears to be, in the words of P.T. Forsyth, that "the exact point of the Lord's Supper is that such symbolism [does] not lie in the elements but in the action, the entire action—word and deed...It [is] the action that [is] symbolical, the breaking rather than the bread, the outpouring rather than the wine."[26]

Let us keep the "twin dangers" in mind as we begin our "guided meditation" through the liturgy, remembering that neither a liturgical fundamentalism nor an "anything goes" relativism will work. Instead we need to do the hard and careful work of listening, trying, and revising, remembering that no matter how educated or experienced we become, all of our varied expressions are but feeble attempts to express our experience of a God who is ineffable Mystery.

What Do We Celebrate?

How do we, Catholics, Protestants, and Orthodox, use these liturgies to heal and to make whole? How do we transform a rite that has for most of our lives been used to glorify sacrifice and death, honoring spirit over matter, men over women, heaven over earth? As Rabbi Gottlieb asks, "What are the words we want to sing talk scream whisper together?" What threads of the past should we resurrect? What new threads need to be developed?

The World Council of Churches formed the Faith and Order Commission to study liturgical convergence among the various denominations, and in the 1970s issued a document, "The Eucharist in Ecumenical Thought." The Commission named seven different "threads" or currently viable approaches to the Eucharist, many of which will already be familiar from our historical studies (corresponding threads are noted in parenthesis):

1. The Eucharist: The Lord's Supper (Jesus' table fellowship)
2. The Eucharist: Thanksgiving to the Creator (Brachot)
3. The Eucharist: Memorial of Christ (Memorialist)
4. The Eucharist: Gift from the Spirit (Divinization)
5. The Eucharist: Communion in the Body of Christ (Real Presence)

6. The Eucharist: Mission to the World
7. The Eucharist: End of Divisions[27]

The "Dombes Agreement" (1973) is the product of French Reformed and Roman Catholic dialogue. This document affirms most of the categories above, but adds to them the following:

8. The Eucharist: Sacramental Presence of Christ (Realist)
9. The Eucharist: Banquet of the Kingdom (Eschatological)[28]

The above approaches are invaluable as starting places for ecumenical discussions of the Eucharist since all of them are ancient and "valid" approaches to the Eucharist. Yet for all of our appeal to the authority of the past, it is also clear that the churches' evolution has not ceased; it is in fact, hurtling forward at a dizzying rate. The above "threads" affirmed by scholars of various denominations expand our repertoire of Eucharistic themes well beyond the sacrificial myopia of most current Eucharistic prayers. I would like to focus on four that I believe are particularly useful for addressing the church's current crisis of power, three of which are found in the list above: Life and Joy (#1 above, *Brachot*); Liberation; Unity (#7, End of Divisions); and the Eschatological Feast (#9).

Feast of Life and Joy

Life and joy as a basis for Eucharistic celebration is especially appropriate. It is congruent with the rite as a "Great Thanksgiving" and hearkens back to the very beginnings of the Church's history, the *Brachot* thread. St. Luke tells us that the early Christians broke bread in their homes and "partook of food with glad and generous hearts" (Acts 2:46). The *Didache* liturgy certainly falls into this category. A close study of this text will reveal no sacrificial language, no propitiation for sin, nothing other than a grateful celebration of the gifts of life and wisdom:

> We give thanks to thee, O Holy Father, for thy Holy Name which thou didst make to tabernacle in our hearts, and for the knowledge and faith and immortality which thou didst make known to us through Jesus thy child; to thee be glory forever. Thou, Lord Almighty, didst create all things for thy Name's sake, and didst give food and drink to people for their enjoyment, that they might give thanks to thee, but us hast thou blessed with spiritual food and drink

> and eternal light through thy child. Above all we give thee thanks that thou art mighty. To thee be glory for ever.[30]

Edward Schillebeeckx points out that in the Eucharistic elements themselves, we find the perfect symbols for both Life and Joy: "...bread is the symbol of life and wine is the symbol of the joy of life."[31] Another outstanding theologian, Frederic Debuyst, holds that a truly joyful feast requires three qualities: "universality, unanimity, and a participation in eternity beyond the boundaries of time."[32] As Davies explains,

> The universality means that there are no strangers at the festive board. If, in fact, a stranger appears at the door, he must become a guest, for if he is turned away or prevented from entering, this becomes a sin against openness and can ruin the spirit of the celebration. The second characteristic is unanimity; it clearly requires everyone to share the same intentions and values... Debuyst cites a text of St. John Chrysostom to make the point that a festive occasion makes its own communion... "Where charity radiates its joy, there we have a feast." It is agape—the divine love—that finally makes the feast.
>
> The third trait necessarily concerns the temporal duration of the festivity. Even if every human festive occasion has a beginning and an end, it is still possible to think of a perduring festival that is interior to the guests at the temporal feast—grounded in the sheer goodness of creation and the deeply rooted brotherhood and sisterhood of humanity.[33]

Davies likewise points out that for ancient peoples, the expression of joy was not considered a base or forbidden thing in liturgical worship. Long predating our Western dualism, the soul and body were not yet divided in people's imaginations, and "joy was seen as a gift of God and was often associated with religious feasts and liturgical worship."[34]

The contemporary celebration of Easter is probably the closest modern Christians have come to knowing the joy found in the most ordinary of early Christian liturgies. Yet we should seek to make such joyful celebration normative in our rites, emphasizing in the texts of our prayers not the gloominess of medieval piety, but the life and joy that we receive from God in our ordinary lives, in the blessedness of creation, in the dignity of our labor, and in the communities and loved ones that nurture and affirm us.

The German Lutheran Church includes in its Eucharistic prayer the following section, which is full of hope and affirmation:

> We praise you for the wonder of your creation. You bless human labour and endow us with life and joy. You have given us bread and wine that we may celebrate the supper of your Son. We thank you for the mystery of your love. Receive us anew as your own that our conduct may honour you, through Jesus Christ, our Lord.[35]

The Festival of the Holy Names expands upon this theme in their first Eucharistic Prayer (Life and Joy):

> Sacred and Immortal One, throughout the history of the world, it has always been your way to bestow rich blessings upon your children: in the ongoing weaving of the world, O God, you give to us life. In the gift of our communities and families, you give to us joy. In Jesus of Nazareth you give to us an example of genuine living. In his death and resurrection, you give us the hope of eternal life. Through the gift of your Holy Spirit, you give us the courage and the power to remake the world.

The prayer continues with the following institution:

> When once he walked among us as a human being, Jesus said to his friends "I am the Bread of Life," and indeed, Divinity is our substance and our sustenance. "Anyone who follows my teaching, though they have nothing, yet never shall they hunger."
>
> Jesus likewise said, "I am the True Vine..." and indeed, Divinity is the source of our hope and our joy. "Those who abide in me, and I in them, shall bring forth much fruit."

Affirming the goodness of creation in our prayers will for us today also bring with it an acknowledgement of our responsibility to care for and protect the earth. This mixture of joy and wonder in God's creation, and our sin in destroying it, is also appearing in an increasing number of liturgies as Christians all over the world begin to take our ecological crisis seriously. Prayer C from the 1979 Episcopal *Book of Common Prayer* contains the following *anaphora*:

> God of all power, Ruler of the Universe,
> you are worthy of glory and praise.
> **Glory to you forever and ever.**

At your command all things came to be:
the vast expanse of interstellar space,
galaxies, suns,
the planets in their courses,
and this fragile earth, our island home.
By your will they were created
and have their being.

From the primal elements
you brought forth the human race,
and blessed us with memory, reason and skill.
You made us rulers of creation.
But we turned against you and betrayed your trust;
and we turned against one another...[36]

The Festival's third Eucharistic prayer (Servants and Priests) is more explicit in regard to our treatment of the earth:

> Holy God, we bless you for your creation, for beauty that astounds us and for goodness that humbles us; for the canopy of stars that blankets this blue-green jewel and for the deliciousness of fruit and cool-running water. In every way you have made our home a blessing to us, and charged us with responsibility to care for and nurture it...
>
> We confess that we have not always been kind to your creation: we have sullied the waters and air, and taken life that was not ours to decide. Time and again we tried to build towers to reach the heavens, setting up dominions for ourselves, pretending to be rulers over the earth, enslaving the peoples, abusing our families, and exploiting the poor.
>
> *All* **We forgot that we were a holy people, servants of this earth and of one another, and we forsook our holy duty to make justice and teach peace to the nations.**
>
> *Presider* But you did not forget us: in your compassion you brought forth Jesus of Nazareth; who taught us to dream of a community where none are seen as diseased or forgotten, where power is forsaken for intimacy and where the presence of God is radiant.

Joyful thanksgiving and grateful praise: these are the most primitive, and perhaps the most worthy, reasons to celebrate the Eucharist. In writing prayers that reflect this orientation we have both rich precedent in the church's history, and the inexhaustible fourth wing of Wesley's Quadrilateral—our own experience—to draw upon. Such an emphasis would remove much of the medieval gloom and morbidity that has long hovered over Eucharistic celebrations in the West, and replace it with a moving expression of praise and thanksgiving, which is the proper attitude for something called "Eucharist" ("Thanksgiving").

Liberation Feast

This thread, which owes its genesis to the Latin American Liberation theologians of the 1970s, sees the Eucharist as a political statement, and a commitment for the participants to end hunger and injustice. Liberation Theology's "founder" is Gustavo Gutiérrez, whose book *A Theology of Liberation: History, Politics and Salvation* turned the theological world on its ear. According to Davies,

> Gutiérrez correlates the Eucharist with human brotherhood. He sees the life of Christ as a total self-giving for others, vividly recalled in the chief sacrament. He also views the Eucharist as a feast of joy that the church shares and wishes others to share. Its very reason for existence is to create brotherhood and sisterhood, and its background is the Jewish Passover that celebrates the liberation from Egypt and the covenant established by God on Sinai. Furthermore, Gutiérrez acknowledges that liberation from sin is at the very root of the need for political liberation and socio-economic justice. Finally, he argues that true communion with God and others presupposes the abolition of all injustice and exploitation.[37]

Gutiérrez pinpoints three levels of liberation proclaimed by the Gospel: (1) "liberation from social situations of oppression and marginalization," (2) "a personal transformation by which we live with profound inner freedom in the face of every kind of servitude," and finally (3) "there is the liberation from sin, which attacks the deepest root of servitude; for sin is the breaking of friendship with God and with other human beings, and therefore cannot be eradicated except by the unmerited redemptive love of God whom we receive by faith and in communion with one another."[38]

Though a fairly new thread, the Liberation-oriented Eucharist has surfaced now and again in the Church's history. St. Paul warns the rich and powerful Corinthians against taking the supper before the poor can arrive, shaming them for their sinful behavior. Later, St.

Cyprian, Bishop of Carthage, likewise upbraided the wealthy for their mean-spiritedness and lack of regard and towards the poor. He even went so far as to deny the rich communion until they had made an offering for the poor! "Do you rich and wealthy," he wrote, "think that you celebrate the Lord's feast without a sacrifice, who take part in the sacrifice that the poor person has offered?"[39] St. Theresa of Avila extends the justice teaching to include a powerful interpretation of the resurrection. As Davies explains:

> Returning Jesus to life, which the powerful of his time had taken from him, [God] "topples the powerful from their throne," annihilating the worst they could do to the struggle for justice. The annihilation (negation) thus placed in the hands of all those who had been wronged the most powerful weapon to continue the struggle. The resurrection is, therefore, the ultimate basis for rebellion.[40]

Denounced by the Roman Catholic magisterium for being tainted by Marxism, Liberation Theology has restored the Gospel emphasis on freedom to the church's worship. And in the late 1960s and '70s, a time when technology was for the first time in human history exposing the inner workings of tyrannical governments and organizations to public view (and thus critique), a time when public consciousness of peace and justice issues was at a historic and watershed level, Liberation Theology not surprisingly struck a chord with Christians of all stripes around the world, as clergy and laity rediscovered Jesus' teachings on human dignity, political and personal justice, and the imperative for peace. Besides Gutiérrez, Liberation Theology has also been embraced by such notable figures as Leonardo Boff, Archbishop Avaresto Arns, Jürgen Moltmann, J.R.M. Tillard and Nicholas Lash. Adapting liberation theology for women's issues, Mary Collins, Monika Hellwig, and Elisabeth Schüssler Fiorenza have made great contributions. Even Protestant theologians such as Robert McAfee Brown, Walter Brueggemann, and John Howard Yoder[41] have carried the torch. In liberation theology, the widely separated church has found scriptural and traditional support for meeting the very real and vital issues coming to light in a newly global culture.

Unfortunately, although much has been written on Liberation Theology, little has been done to incorporate it into the Eucharistic liturgy. This is tragic since the Eucharist lends itself readily to the task. The offertory is an opportune time to remind participants of their mutual interdependence. And the Institutional Narrative is as stark a story of bravely met injustice to be found in the Western canon. Few of our "new" threads are as clear, or even as important, as this one.

The Festival has adapted a prayer from the Unitarian Universalist Abraxis group as their second Eucharistic prayer (Liberation), which summarizes the feast's origins in the Passover and the justice teachings of Jesus:

> We thank you, O God, that in every time and place you have made your home with the poor and the powerless. With your mighty hand, you led your people Israel out of bondage to Egypt. Through your prophets you taught your people to do justice, to love mercy and to walk humbly in your Spirit.
>
> In Jesus of Nazareth you made your home with us, and taught us that it is the meek who shall inherit the earth; that those who suffer for what is right are blessed in your eyes. Through him you lived and died as one of us, preaching the Good News of liberation to the poor and the oppressed.
>
> And even now you embrace us in love, and give us strength to bring this Good News to all...

The prayer continues with the Institutional Narrative and a brief *epiclesis*, after which is said:

> Blessed are you, Eternal Sustainer of the Universe; for through your miraculous creation, you bring forth grain from the Earth. As these kernels were scattered upon the mountains and were gathered and made one loaf, even so do you make us one, for we are children of one Earth, and partake of one bread.
>
> *The bread is broken.*
>
> Therefore, when the bodies, spirits, and homes of others are broken, we are broken.
>
> Blessed are you, Eternal Sustainer of the Universe; for through your miraculous creation, you bring forth the fruit of the vine. As the fruit of many vines is put into one press to be crafted into one vintage, even so you have made us all one family, sharing one blood.
>
> *The wine is poured from the cruet into the chalice.*

> Therefore when the life-blood of any creature spills, our blood is spilled.
>
> Today/Tonight, we break bread for the suffering of the Earth, for those whose habitats have been destroyed, for those who struggle for justice, who have paid the price for freedom with their own flesh and blood, and for the millions who suffer oppression, sickness, and distress. And we break bread for those we love not present, especially...[42]

The Festival's prayer is a powerful liturgy, and very moving whenever it is celebrated. It is but a harbinger of prayers to come, however, as peace and justice become more and more the focus of many contemporary Christians. As both a theological orientation and a basis for liturgy, the Liberation Feast speaks to many of the issues discussed in Part Two, and Christians everywhere would do well to embrace it. This is certainly my hope, for as Gutiérrez writes,

> Without a real commitment against exploitation and alienation and for a society of solidarity and justice, the Eucharistic celebration is an empty action, lacking any genuine endorsement by those who participate in it... "To make a remembrance" of Christ is more than the performance of an act of worship; it is to accept living under the sign of the cross, and in the hope of the resurrection.[43]

A Liberation Eucharist demands justice, not just in the world at large, but in the performance of the ritual as well. For a community to taste real justice in its midst, in its community life, and to celebrate itself consciously in its common worship holds great promise for the fate of the church and the world. If we truly "pray what we believe," then we shall be teaching peace and justice wherever we worship, and we shall be demonstrating it in our worship lives as well. A Liberation Eucharist celebrated by a community who lives out its liberation will bear a living and powerful testimony for the Gospel of Peace.

Feast of Unity

The Eucharist as a Feast of Unity is probably the most ancient of the Eucharistic themes, as it harkens back to the table-fellowship of Jesus' own ministry (see the *Brachot* Thread in Part One). As we have seen, it was in welcoming even the most despised "sinners" to the table that Jesus affected his redemption, restoring dignity and self-worth to those whom society said had none. His enemies called him a "glutton and wine-bibber." His friends, however, called him Rabbi, and later, God. The power inherent in this thread is not lost to us; in fact, in a reactionary age in which our politics is leading to an ever-growing social stratification, the significance of this thread has rarely held so much promise. The "radical egalitarianism" of Jesus' table fellowship is vitally important to the church today, especially if we are committed to being Jesus' hands in this world, and not just to being an exclusive country club.

Indeed, Jesus' prayer in John's Gospel reveals that unity solidarity was one of Jesus' primary concerns, "The glory that you have given me I have given them, so that they may be one, as we are one, I in them and you in me, that they may become completely one, so that the world may know that you have sent me and have loved them even as you have loved me" (John 17:22-23). This is in stark contrast to the practice of many Christians today, from the Eastern Orthodox who refuse communion to anyone not baptized by them to the conservative Baptist church which practices a "closed communion," denying anyone who is not a member of their own local church! It is shocking how such practices can even begin, let alone continue, when they are in such direct opposition to both the letter and the spirit of the Gospel. Mary Collins writes,

> The strong sign of the assembly of outcasts and strangers—people so unlike that they would never choose one another's company—being invited to welcome and to forgive one another in Jesus' name, to be at peace, to sin no more—is supressed when we reject ambiguity and demand clarity and coherence in our ecclesial relationships before we can celebrate Eucharist.[44]

Instead of the infighting and bickering over "correctness" or "jurisdiction," a return to Jesus' radical practice would take no notice of such things and might even return us to a time when it was said of Christians, "How they love each other!"

Fortunately the concern for unity did not die out with the end of Jesus' ministry, and subsequent followers tended to see the unity of the church symbolized in the bread of the Eucharist. St. Paul instructs the Corinthians, "Because there is one bread, we who are many are one body, for we all partake of the one bread" (1 Cor. 10:17). We have already encountered, in Part One, the beautiful prayer from the *Didache* liturgy (second century): "As this bread that is broken was scattered upon the mountains and gathered together and became one, so let the church be gathered from the ends of the earth into thy Kingdom."

Such prayers for unity are still among us, although they are not usually the focus of the celebration. Prayer "D" from the 1979 Episcopal *Book of Common Prayer* says, "Grant that all who share this bread and cup may become one body and one spirit, a living sacrifice in Christ, to the praise of your name" (375). While the emphasis on unity here is welcome, the emphasis on Christians becoming a "living sacrifice" remains problematic.

In a communion of unity we remember that we are not only celebrating our union with Christ, but with each other, and not only with those immediately gathered, but with all those around the world who eat this same meal, and with all the saints who have gone before and have celebrated this meal in their own times and according to their own traditions. This "transcendental" unity of the church is not often preached, but it is still there, exerting its subtle influence if only by virture of its truth.

The American *Lutheran Book of Worship* certainly incorporates a vivid sense of the communion of saints when it prompts the following prayer: "Join our prayers with those of your servants of every time and every place and unite them with the ceaseless petitions of our great high priest until he comes as victorious Lord of all" (70-71).

The United Reformed Church (U.K.) has a beautiful and powerful *epiclesis* that extends this unity from Christians to the whole of the world: "We beseech you, send among us your Holy Spirit and give a new face to this earth that is dear to us. Let there be peace wherever people live, the peace that we cannot make ourselves and that is more powerful than all violence, your peace like a bond, a new covenant between us all, the power of Jesus Christ here among us."[45]

The third Eucharistic prayer from The Festival of the Holy Names (Servants and Priests) derives its Institution from the Last Supper scene in the Gospel of John, which reminds us that divisions of power or rank have no place in the Gospel:

> When they met to celebrate the Passover, Jesus said to his friends, "You who would be the greatest amongst you

> must be the servant of all." And then their reverend teacher wrapped himself in a towel, and carefully washed their feet.
>
> Still a dispute arose among them as to which of them was to be regarded as the greatest. But he said to them, "The rulers of the Gentiles exercise power over them but it shall not be so with you; rather the greatest among you must become like one who serves. For who seems greater, the one who is at the table or the one who serves? Is it not the one at the table? but I am among you as one who serves."
>
> And then while they were eating the meal of the covenant, Jesus used familiar symbols of bread and wine to celebrate a new relationship between God and the earth; a relationship of grace and friendship with the potential to remake the world.

There are many ways that the theme of unity can be stressed in our celebrations, not only through the Eucharistic prayer but also through our actions. A 1979 forum meeting at the church of St. Lawrence in Nuremberg made the following suggestions for creating solidarity in our celebrations of the Eucharist:

> - We give space...to remembering hunger and oppression.
> - We express in concrete intercessions our hope for God's justice.
> - We look for forms of a credible thank-offering and bring to the meal what we want to share.
> - We invite strangers and aliens to the meal and take account of their presence in the forms of our celebration.
> - We go to the sick and the lonely and celebrate the meal with them.
> - We also use grape juice for the sake of alcoholics.[45]

We can also involve more people in our liturgies, sharing the power and responsibility of the minister with the congregation and dismantling the structure of hierarchical privilege that priests and ministers have always enjoyed. It is especially important to address the very appearance of power-over, especially in our ritual. As Procter-Smith says,

> ...most liturgical actions and gestures have more in common with gestures and symbols of dominance than of inti-

> macy or equality. The clergy occupy official sacred space, which is often also physically elevated above the congregation. The clergy are also elevated when they stand while the congregation sits. Clergy may wear authoritative clothing or other symbols of authority. They are regarded as having the license to address parishioners by familiar names while being themselves addressed by title. Similarly, clergy normally touch parishioners in the course of religious rites or as part of their more general pastoral duties. Lay people do not normally touch their clergy, beyond a polite handshake, and may feel some degree of anxiety if expected to do so...
>
> Emancipatory body language must work to eliminate gestures and symbols of dominance from the liturgy and to generate symbols and gestures of mutuality and egalitarianism. At stake here is a principle dear to both the liturgical movement and the feminist movement, that of the full and free participation of the whole people of God in their liturgical work.[47]

Attention to these non-verbal symbols of rank and domination require careful investigation, for such actions also embody the long-held expectations of laity and clergy alike, for whom they are valued acts of piety, surrounded with much sentimentality.

Simply taking away the very things that make church feel like church to some is not the answer, but struggling toward actions and words that work for everybody is. As Sheila Redmond reminds us, the creation of liberated liturgies

> ...requires an understanding of contextuality, a commitment to an ongoing process, a willingness to experiment, an explicit rejection of hierarchical forms of litugical leadership, and a corresponding commitment to shared leadership, pluralism, and ecumenicity. The major problem...is the integration of these values into mainstream liturgies. Our perspective of wholeness, the idea that personal stories tell us something about spirituality on a broader level, is a positive value that must be shared. But care must nonetheless be taken.[48]

The United Church of Christ's *Book of Worship* gives a fine example of how to turn a rite of dominance into one of mutuality. After the confession of sin, the minister pronounces the absolution: "Almighty God has forgiven you all your sins and has promised to bring you to everlasting life," to which the people respond "Amen." What is striking is that the people then return the favor, saying to the minister: "Almighty God has forgiven you all your sins and has promised to bring you to everlasting life," to which the minister then responds "Amen."

In the Festival we have expanded our use of gestures of mutuality by inserting a hand-washing ceremony into one of our Eucharistic prayers. The call to the table of Eucharistic Prayer III: Servants and Priests is as follows:

> We are a beloved priesthood, a holy community, God's own. We are called to proclaim the wondrous acts of the One who brought us through the darkness into light. Let us serve one another with grace, washing each other's hands, feeding one another, and proclaiming Christ's presence wherever two or more are gathered. Come to the feast prepared for you from the foundation of the world.

Then a celebrant takes the first communicant and leads them by the hand to the table, where the celebrant washes the communicant's hands, and offers bread and wine in silence, while the congregation drums and dances. When the communicant has dined, the music stops, and s/he turns to the congregation, proclaiming "Christ is here!," to which the congregation responds: "The Spirit is with us!" Then the first communicant leads the second communicant to the table and repeats the rite.

Liturgical clothing can also be problematic, as it denotes power and privilege. The origin of the chasuble, for instance, was the raincoat worn by military officers and other officials of rank in imperial Rome. Likewise the preaching robe of reformed traditions emphasizes the preacher's superior education.

In the Festival we do employ chasubles, but they are at the discretion of the presider, and since everyone who wishes may take a turn as presider, the power of symbolic privilege is deflated. More appropriate to rites of unity and equality are the simple alb (white robe) and stole (a scarf which goes over the neck and hangs down to the knees), which are both simple and proper in most liturgical traditions. It is all the more fitting because the stole is the liturgical remnant of the towel Jesus wrapped himself in to wash the disciples' feet.

The Feast of Unity may be the most difficult of the new directions to employ, but it is also one of the most ancient and rewarding. It is most important to engage interested laity in the writing and revisioning of such a rite if it is to be genuine. But if attention can be given and prayerful listening can occur, the assembly may be able to pray with a whole heart:

> Eternal God, make your Holy Spirit known in our midst. In the sharing of this meal make of us a community of friends, a discipleship of equals, teaching us to be servants and priests one to another, proclaiming the Good News of the Community of God amongst us.[49]

Eschatalogical Feast

The early Christians saw their community as a foreshadowing of the coming "Kingdom" that Jesus preached about, and the Eucharist as a foretaste, or a sacrament, of the eschatological feast: the banquet—or eternal party—to be held at the end of this age, when all tears shall be dried, and humankind's longing for a world at peace and in harmony with God's will is finally manifest. Jesus is to be the host of this feast, and all nations shall partake of its bounty. As Davies says,

> Each celebration of the Eucharist points beyond itself to the final coming of Christ at the end of time. Each Eucharist is, as Jeremy Taylor expressed it, "an antepast of heaven." While the followers of Christ already share in his Kingdom, yet this Kingdom must expand until its fellowship is complete in the heavenly Jerusalem.[50]

This is a most important meaning for the Eucharist, for it orients us not towards a sentimental memorial of the past, but points us towards the future, and provides us with a compelling vision that is promised to be the fulfillment of all of our efforts. In this orientation, the Eucharist cannot be celebrated as a mournful or solemn event, but instead it is infused with hope, expectancy, and responsibility. As a foretaste of the great coming "party" it can take on a carnival air, becoming a joyous, even raucous event.

Evangelical mythology of the end times is highly apocalyptic in tone, envisioning a "rapture" when God takes all of the Christians out of the world, and those left behind are left largely to Satan's mercy. At the end of seven years, Jesus and the host of heaven are expected to ride out of the sky and to defeat the armies of Satan and the nations at the Valley of Meggido. After Satan and all those who have not confessed Jesus as Lord have been thrown into the Lake of Fire those who are left will celebrate the messianic feast, which will last for a thousand peaceful years, with Christ ruling as "King" in Jerusalem.[51]

For liberal Christians, the eschatological hope is very different. Instead of dividing the world into "us and them," liberal Christians see humanity as in the same boat, with shared responsibility to educate and reform present economic and political systems. For us, the Second Coming is not a physical, bodily return of the historical Jesus, but a figurative return, when the teachings of the historical Jesus finally take root in history, and the Community of God is ultimately made manifest on earth by the inspiration of the Holy Spirit and the hard work, sweat, and prayers of all peoples of faith, of every tradition. Thus the Eschatological Feast is not just something God promises, but is itself the fulfillment of the great commission. It is a reminder of our responsibility to get to work creating peace, justice, and equality, and a promise that ultimately our efforts will find fertile soil and will flourish. As Jürgen Moltmann writes,

> From first to last, and not merely in the epilogue, Christianity is eschatology, is hope, forward looking and forward moving, and therefore also revolutionizing and transforming the present. The eschatological is not one element of Christianity, but is the medium of Christian faith as such, the key in which everything in it is set, the glow that suffuses everything here in the dawn of an expected new day.[52]

This understanding is not dissimilar to the understanding of liberal Jews, who view the coming of the Messiah in nearly identical terms: as an ideological, not a physical arrival, and regard their responsibility in bringing about the Messianic age as "*tikkun*," the remaking of the world. Liberal Christians and Jews have much in common, if not in liturgy, then certainly in eschatological theology. This is a tremendous ground for cooperative efforts, for our goals are the same.

Advent is a perfect time for Eschatological emphasis, since in that season we await not just the arrival of the Christ Child, but the Second Coming as well. The air of expectancy, hope, joy and yes, even penitence, are perfectly suited to such a Eucharistic orientation.

Unfortunately, although many Eucharistic prayers make mention of the Eschatological Feast in passing, few of them use the Eschatological thread as the foundation for the prayer. The most explicit reference, for instance, in the 1979 Episcopal *Book of Common Prayer* is in Eucharistic Prayer III:

> In the fullness of time, put all things in subjection under your Christ, and bring us to that heavenly country where, with *N.*, and all your saints, we may enter the everlasting heritage of your sons and daughters (369).

Though it is sad that so little is being done with this thread, there has been some creativity around it. In his *Parole Visible*, French theologian Leenhardt suggests switching the symbolism of the cup to correspond to the Eschatological Feast:

> The restitution of the eschatological sayings to the liturgy of the supper oblige one to fill a gap in our actual practice. The bread and cup have been confused in the same theological and liturgical movement, by referring them both to the coming death. But we have previously noted that the cup of the new covenant inaugurated by the death of Jesus is a new rendezvous given to the communicants, the assurance of their participation in the Messianic feast. Liturgically it must be marked that the two perspectives should be distinguished: that of the cross and that of glory: that is to say to separate the distribution of the bread and the circulation of the cup. Each of these acts, reattached to the words of Jesus which supports it and nourishes the sense, should liturgically be a whole.[53]

In the usage of the Festival, there is not as yet a prayer devoted exclusively to this thread, but elements of it do appear in the existing prayers. In the Liberation Eucharist (Prayer II), for example, we make the following covenant in place of a post-communion prayer:

> Therefore we covenant with one another to work until bodies are broken no more, to act until blood is no more spilled, to practice peace until all can dance on the land beneath the sun, eating their grain with joy and drinking the fruit of the vine with a merry heart. One day there shall be peace! One day all—*All*—shall rejoice!

With so little use being made of the Eschatological thread, there is obviously much creative work to be done here, and important work at that, as this thread provides a potent vision of the future capable of uniting and inspiring people to work for a better world.

As should be obvious by now, the Eucharist has an inexhaustible range of meaning. The four Eucharistic Feasts briefly commented on here are only a starting point, perhaps the most obvious ways to heal the crises facing us. We need Life and Joy because we have forgotten how to wonder and have been told by our tradition that the body and the world are corrupt. Liberation is important, as it is the most immediate task before us, one on which the world is already fixated, in an ironic way. Recall, for instance, the myth of the United States of America—"Give me liberty or give me death!" Less ironically, this thread is also of immense importance for women, oppressed peoples, and those in recovery (substance abuse, etc.). The Feast of Unity speaks to us powerfully because of the dreadful state of Christ's churches, and the racial and national sins that separate us. Finally, the Eschatological Feast serves to provide a sorely needed vision of all the peoples of the earth as one people, a goal within our grasp worth working for.

While I believe that these four are the most important threads for the Christian community at the present time, other, even more appropriate threads will emerge as local communities begin to feel free to experiment, to ask such questions as, "What does the Eucharist mean for us?" and to put into words the deepest longings of their lives of faith. And as the Sacrifice Thread comes to be seen as one among many, we may well see a renaissance of vibrant and original new prayers which will speak to the church in its time of crisis—and lead it out into a new day.

What Words Do We Use?

In the remainder of this section we shall take the Eucharistic liturgy (including the Liturgy of the Word) section by section and discuss the many issues inherent in its present form, especially as it is found in Roman Catholic and American Episcopal forms of prayer. We shall take a hard look at how the present forms are hurtful to many and in some cases antithetical to the Gospel. Then we shall suggest some ways ahead as suggested by theologians and liturgists as well as the experience of the Festival of the Holy Names.

The Liturgy of the Word

The first part of the Eucharistic service is usually the Liturgy of the Word. Modeled on the Jewish Synagogue service, it emphasizes the reading and interpreting of scripture and the corporate saying of prayers. In the ancient church, it was the part of the service that was open to everyone. The Liturgy of the Word is often divorced from the Liturgy of the Table in Protestant worship, providing by itself the normative ritual of many denominations. Ideally, however, it prepares the congregant for a proper, thoughtful reception of the Eucharist, and provides liturgical time for the reading of scripture and exhortation.

The Greeting

We no sooner begin than we run into trouble. The opening words of the Roman Catholic Liturgy of the Word are "In the name of the Father, and of the Son, and of the Holy Spirit. Amen."[54] The 1979 Episcopal *Book of Common Prayer* begins similarly, albeit in a more characteristically Judaic form: "Blessed be God: Father, Son, and Holy Spirit. And Blessed be his Kingdom, now and forever. Amen" (335).

Both of these greetings employ standard Trinitarian language, and therein lies the problem. From the outset in this liturgy we are confronted with "the all male one-parent family with a whoosh of vapor."[55] As we have already noted, there is great value in the doctrine of the Trinity, but the fact that the Trinity is pictured as exclusively male is unacceptable to many women and men of conscience. Partly because it is not true (few people would actually argue a case for God the Father sporting human reproductive organs), but mostly because of the exclusionary messages such an image sends to women. From the very beginning we need to deal with the serious issues of inclusivity. As Janet Schaffran and Pat Kozak remind us,

> Inclusive language is not a fad. It is not this year's "cause," to be soon replaced by another. The growing use of inclusive language is the result of a serious commitment on the part of many people to use words more responsibly, to speak more precisely, and to communicate more truthfully and sensitively.[56]

That the cry for inclusive language is being heard in a number of churches means that there is a growing number of people for whom our old ways of speaking about God, and the messages implied in those ways, are inadequate to express the lived experience of God in the lives of both men and women.[57]

So how do we begin? What do we change that will break open the liturgy to the experience of women and others who have had little or no say in the worship life of the church? There are a number of ways to approach this problem. Liturgists have been experimenting with several options, such as non-gendered language, balanced language, and balanced imagery. Let us examine each of these.

Non-Gendered Language. Non-gendered language accomplishes its task by substituting gender-blind terminology. With this approach, masculine pronouns are avoided by referring to God in the second person as "you" rather than talking about God in the third person ("he" or "she"). "Man" is replaced by "humanity" or "people," and instead of speaking of humanity in the third person ("for the salvation of all men"), we speak in the first person ("for our sake").

So how might we address the Greeting above? One way is to substitute gender-neutral names for the persons of the Trinity that are *functional* rather than *relational*. "Father" and "Son" are not names so much as descriptions of a familial relationship that has meaning for us. But God is much more than simply a "Father" or a "Son." God is also the Creator, the Liberator, the Redeemer, the Inspirer, and so on. Thus to retain the Trinitarian formula, we might try "Creator, Word, and Holy Spirit." The Festival models its Greeting after the Episcopal form: "Blessed be God: Creator, Liberator, and Comforter. And blessed is Creation, now and forever." Note that in this usage, the masculine and archaically monarchical "Kingdom" has been replaced by a properly liturgical affirmation of the goodness of the earth and the universe.

Such shifts may be difficult for many. Sally McFague has compiled a list of stages of metaphor:

> In the first stage, a newly coined metaphor seems inappropriate or unconventional and may be rejected. At a second stage, a living metaphor has both literal and metaphorical meaning and is insightful. The challenge to liturgical revisers is to present new metaphors that can overcome the initial shock and become living metaphor that stimulate imaginative thinking in the church. Experimental use of texts may be the best way both to provide sufficent familiarity to allow new metaphors to move to the second stage and to weed out metaphors that are widely rejected. In this way, new metaphors can become the prayer of the people.[58]

Obviously, metaphors that will work in one community may not work in others, as people of various professional backgrounds, subcultures and ethnic derivations will find meaning in different images. But the key is to "try them on for size" long enough to get past the initial shock and to see if they can be meaningful for the community.

Gender-Balanced Language. Non-gendered language is not the only answer. Using functional language instead of relational language confuses the role of persons in the Trinity. For instance if we ascribe

"Creator" to the person traditionally called the "Father" does that mean that the other two persons of the Trinity do not create? Also, some people consider non-gendered language cold, or even not corrective *enough*:

> For some, however, calling God "Source of Mercy, Fountain of Life, Eternal One, Divine Presence, Teacher and Friend" is not yet inclusive enough. At worst, even though the liturgy now uses "Eternal One" for "Lord" and "Ruler" for "King," people still *think* of God as male. Why else would many still scream "Idolatry!" when a female image for God is used? Eliminating masculine pronouns and names for God does not eliminate people's well-established masculine associations with the word "God." As a five-year-old girl put it, "God is [still] a boy's name."
>
> At best, gender-neutral language, while removing a barrier to women's identification with God, does not encourage either girls or boys, women or men, to see themselves in God's image. For we are not gender-neutral. We are male or female.[59]

According to Procter-Smith, unless God can be specifically named as female, the innovation is not emancipatory for women. To truly emancipate our liturgies—and women—we are required to use gender-specific language. Gender-neutral strategies will not help us here, but Gender-balanced language can.

This strategy continues to use gendered pronouns and names, but is careful to make sure that an equal number of female and male terms are used. This approach can be especially jarring, alternately using "him" and "her," and can easily feel contrived. One way to pursue this approach is to resurrect names for God that are Biblical but unfamiliar. Procter-Smith writes,

> Feminist liturgical anamnesis also remembers the name of God as many names, especially as female names. Naming God as female and as varied makes it possible to affirm particularity in encounters between people and the Holy One. Naming God as female also affirms the value and sacredness of women who are varied...If the Holy One can be named female, then female bodies and experiences can be holy.[60]

It is for this very reason that the Festival of the Holy Names adopted its name, striving as it does to celebrate all of God's names in both genders.

In pursuit of this kind of balance, some communities (especially Women-Church groups) have experimented with balancing references to "God" with references to "Goddess." Although many communities might find this too shocking at first, it may yet prove a rewarding experiment. Edwina Gately has even suggested the intriguing and sexually ambivalent Old English spelling "Godde"! Some communities may find, however, that referring to "God our Mother and God our Father" better affirms the Christian faith in one deity, as the Festival does in its version of the Lord's Prayer (called Jesus' prayer in the Festival), which renders the first two lines "God our Father, God our Mother, holy are your names."

Others, in an attempt to "emancipate" God from patriarchy, would simply substitute "Mother" for Father, without attempting balance. This kind of overcorrection cannot be an ideal or ultimate answer for either women or men since it does not promote inclusivity for all.

Perhaps God should not be named in parental terms at all, since it distresses both those who have grown up with abusive parents as well as those who are parents themselves, but cannot possibly live up to this deified ideal. As Redmond points out,

> Deification of parents is dangerous. Using parents as models or symbols of God creates a burden and responsibility for the parents that can only induce guilt or denial and self-doubt when they fail to meet the standards set by a human conception of God. Whenever we create new symbols or models for God, we always run the risk of doing harm, even if that is not our intent.[61]

Another way to approach the gender-balanced language perspective is to name either the second or the third person of the Trinity as female. This might sound shocking and even heretical to some, but it has plenty of precedents in the church's history:

> The apostle Paul calls Christ the Wisdom of God (1 Cor 1:24). In the original Greek text the word for "wisdom" is the feminine Sophia. The Gospels of Matthew and Luke compare Jesus to a mother hen (Mat 23:37; Lk 13:34). In the middle ages, St. Anselm prays to "Christ Mother"; Julian of Norwich praises Christ as "All-Wisdom, our kindly Mother"; and Thomas Aquinas refers to Christ as "our Mother, Wisdom of God."[62]

Jesus-as-female, especially as conceptualized in the Sophia Christology, has garnered much scholarly attention in the last fifteen years, and with good reason. The influence of Sophia upon early Christians and their interpretation of Jesus' life and message have been largely forgotten. Johnson explains:

> Found in the Jewish Scriptures and intertestamental literature, Wisdom is a complex female figure who personifies God's presence and creative action in the world. She comes forth from the mouth of the Most High, pervading and connecting all things. In texts of great variety Sophia creates, redeems, sanctifies, establishes justice, and protects the poor. Searching the world for a dwelling place, she pitches her tent in Jerusalem. Themes of light and dark, finding and seeking, bread and wine, life and death are woven into her symbol. Obviously transcendent, this personified figure comes toward human beings, challenges and comforts them, and lures them to life: "Whoever finds me finds life" (Proverbs 8:35). We are dealing here with the mystery of God in graceful, powerful, and close engagement with the world.[63]

Barker points out that it was through the influence of Philo that the Hebrew figure of Holy Wisdom was Hellenized and stripped of her femaleness.[64] Philo equated Sophia with *Nous* (mind) and with *Logos* (word or idea). Barker says, "In this transaction...she emerged as a male hypostasis, the Logos, while retaining the divine functions of her earlier persona."[65]

Thus she who came "forth from the mouth of the Most High," became the Logos: "In the beginning was the Word, and the Word was with God, and the Word was God" (Jn 1:1); she who was "pervading and connecting all things" became the cosmic Christ in whom we "live and move and have our being" (Luke 17:28); she who "pitches her tent in Jerusalem" became the one who "became flesh and pitched his tent among us" (Jn 1:14).

So pervasive was this belief that Sophia was the pre-incarnate Christ that both sides of the Arian controversy (which instigated the formulation of the Nicene Creed) appealed to Christ-Sophia theology to prove their points.[66]

For some, naming the Holy Spirit as female is preferable. It is also helpful that Sophia has been historically associated with the Holy Spirit. In early Syriac manuscripts, in fact, female imagery for the

Holy Spirit is found in many liturgical sources. There are also some modern Pentecostal churches that have taken up the idea of the Holy Spirit as female, although these are far beyond the mainstream of evangelical Christianity and would probably not be interested in other aspects of inclusivity. In fact, as Elizabeth Johnson has pointed out, when the Holy Spirit has been given the female gender it has usually been for the purpose of reinforcing stereotypical feminine roles, especially since the top two rungs on the God ladder remain firmly male.[67]

If done with care, re-discovering Christ-Sophia theology or naming the Holy Spirit as female can be helpful, but the "shock factor" (of praying to Sophia, for instance) will be difficult for many to overcome. A community seeking to use balanced language as its primary strategy will have tough going. Gender-balanced language is better used as just one of many strategies to be employed on occasion.

Gender-Balanced Imagery. A much more popular approach is gender-balanced imagery. Gender-balanced imagery differs from gender-balanced language in that it does not strive to be inclusive in language, but instead seeks to "balance" language with feminine imagery. This is the approach finally decided upon by the Episcopal Standing Committee on Liturgy, which, in at least one experimental liturgy, retains the typical androcentric names for God (Father, Son, and Holy Spirit), yet "balances" these by using scriptural imagery that describes God's actions towards us as being maternal. The following Eucharistic prayer from the Supplemental Liturgical Materials issued by the Episcopal Standing Commission on Liturgy is an excellent example of a gender-balanced approach:

Celebrant The Lord be with you.
People **And also with you.**

Celebrant Lift up your hearts.
Peopel **We lift them up to the Lord.**

Celebrant Let us give thanks to the Lord our God.
People **It is right to give God thanks and praise.**

Celebrant We praise you and we bless you,
holy and gracious God, source of life abundant.
From before time you made ready the creation.
Your spirit moved over the deep
and brought all things into being:

> sun, moon, and stars; earth, winds, and waters;
> and every living thing.
> You made us in your image, male and female,
> and taught us to walk in your ways.
> But we rebelled against you,
> and wandered far away;
> and yet as a mother cares for her children,
> you would not forget us.
> Time and again you called us
> to live in the fullness of your love...[68]

Note that in the above prayer we still "lift our hearts to the Lord," yet God's actions are "like a mother..." This approach has appeal for a number of reasons. First, it doesn't rock the boat too much. Traditionalists can be soothed by pointing out that the proper form is adhered to and that the feminine imagery is strictly biblical. It may be an ideal "compromise" position, but it is definitely a compromise. One woman I interviewed disdained this approach, saying that what it said to her was: "God is still a man, but he acts like a woman."

Indeed, the figure of a cosmic transvestite does not evoke a feeling of awe and worship for most of us. It is also not, as Procter-Smith points out, emancipatory for women. When God cannot be named as a woman, women cannot be liberated by such a god. As the Orthodox say, "God cannot save what God does not assume." Like the other two approaches above, gender-balanced imagery is not a stand-alone answer to the "problem" of making liturgies inclusive. It is one tool to be employed in tandem with the other approaches.

In addition to the above methods, we would do well to remember that God is above all Mystery, and that any name we give is somewhat arbitrary and partial. Thus the multiplicity of names and images in scripture (God as "hiding place," "sword and shield," etc.) lead us away from formulaic "names" such as Father or Mother, and towards a cacophony of attributions that are all true, and all partial. And we also need not limit ourselves to word-images. As Schaffran reminds us, "These images can be evoked in a variety of ways: through dance and storytelling, mime, journaling, nature, music and art. Images are invoked or sustained in virtually every human experience."[69]

Ware suggests such descriptions as "God, arrayed in justice," "God of all generations," "God of light and sun," "Heart's delight,"

"Inspiration to goodness," "Searcher of hearts," etc.[70] All of these ways of naming God—and many more besides—have been used during the past twenty years in experimental liturgies in many communions, and for some the shock value is diminishing, being replaced by a comfortable familiarity and real spiritual value. The Daily Office produced by the Society of St. Francis includes this alternative to the *Gloria Patri:* "Glory to God, Source of all being, Eternal Word and Holy Spirit: as it was in the beginning, is now, and shall be forever. Amen." The fact that now many of us could gloss right over something so worded without it triggering any negative responses is evidence that the shock value of some alternative forms is diminishing. This is a very positive sign.

The United Church of Christ in its 1985 *Book of Worship* has legitimated the use of new images in its own version of the liturgy's Greeting: "In the name of God: Creator, Redeemer, and Comforter." Or this non-trinitarian alternative: "Peace be to this house and to all for whom this is home" (79).

Although the United Church of Christ is admittedly on the far edge of Christian liberalism, the fact that such greetings have been approved for the church's official liturgy is heartening. It is evidence that, at least in this denomination, the hard work is being done.

The Confession and Absolution

Corporate confessions are a relatively late innovation to the Eucharistic liturgy. The Council of Nicea even forbade their use on Sundays and during the whole of the Easter season. The confession did not become standard practice until the sixth century.[72] Its heyday was certainly the Middle Ages when it was required as a preparation for the people's infrequent reception of communion.

But as people's fear of the Eucharist is replaced by an understanding that the rite is not "magic" but rather an expression of community, more and more the Confession is disappearing from formal Reformed worship, even being omitted from the main Sunday Eucharist at Grace Cathedral in San Francisco (Episcopal). But if we shift our gaze from private to societal sin there is good reason to retain—and re-vision—the Confession of Sin.

The Roman Catholic Rite places it directly after the Greeting, though in some other communions it serves as the conclusion to the

Prayers of the People. The Rite I confession from the current Episcopal Prayer Book reads:

> Almighty God, Father of our Lord Jesus Christ, maker of all things, judge of all men: We acknowledge and bewail our manifold sins and wickedness, which we from time to time most grievously have committed, by thought, word, and deed, against thy divine majesty, provoking most justly thy wrath and indignation against us. We do earnestly repent, and are heartily sorry for these our misdoings; the remembrance of them is grievous unto us, the burden of them is intolerable. Have mercy upon us, have mercy upon us, most merciful Father; for the Son our Lord Jesus Christ's sake, forgive us all that is past; and grant that we may ever hereafter serve and please thee in newness of life, to the honor and glory of thy Name; through Jesus Christ our Lord. Amen (331).

Though such "worm theology" is no stranger to Anglican worship, rarely do we find such a concentrated dose of it as in the above confession. There are a number of things with which to take issue. Besides the obvious sexism, there is also the issue of power. This prayer does not work for those who no longer accept a medieval model of the universe where God is a magnified King who metes out punishment upon those who upset the established order.

In one alternative model, Process Theology, God is not "Almighty," but mightier than anything else in the universe. God does not have the power in this system to coerce, but only to inspire and suggest. The above prayer speaks of an all-powerful King in the sky who is hopping mad at all of us, while Process thought speaks of the "fellow sufferer who understands," the Divine Companion on our journey.

Fortunately, the "monster God" imaged in the Rite I prayer is becoming a museum piece. A highly original prayer that retains the monarchical imagery but is gratefully lacking any trace of "worm theology" is found in the liturgy of the Theosophical Liberal Catholic rite:

> O Lord, thou has created man to be immortal and made him to be an image of thine own eternity; yet often we forget the glory of our heritage and wander from the path which leads to righteousness. But thou, O Lord, hast made us for thyself and our hearts are ever restless till they find their rest in thee. Look with the eyes of thy love upon our

> manifold imperfections and pardon all our shortcomings, that we may be filled with the brightness of the everlasting light and become the unspotted mirror of thy power and the image of thy goodness; through Christ our Lord. Amen.[72]

Though an enormous improvement, the above prayer does seem to relegate all personal sin to the category of "mistake," which, if any of us is honest, is not entirely correct. And like the Anglican prayer that preceeded it, it also seems oppressively long. Consider the much-improved confession found in the Roman Catholic rite:

> I confess to almighty God, and to you, my brothers and sisters, that I have sinned through my own fault (they strike their breast) in my thoughts and in my words, in what I have done, and in what I have failed to do; and I ask blessed Mary, ever virgin, all the angels and saints, and you, my brothers and sisters, to pray for me to the Lord our God.[73]

While this rite does not confer forgiveness, which in Roman practice can only happen in private confession, it is a great improvement over older formulations. Many women will take offense at the apparently arbitrary and out of place insistance upon Mary's virginity, but the prayer is for the most part void of gratuitous brow-beating and intimations of divine cruelty.

The chief complaint against such a prayer is not the language *per se*, but the prayer's myopic focus on individualized sin. While it is true that from time to time most of us do intentionally hurt one another, our gravest sins are not usually ones of personal volition but of societal complicity. Such grave sins as the rape of the Earth, the abandonment of the poor, the exploitation of native peoples and pre-industrialized nations are rarely the subject of our litugical confessions, yet they are certainly the ones of which we are most in need of repentance and from which we are most in need of conversion.

The following confession is a fine example of an attempt to address societal sin, and comes from the United Nations' Environmental Sabbath:

> Gracious God,
> who made the covenant promise with our ancestors,
> we gather here today a rebellious people.
> We want to act out your intentions for us,

> but we keep getting mixed up
> by all the glitter of the world around us.
> You tell us to honor creation,
> and we use other people and animals and plant life
> only to meet our wants.
> You offer daily bread to every living creature,
> and we steal that bread from our brothers and sisters
> in the name of our greed.
> You promise us new life,
> and we shrink back from it in fear.
> Heal us, God, lest we destroy ourselves.
> We need your presence among us. Amen.[74]

In the Festival we use a sung confession composed by one of our members. Though it has been criticised for being "new age-y" and somewhat pantheistic, it succeeds in combining personal and societal concerns by virtue of its presumption that the societal *is* personal:

> For my resistance to being all I'm created to be,
> For my denial of life, of life abundantly
> For the discord I bring into the harmony
> I beg the indulgence of Earth, sky and sea,
> Of All-that-I-Am, of All Who Are,
> of All in All in All.[75]

The absolution that follows this prayer is simply a proclamation of peace as the presider signs the absolution and sings, "Shalom." Another fine absolution, as we have seen previously, is found in the United Church of Christ's *Book of Worship,* in which the presider says, "Almighty God has forgiven you all your sins and has promised to bring you to everlasting life;" to which the congregation responds reciprocally, "Almighty God has forgiven you all your sins and has promised to bring you to everlasting life" (64).

An alternative to a confession in traditional Catholic worship is the *Asperges*, or the blessing with water. Usually thought of as a reminder of one's baptism, it can replace the rite of confession, and provides a ritual opportunity rich with symbolic import for creative faith communities.

Traditionally the blessing is done with holy water, over which an "exorcism" has been performed to cleanse it of any evil. This presupposes a universe where evil is the primary reality, which is about to overwhelm and overcome goodness, which is trying to find a foothold. In a Cosmic Christ theology, however, as in the Eastern

Church, where goodness is the primary reality against which evil has a hard time holding its own, water is already blessed and doesn't need to be exorcised.[76] Nature is itself divinized. The Festival liturgy makes use of both the Confession and the *Asperges*, placing the Confession after the Prayers of the People, and allowing the *Asperges* to retain its proper place at the beginning of the rite. This prayer affirms the holiness of creation, with which we and all the earth are continually blessed:

> Dear friends, this water will be used to remind us of our origins, of the waters of the womb from which we were born, and the waters of the Earth that refresh and sustain all beings. May God bless me as I perform this service. With the Earth's hallowed waters do I consecrate this holy altar and sanctuary. And bless also this people, who gather to celebrate an astounding love.

While the *Asperges* is not celebrated by Protestant churches and is rare enough in Catholic services nowadays, many churches may find the *Asperges* to be a valuable ritual to recover, either as a substitute for, or augment to, the Confession and Absolution.

The Readings

One of the most frequent surprises Evangelical Christians encounter when they first attend a liturgical service is the enormous amount of scripture read. While most Free Churches use only a single (usually short) passage from which the minister preaches, liturgical churches incorporate separate readings from the Hebrew scriptures, the Psalms, the Epistles, and the Gospels. In addition, it should be said that a large percentage of the liturgy itself is derived from scripture.

The riches of scripture are either a boon or a liability, depending upon how one looks at it. Having so much scripture is comforting to most of us, but it also serves to diffuse the message of any one of the readings. It's simply too much for anyone to hold in their mind at once. Add to this the oblique "connections" of one reading to another as directed by the lectionary, and one begins to see the wisdom of the Free Church approach. It often takes a great feat of imagination to find some alleged "theme" running through each of the prescribed readings.

In addition, since scripture is decidedly androcentric and patriarchal, more scripture means that the preacher's job is that much tougher. One reading isn't so difficult, but if one intends to take a critical approach to scripture, it is difficult to let a blatantly patriarchal passage go by uncommented on.

In some Free Church circles, members are questioning the primacy of scripture over other inspirational writings that often don't need so much explanation. Suddenly poems by Adrienne Rich are taking their place beside the Gospel reading. The Festival, with both liturgical and Free Church members, has steered a middle course, usually combining one to three carefully chosen scripture readings with a contemporary source.

Liturgical churches usually set the Gospel reading apart from the others by means of the Gospel acclamation. In the Roman rite this begins with the reader (the priest or deacon) saying, "The Lord be with you!" to which the people respond "And also with you." The priest then crosses himself and says "A reading from the holy Gospel according to ——." The people then respond, "Glory to you, Lord." After the reading, the priest finishes by saying, "This is the Gospel of the Lord." The people respond, "Praise to you, Lord Jesus Christ."

Inclusivising the language of the Gospel acclamation is relatively easy. "The Lord be with you," can easily become "God be with you," or "Godde be with you." But a more traditional and wonderfully inclusive substitute comes from the Liturgy of St. John Chrysostom of the Eastern Orthodox chruch:

Priest Wisdom! Attend!
Let us hear the holy Gospel. Peace be to all.
Choir **And to thy spirit.**[77]

This is the best I have come across, in that it does away with the sexist and imperial language ("Lord") and replaces it with "peace," which never changes, even when our systems of government do.

"Christ" may easily be substituted for Lord in the next part ("A Reading...") without much dissonance. As is the way with liturgy, it doesn't take long for the new formulation to begin to feel natural, and soon you have people asking each other, "What was it we used to say there?" This is a true sign that liturgical change is taking hold.

Other communities may want to compose their own acclamations. In the Festival we adapted a song by Willard Jabusch set to a traditional Hasidic melody:

Cantor Open your ears, O faithful people
Open your ears and hear God's Word
Open your hearts, O royal priesthood,
God has come to you.

Gospel Reading

Cantor God has spoken to the people, Hallelujah!
And the words are words of wisdom, Hallelujah!

Although in the Festival the above acclamation both introduces and caps all of the readings, I prefer it as simply the introduction to the Gospel, since the way we use it now gives equal weight to all of the readings. (Remember I am just one voice at the Festival planning meetings—I often get voted down!) I believe that the Gospel acclamation is a very meaningful ritual, in that it ideally sets apart the Gospel as somehow special, which indeed it is. Of all of the Hebrew and Christian scriptures, the synoptic Gospels are the least problematic and the most meaningful for followers of Jesus. M. Scott Peck has said that "the Gospels are the best-kept secret in Christianity."[78] The Gospel acclamation ideally should break this secrecy, to say to people, "Wake up! The really important stuff is coming up!" I have even seen the Gospel Acclamation enthusiastically embraced in a Free Church setting that uses little or no additional ritual. The people felt that what they most treasured in their scripture was being honored, and that this honored God.

The Homily

The homily, or sermon, which immediately follows the Gospel reading is inherited from Judaism and was part of the Christian liturgy from the very earliest times. Its purpose is to explain the readings in terms relevant to the congregation. Current fashion in liturgical churches limits the homily to between twelve and twenty minutes. The homily is meant to provide insights for practical living from the Gospel. For Evangelical and Free churches, on the other hand, where there is no Liturgy of the Table, the sermon is the "main course" and can run from between a half hour to over an hour in length, its main purpose being to exhaustively explicate the text and to move people to convert and embrace Jesus' sacrifice for their sins.

One difficulty with preaching is that it seems to assume a hierarchical stratification wherein the minister is deemed to have authority not given to the laity. One way to avoid this is to share preaching responsibilities with the laity. Amongst some evangelical sects (such as Appalachian Baptists) preaching is a sign of spiritual maturity, a rite of passage in which all men (of course) are expected to participate.

This is indeed an area that deserves reflection and creativity. Procter-Smith gives some guidelines for what she calls emancipatory preaching:

> Emancipatory preaching must discover gestures that establish and reinforce not dominance and submission but mutuality between preacher and community. The arrangement of space for speaking and hearing must allow for both audibility and reciprocity. The community may be encouraged in part by the space itself to see themselves as part of the proclamatory event and enabled to participate in the event by responding verbally to the sermon either in the course of or immediately following the sermon. The preacher may choose to stand, sit, or to move around while delivering the sermon but the choice will be made or at least principally based on the community's need to be engaged in the process of preaching. The authority of the sermon depends not on the use of traditional symbols and gestures of dominance, but on the authenticity of what is preached, and its accountability to women.[79]

This model is followed by St. Gregory Nyssan Episcopal Church in San Francisco, where a very short sermon is delivered, and then any who choose may respond either to the sermon or from their own experience of the scripture. Visitors to St. Gregory's remark upon what a liberating experience it is to have the floor offered to them to have the "last word" after the priest has spoken.

At the Festival of the Holy Names we dispense with a formal sermon altogether (except on special occasions) and introduce the "Sharing the Gospel" period by saying:

> We have heard the scripture of our tradition. Now we invite you to share from the scripture of your life. We open ourselves to hear your personal truth without judgment or interruption.

We also call this time "Midrash" after the Jewish practice of explicating and re-interpreting their faith. And re-interpret we do! While scripture is almost always our beginning point, often a Festival midrash will begin by saying what irritates us about the readings, processing together the issues that they raise for us and sharing with each other the pain we feel around them. By the end of the time we have usually found a few gems of meaning and inspiration in the texts as well. What feels so liberating about this approach is, as the presider's introduction states, scripture and personal experience are given equal weight. One might even go so far as to say that, in practice at least, the scriptures are even accountable to our experience.

Since this is a non-structured time, there are often long stretches of silence while we each sit quietly with our thoughts until someone is moved to speak. We try to take after the Quaker tradition here, honoring the silence as being equally sacred, or even more sacred than words. When the Spirit moves someone to speak, that person is given the full attention of all present, regardless of who the speaker is, or whether he or she has ever been to the Festival before. All are given the right to speak, and are listened to with reverence.

Frequently (since there is no doctrinal statement or creed embraced by the Festival) a great number of opinions are expressed. We see this as healthy and no one is interrupted or told that they are wrong, since we are commited as a community to support one another on our spiritual journeys.

The few times we have had to confront or challenge someone during these times is when people have (very infrequently) responded inappropriately to someone else. Inappropriate responses encountered at the Festival usually take one of two forms: the pronouncement of judgment upon someone else's experience (such as yelling out, "You're wrong!" in the middle of someone's sharing, or speaking condescendingly of someone else's sharing); or the offering of advice intended to "help" the person who has just shared. Clergy are particularly susceptible to the latter—in fact I don't know of a priest or bishop yet who has visited and not made this blunder! It is telling because it reveals quite clearly the assumption of the clergy that they "know better" than the laity. Consequently I have begun to take visiting clergy aside before the service in order to give them a good explanation of the midrash time, giving explicit instructions of what is intended and expected. Alas, however, some habits die hard! The assumption of authority is certainly one of them.

The Creed

The Nicene Creed presents a formidable challenge to inclusive liturgy. Because it is a historical document of the fifth century CE (there is little history of the Nicene Creed "evolving" over time, except perhaps for the addition of the "filioque" clause, which adds the words "and the Son" to the Creed), it is not subject to revision. In many progressive Episcopal churches I have attended, the Nicene Creed is the litmus test of how far one has gone in re-visioning Christianity. If you can say it with a straight face—with all the justifications and alternate meanings rattling off in your mind as you do it—then you've "made it." Pity the poor liberal who keeps his or her mouth shut during the recitation of the Creed: they still have work to do.

The text is as follows:

> We believe in one God,
> the Father, the Almighty,
> maker of heaven and earth,
> of all that is, seen and unseen.
>
> We believe in one Lord, Jesus Christ,
> the only Son of God,
> eternally begotten of the Father,
> God from God, Light from Light,
> true God from true God,
> begotten, not made,
> of one Being with the Father.
> Through him all things were made.
> For us and for our salvation
> he came down from heaven:
> by the power of the Holy Spirit
> he became incarnate from the Virgin Mary,
> and was made man.
> For our sake he was crucified
> under Pontius Pilate;
> he suffered death and was buried.
> On the third day he rose again
> in accordance with the Scriptures;
> he ascended into heaven
> and is seated at the right hand of the Father.
> He will come again in glory to judge
> the living and the dead,
> and his kingdom will have no end.

We believe in the Holy Spirit, the Lord, the giver of life,
who proceeds from the Father [and the Son].
With the Father and the Son he is worshiped
and glorified.
He has spoken through the Prophets.
We believe in one holy catholic
and apostolic Church.
We acknowledge one baptism
for the forgiveness of sins.
We look for the resurrection of the dead,
and the life of the world to come. Amen.

More and more churches are opting to replace the Nicene with the easier-to-swallow (and more ancient) Apostle's Creed (see Appendix C). The 1979 Episcopal *Book of Common Prayer* even makes allowances for this. But even the Apostle's Creed is hardly usable as-is in a "liberated" liturgy.

One answer is to omit the Nicene Creed altogether. This is defensible on the grounds that, as-is, the Creed does not speak the truth about our faith (God is not all-male, for instance). Secondly, the creed was created as an instruction against heresy and was never intended for liturgical recitation. It was incorporated into the liturgy for "blatant schismatic reasons,"[80] to justify the monophysite patriarch of Antioch in 473. Episcopal priest Richard Fabian (co-rector at St. Gregory Nyssan in San Francisco) advises ordinands that "if they must use the Nicene Creed in their parishes, they might march about waving American and Episcopal Church flags, while their church wardens tear up photographs of the Mormon Tabernacle: these gestures would express the custom's fundamental spirit...."[81]

It has thus been a stumbling block to ecumenism ever since the fifth century, especially with the bishop of Rome's insertion of the "filioque" clause ("We believe in the Holy Spirit, the giver of life, who proceeds from the Father *and the Son*"). With the insertion of the "and the Son" portion, Rome schismed itself from the rest of the historical church, as it takes an ecumenical council of the whole church to make such a change; no bishop, not even the bishop of Rome, has the power to change a historical document of the church. Thus, over this and other issues of power, Rome and the Eastern churches continue to be in schism.

The Congregationalist tradition offers another alternative. Very early in their formation they began a practice of drafting a church covenant for each congregation. Thus each local gathering of believers drafted a statement of faith that was true for them, and that was unique to them. This is a truly liberating option, for in reciting a common covenant, the community affirms for itself its mission and its commitment to God and to one another. For example, here are two such church covenants, one from a very old church (Salem church) and one from a contemporary Congregational church in Berkeley, CA.

Salem Church Covenant
We covenant with the Lord and one with another
and deo bynd our selves in the presence of God,
to walke together in all his waies,
according as he is pleased
to reveale himself unto us
in his blessed word of truth.[82]

Grace North Church Covenant
We are united in striving to know the will of God,
and our purpose is to walk in the ways of the Lord,
laboring for the progress of knowledge and justice,
the reign of peace and universal friendship;
depending as did our ancestors
upon the continued guidance of the Holy Spirit
to lead us into all truth.
Generations pass, but the Life we celebrate
and the Grace we trust are eternal and unchanging.
Christ is the Lord who redeems and enlightens
all who trust his grace;
and his Holy Spirit is still poured upon us
as we gather to share the Supper of the Lord.
By this Grace we choose to live
for those for whom we care
and in this Way of Christ we desire
to become a true Community of Grace.

The United Church of Christ, which emerged from the Congregational and Reformed traditions, has incorporated several covenants, or "statements of faith," into its *Book of Worship*, some of which are intended to be inclusive (see Appendix C).

The Festival has had difficulty with this particular element (the Creed) in that by virtue of its experimental and fiercely non-creedal character, finding a statement that everyone in attendance can agree to is almost impossible. One member has suggested that we compile a "Creed of Questions" that reflect the issues with which the Festival struggles, or a loose-leaf binder—open for public perusal at any Festival service—filled with our individual "Statements of Faith." Since everyone at the Festival is different, let's just have a book of Creeds! Early on we did experiment with a couple of "Earth Creeds," and still provide a rubric for inserting a "Statement of Faith" in the liturgy, but for the most part the practice has been dropped.

The Creed is not an insurmountable problem. There is good historical reason to omit it entirely (Jesus certainly wouldn't have been able to make heads or tails out of it), and plenty of precedent in Protestant traditions (such as the Congregationalist Covenant) for alternatives.

The Prayers

Since the Prayers of the People have historically varied from place to place, there is little difficulty in making them inclusive. The Prayers do not have a history of being a rigidly fixed text as so many other elements in the liturgy do. Pueblo Publishing has even published a liturgical resource, *Prayers for the People of God*, which offers full Prayers of the People in a reasonably inclusive fashion for each week of the three-year lectionary cycle, thematically tied to the lectionary readings.

The guidelines laid down by the 1979 Episcopal prayer book instruct that the Prayers should contain at least the following elements:

> The Universal Church, its members, and its mission
> The Nation and all in authority
> The welfare of the world
> The concerns of the local community
> Those who suffer and those in any trouble
> The departed (with commemoration
> of a saint when appropriate) (303).

It is not difficult to make the prayers inclusive, even deeply meaningful, since one does not have to follow a set traditional form. Consider the following (rather lengthy) form in use by the Festival:

> *Reader* We believe that silence and dance are appropriate forms of prayer. Therefore with all our hearts, minds, and

bodies, let us pray to our Creator in word, song, silence, and movement, singing:

Inhabit our prayer, O God.
or this **God hear our prayer.**

Reader For the cleansing, healing and rest of the Earth and all her creatures, the waters, soil and air, we pray... **R.**

Reader For a world-wide awakening to justice, liberation, and love, we pray... **R.**

Reader For increasing accountability and integrity of leaders in the church, the nations, and local social and political positions of power, we pray... **R.**

Reader For creative justice in our personal and public lives, for the helpless, for the downtrodden, for the betrayed, abused, and afflicted, we pray... **R.**

Reader For courage to confront evil, to live true to our divine natures, for the ability to hear God's voice, we pray... **R.**

Reader For the healing of all creatures sick and suffering, poisoned, disrespected and dying in our midst, known and unknown to us, we pray... **R.**

Reader For the welcoming of the Christ Spirit with every breath we breathe, we pray... **R.**

Reader Let us now offer up our own needs to God...

Prayers commemorated by sounding a bell and/or lighting a candle.

Reader With all our hearts, minds and bodies, let us praise our Creator, singing:

Inhabit our praise, O God ...
or **God, Hear our praise!**

Reader For the times we have been aware of your presence in our lives, we are grateful! **R.**

Reader For the wonder, intricacy, beauty and mystery of Creation and of the sacredness of our own existence, we are exuberant! **R.**

Reader For the true existence of love and compassion in the midst of suffering and evil, we acclaim your presence! **R.**

Reader For the growing awareness worldwide of our selfishness to this Earth and for the actions being taken to heal her and repent, we thank you! R.

Reader For creativity, beauty, justice, variety, emotion, ritual, sensuality, rivers, rocks and trees, love, solitude, change and trust, we are amazed! **R.**

Reader Let us now offer up our individual praises and thanksgivings.

Praises are offered and are commemorated by cymbals and bells and/or lighting a candle or other.

Reader Ever present and eternal God,
hear the prayers and praises of your people.
Help us to live in hope, to build your community,
and to be bearers of grace to all. **R. Amen.**

The Peace

The kiss of peace in most churches is simply a chance for the congregation to shake hands. Liturgically, however, it arose in keeping with Matthew 5:23-24: "So when you are offering your gift at the altar, if you remember that your brother or sister has something against you, leave your gift there before the altar and go; first be reconciled to your brother or sister, and then come and offer your gift." Thus in such ancient authorities as Justin, the Kiss of Peace was an opportunity within the celebration itself for reconciliation between worshippers, so that they may share at God's table with good will toward one another.

Reclaiming the meaning of this rite can be very powerful and very useful. It is a reminder, each time we come together, that our feelings are important, that loving confrontation, reconciliation, and forgiveness are not just theological ideas, but the very stuff of daily congregational life. The Kiss of Peace offers us an opportunity not to simply "stuff" our feelings, allowing tension and resentment to grow between us and our brothers or sisters. Instead it invites us to speak our pain, to ask for acknowledgement and apology, and to move ahead together with forgiveness and love.

Today there is more handshaking than kissing, although in more demonstrative congregations, one may see some hugging. As Fabian reports of the early church,

> Public kissing was a Christian innovation, originally baptismal: the bishop kissed the newly baptized to symbolize the gift of the Holy Spirit, just as God breathed life into Adam's mouth (Genesis 2) and the risen Christ breathed on the disciples (John 20).
>
> Anciently, therefore, Christians exchanged the Peace by kissing on the mouth, and men and women exchanged this kiss only with members of their own sex, to avoid scandal. (How times have changed!) Later it became a kiss on the cheek, or on both cheeks, or three kisses on two cheeks: in these forms eastern Christians have continued the practice uninterruptedly, using it inside and outside the liturgy.[84]

In Roman Catholic churches, the Kiss comes after the Eucharistic prayer and right before reception of communion. This innovation occurred around the fifth century. Most Protestant bodies retain the more ancient position of exchanging the Peace after the Prayers of the People and just before the Offertory. This does not seem to break up the flow of the Communion quite so much as the later placement, and also, if one needs more than a few seconds to say "I'm sorry" to someone, the earlier placement gives one the leeway of the Offertory to continue one's reconciliation.

As far as making the Kiss of Peace inclusive, it is a simple matter of replacing "The peace of the Lord be always with you" with "God's peace be always with you" or "The peace of Christ be always with you," or even simply, "Peace be with you!"

The Offertory and Transfer of Gifts

With the Offertory we transition from the Liturgy of the Word to the Liturgy of the Table, and whether it belongs to the first or the last half of the service is a matter of some disagreement. It is, in any case, certainly a preparation for communion and an opportunity to incarnate our worship, turning our words about justice into deeds. Justin wrote that the most important part of the Eucharist was the Offertory, when people brought forth the fruit of their "lives and labor" in order to assist "the orphans and widows, and those who are in want because of sickness or other cause, and those who are in bonds [prisoners], and, in short...all those in need."[84]

At the Festival, the Offertory is not just a time to "pass the plate" but also to bring forth canned goods for the local food bank, to offer "volunteer slips" promising a certain number of social service hours for the week to come, or any other "offering" of one's time or other resources towards the manifestation of the Community of God. The Offertory is the ideal point in the service to promote social justice, and to encourage people to be involved in making justice in their communities, both within the service and outside of it.

Finally, there is the Transfer of Gifts, where, after the Offering has been taken, we symbolize the returning of our money, time, and other "fruits of our hands" back to God by bringing forth the bread and wine to the Holy Table. As Fabian tells us,

> The Transfer of Gifts from sideboard to altar table was originally a homely part of a rabbi's dinner with his close disciples—a formal but intimate routine called *Chaburah*, or Feast of Friends. The students brought gifts of food and placed them on the sideboard; when all had assembled the doors were closed, and one after another the dishes were carried to the table, blessed, and served while the company discussed the scriptures. Christians continued this simple usage for centuries: as their congregations grew, the deacons chose bread and wine from the people's many offerings on sideboards, and carried these to the table while the people exchanged the Peace.
>
> With the advent of crowded public church buildings, this simple Transfer of Gifts became a procession with chants and prayers extolling God's awesome presence and creative bounty toward us, from which we offer gifts of bread and wine. In the East this ritual swelled to a juggernaut dwarfing and finlly eclipsing the Entry Procession. On medieval Sundays at Haghia Sophia, 600 clergy marched in the Transfer of Gifts! No weekly liturgy could bear two such extravagnzas, so the distinctively participatory Byzantine Entry Procession atrophied. In Byzantine churches today a mere vestige of the Entry Procession crops up amid the opening hymns and readings, and is called "Little Entrance"; the title "Great Entrance" now belongs to the Transfer of Gifts.[85]

The Transfer of Gifts is by comparison a small affair in Western churches, and usually consists of two laypersons processing with the bread and the wine at the same time as the Offering plate is being brought forward for the blessing. These are our "gifts" in various forms, being given back to God by us all.

The Preparation of the Gifts

When the gifts have been received by the minister at the Holy Table, thanks are given for the bread and wine, for their symbolic import, and for the ritual we are about to perform. The Roman Catholic Preparation is as follows:

> *Priest* Blessed are you, Lord, God of all Creation.
> Through your goodness we have this bread to offer,
> which earth has given and human hands have made.
> It will become for us the bread of life.
> *People* **Blessed be God forever.**
>
> *Priest* Blessed are you, Lord, God of all Creation.
> Through your goodness we have this wine to offer,
> fruit of the vine and work of human hands.
> It will become our spiritual drink.
> *People* **Blessed be God forever.**[86]

This is a beautiful, creation-centered prayer which is easily made inclusive. While most Protestant bodies have omitted the Presentation of the Gifts owing to the Reformer's overreaction to the Mass as a repetition of Christ's sacrifice, it is slowly being rediscovered as an ideal opportunity to give thanks for the offerings, to acknowledge our dependence upon God, and to set the mood for the Eucharistic Prayer, which immediately follows.

In the Festival of the Holy Names we have adapted the above text and two other texts for use during the Preparation. One is from the *Didache*:

> *Presider* Blessed are you our Creator,
> for the life and wisdom and transforming love
> that you have made known to us
> through your child, Jesus.
> *People* **Glory to you forever!**
>
> *Presider* Blessed are you, our Creator
> for you have called us to be branches
> of the true vine that you have made known to us
> through your child Jesus.
> *People* **Glory to you forever!**
>
> *Presider* As the grains of wheat once scattered
> were gathered to become one bread,
> so may all your people from the ends of the earth
> be gathered into your community.

Beloved, this is the joyful feast
of the people of God.
Come from the East and the West,
and from the North and the South,
and gather about the table of God.

Another Presentation of the Gifts comes to us from the writings of Teilhard de Chardin. Adapted originally from an Australian *Creation Eucharist*, it is presented here as adapted to the Festival of the Holy Names' usage:

> *Presider* With this bread, O Christ, we place here all the creative action of the peoples of the Earth, their aspirations, their joy, their achievements, and their work.
>
> With this wine, we behold the sorrows, the pain and the suffering of all your Creation.
>
> Into this offering of the world we would gather those closest to us, our beloved and those at enmity with us, and with these we unite the great multitude of souls in Creation. With deepest compassion we join ourselves with the ceaseless journey of the universe, past, present, and future, with its joys and sorrows, hopes and fears, that we may be one with it all.
>
> We draw into this offering every form of life, animals and plants, rocks and fire, planets and stars, winds and waters; and we offer ourselves, all we have, and all that we are. Let all existence be now placed here on our altar that with joy and gratitude we may offer it to you.[87]

The Preparation of the Gifts is an ideal place to remind ourselves of our connection to creation, that all we have to offer to God comes only from this earth. With this prayer the table is set and the Eucharistic Prayer is ready to begin.

The Liturgy of the Table

We now shift our focus from the Liturgy of the Word to the Liturgy of the Table, the most important part of which is the Eucharistic Prayer. This half of the service is called the "Mass of the Faithful" in Orthodox Churches, and in imperial times, only the baptized were allowed to witness it.

Most prayers since imperial times have assumed a trinitarian form. After the preface, the presider begins the Eucharistic prayer proper, which has three parts, one for each person of the trinity: First there is the *anamnesis*, the "remembering" of God's gracious acts on our behalf, as well as a thanksgiving for the glories of Creation. Next there is the Institutional Narrative (also sometimes referred to as an *anamnesis*, for both parts are involved in *remembering*), which is chiefly concerned with Christ Jesus, and the retelling of the last supper. Finally the Holy Spirit is addressed in the *epiclesis*, requesting the blessing of the offering (both ourselves and the gifts of bread and wine). Most contemporary Eucharistic prayers follow this threefold format: thanking the Creator, remembering Christ, and inviting the Spirit.

The Sursum Corda

"*Sursum Corda,*" Latin for "Lift up your hearts," provides the name for this part of the ritual.

The Liturgy of the Table begins in a most ancient way, in a dialogue that is derived from scripture and has its ritual origin in the Jewish Sabbath Supper:

Celebrant The Lord be with you.
People **And also with you.**

Celebrant Lift up your hearts.
People **We lift them to the Lord.**

Celebrant Let us give thanks to the Lord our God.
People **It is right to give him thanks and praise.**

Although its basic form goes all the way back to our second earliest extant Eucharistic prayer, recorded in the *Apostolic Tradition of Hyppolytus* (third century C.E.), there are variations. The Eastern Orthodox liturgy includes the dialogue, "Christ is in the midst of us!," to which the assisting priest responds, "He is with us and will be." This is at the end of the Eucharistic prayer in Orthodox liturgy, but the Celtic church (and more recently, Anglican prayers) made this part of the Sursum Corda:

Presider The Lord is here.
All **His Spirit is with us.**

Presider Lift up your hearts...[88]

The Festival has taken advantage of the inclusive possibilities of the Celtic usage, and renders the *Sursum Corda* thus:

Presider Christ is here.
People **The Spirit is with us.**

Presider Open your hearts.
People **We offer them to God.**

Presider Let us give thanks to the Infinite One.
People **We rejoice to give thanks and praise.**

Note that the transcendent language in "Lift up your hearts / We lift them to the Lord" (which suggests that God is somewhere up in the sky) has been amended to reflect what we are really trying to get at, that we are coming to this table with open hearts to offer them—and the rest of us—to God.

The Proper Preface, Sanctus and Benedictus

The traditional Liturgy of the Table then continues, with the presider saying:

> It is right, and a good and joyful thing, always and everywhere to give thanks to you, Father Almighty, Creator of heaven and earth. For you...

At this point a Proper Preface is sung or said. Although the whole first part of the Liturgy, from the *Sursum Corda* through the *Sanctus,* was originally known as the Preface, now this word is usually only used to describe this short, variable, and optional component. It provides the community an opportunity to "customize" each particular celebration, since at the "For you..." the celebrant may extemporize or make use of a previously prepared Preface that reminds the worshipers of the focus or theme of the day's celebration. The Preface usually states in succinct terms precisely what the congregation is thankful for on this occasion.

This opportunity is lost when one is expected to simply use an appointed Proper Preface, which in Anglican and Roman usage may or may not have any thematic connection to the readings or the sermon. Ideally all of the "variable" parts of the service (opening prayer, readings, litanies, sermon, proper preface) would be tied together thematically to give the service both focus and variety.

The proper preface is especially easy to make inclusive and community-specific, since there is not a set historical form to keep. A typical Festival of the Holy Names preface for the theme of "Peace" might be: "...for your peace passes all understanding and it weaves healing and redemption throughout Creation." Proper Prefaces are short, sweet, and quick reiterations of the day's theme.

After the short statement of "why we are thankful today," the presider concludes, saying:

> Therefore we praise you, joining our voices with Angels and Archangels and with all the company of heaven, who forever sing this hymn to proclaim the glory of your Name...

The hymn which follows, known as the *Sanctus*, is derived from Isaiah 6:3 and depicts God's appearance in the Jerusalem temple as a King in "his" court, surrounded by Seraphim shouting "Holy! Holy! Holy!":

> Holy, holy, holy
> Lord, God of hosts
> Heaven and earth are full of your glory.
> Hosanna in the highest.

This is usually followed by a short section from Psalm 118 known as the *Benedictus:*

> Blessed is he who comes in the name of the Lord.
> Hosanna in the highest.

As Fabian tells us, since the Benedictus is found at both the end of the *Didache*'s Eucharist text and is commonly sung at Jewish Sabbath Suppers, it may very well be the hymn sung by Jesus and the disciples at the Last Supper. When sung together with the *Sanctus*, this hymn provides one of the aesthetic high points of the Eucharistic prayer, as many beautiful settings are commonly used for corporate singing. Since the two are usually bundled together, I will refer to the two together as the *"Sanctus."*

If it seems that a hymn like this should more logically provide the climax of the prayer, you are correct. Originally, the prayer was over by the time the *Sanctus* was sung, but in time another, and yet another, prayer was added, until before the end of the fifth century the hymn found itself sandwiched in the middle of the ritual rather than at the end.[45] St. Gregory Nyssan Episcopal Church in San Francisco has restored the Sanctus to its powerful position at the end of the prayer, and while it works just fine there, this change is not likely to start a movement.

A more important innovation has been to change the text of the *Sanctus* to make it as beautiful as its musical setting. The 1979

Episcopal *Book of Common Prayer* expunges its militant language by rendering the beginning of the hymn "Holy, holy, holy Lord, God of *power and might*." This is very helpful, but the transcendent language of "Hosanna in the Highest" is retained, reinforcing the Heaven/Earth dualism inherited from Persian (and later Gnostic) sources. This may or may not be a problem, depending upon how sensitive a community is to such dualisms.

At the Festival of the Holy Names, we have rendered the Sanctus as follows:

> Holy, holy, holy, God of love and power,
> All Creation speaks of your glory, O-God-with-us.
> Blessed are we who come in the name of our God!
> Hosanna, Hosanna from our hearts.

This version, sung to a setting by Ronald A. Nelson from the United Church of Christ's *Book of Worship*, provides one of the emotional high points of the Festival celebration. Militant language ("God of power and might") has been eschewed for the balance of "love and power." Instead of playing into the Heaven/Earth dualism, we simply say "All Creation," which logically includes both. Further, instead of casting our praise into some Heaven-in-the-sky, we address our song to Emmanuel, God-immanent: God-with-us.

For the *Benedictus*, "blessed is he," which has been taken to mean Jesus, and subsequently the priest, is replaced by "we," since we are all priests and are charged to be Jesus for each other. Finally, "Hosanna from our hearts" is again a little closer to home—and heart—than the transcendent original.

While the Festival text may no doubt seem to some to deviate too far from the original, the reader can surely see that, for all of its novelty, the community has sought to retain the meaning and intention of the traditional hymn.

The Anamnesis: Thanking the Creator

Anamnesis means "Remembrance," and in the next two sections we will be remembering the Creator's gifts to us throughout history, up to and including Jesus, for Christians the culmination of God's faithfulness. Jesus is then remembered again in the recitation of the institution of the Last Supper.

The first part of the *anamnesis*, which I call "Thanking the Creator," usually contains themes of gratitude for the gift of creation, and a retelling of salvation history—a remembrance of God's faithfulness to people of faith through time; or simply asking God to remember *us*.

The *anamnesis* of the current Roman Catholic prayer is of the latter variety, and reads:

> We come to you, Father,
> with praise and thanksgiving,
> through Jesus Christ your Son.
> Through him we ask you to accept and bless
> these gifts, which we offer you in sacrifice.
>
> We offer them for your holy Catholic Church,
> watch over it and guide it;
> grant it peace and unity throughout the world.
> We offer them for N. our Pope,
> for N. our bishop,
> and for all who hold and teach the catholic faith
> that comes to us from the apostles.
> Remember, Lord, your people,
> especially those for whom we now pray, N. and N.
> Remember all of us gathered here before you.
> You know how firmly we believe in you
> and dedicate ourselves to you.
> We offer you this sacrifice of praise
> for ourselves and those who are dear to us.
> We pray to you, our living and true God,
> for our well-being and redemption.[90]

We might well ask whether God needs to be reminded of us, or whether it is we who need to be reminded of God. There is also a great deal of stress in the above prayer on the fact that this act is a sacrifice, for which the gifts are offered, and a sense of isolationalism, asking God to bless the leaders of the "Catholic" faith, and not for the souls of all beings or even the leaders of all Christian churches. On the other hand, happily, in this prayer a "sacrifice of praise" rather than one of suffering is offered as being pleasing to God.

Not all *anamneses* have been so limited. Prayer "D" from the 1979 Episcopal *Book of Common Prayer* provides an example of gratitude for the Creation:

> We acclaim you, holy Lord, glorious in power. Your mighty works reveal your wisdom and love. You formed us in your own image, giving the whole world into our care,

> so that, in obedience to you, our Creator, we might rule and serve all your creatures. When our disobedience took us far from you, you did not abandon us to the power of death. In your mercy you came to our help, so that in seeking you we might find you (373).

As awareness of our ecological crisis has risen, more Creation-oriented themes have emerged in the Eucharistic prayers of many churches. This particularly beautiful prayer comes from the United Reformed Church of the United Kingdom:

> We thank you,
> Lord God almighty,
> that you are a God of people,
> that you are not ashamed
> to be called our God,
> that you know us all by name,
> that you hold the world in your hands.
> You have created us
> and called us in this life
> that we should be made one with you
> to be your people here on earth.
> Blessed are you, creator of all that is.
> Blessed are you
> for giving us space and time for living.
> Blessed are you for the light of our eyes
> and for the air we breathe.
> We thank you for the whole of creation,
> for all the works of your hands,
> for all that you have done among us
> through Jesus Christ our Lord.[91]

This prayer is remarkable not only for its message of inclusivity towards the whole of God's creation, but also because it is rendered in lyrical language appropriate for the beauty of its subject.

Another prayer remarkable for its language is Prayer C from the Episcopal *Book of Common Prayer,* which is striking for a number of reasons. Like many Orthodox liturgies, there is a great deal of "call and response" between the presider and the congregation in this prayer. Plus, there is no "proper preface" in this prayer. Derided by many in the Episcopal church as "the Star Wars prayer," many congregations have gotten past the initial shock and have come to appreciate its "cosmic" language:

Presider God of all power, Ruler of the Universe,
you are worthy of glory and praise.

People **Glory to you for ever and ever.**

Presider At your command all things came to be: the vast expanse of interstellar space, galaxies, suns, the planets in their courses, and this fragile earth, our island home.

People **By your will they were created
and have their being.**

Presider From the primal elements you brought forth the human race, and blessed us with memory, reason, and skill You made us the rulers of creation. But we turned against you, and betrayed your trust; and we turned against one another.

People **Have mercy, Lord,
for we are sinners in your sight.**

Presider Again and again, you called us to return. Through prophets and sages you revealed your righteous Law. And in the fullness of time you sent your only Son, born of a woman, to fulfill your Law, to open for us the way of freedom and peace.

People **By his blood, he reconciled us.
By his wounds, we are healed (369-370).**

The church's thanksgiving is not only for the gift of creation, but typically also for God's continued faithfulness. Thus, most prayers also include a "history of salvation," which traces God's action on behalf of humankind from the Old Testament to the New. Prayer "B" from the same prayer book summarizes the history of salvation thusly:

> We give thanks to you, O God, for the goodness and love which you have made known to us in creation; in the calling of Israel to be your people; in your Word spoken through the prophets; and above all in the Word made flesh, Jesus, your Son. For in these last days you sent him to be incarnate from the Virgin Mary, to be the Savior and Redeemer of the world. In him, you have delivered us from evil, and made us worthy to stand before you. In him, you have brought us out of error into truth, out of sin into righteousness, out of death into life (368).

One problem with such histories of salvation is the narrow focus on Israel and the early church as "God's people," ignoring the sheep of Christ's "other" flocks. The idea that God has only been present and attentive to the peoples of Judaic and Christian cultures is sheer hubris. Prayer Three from the Festival of the Holy Names liturgy also contains a history of salvation, but is more welcoming and universal in its approach to people of other faith traditions:

> Eternal God,
> from before the times of our reckoning,
> we have celebrated with a holy meal
> the family you have made of us.
>
> You have come to us in many ways:
> To the children of Abraham and Sarah,
> you came in manna, the life-giving bread
> that appeared as dew upon the ground,
> nourishing and giving witness
> to your faithfulness day after day.
>
> To the disciples, you came in Jesus,
> the Bread of Life,
> feeding the souls of all who have ears to hear.
>
> To Christians you have come
> in the bread of Eucharist,
> uniting a family of faith, now and forevermore;
>
> And to people of compassion everywhere
> you have come in your life-giving Spirit
> to provide a soulful feast
> for the whole of the Earth.

This prayer does indeed tell "our" story as Westerners and inheritors of the Judaic-Christian traditions, but also acknowledges God's faithfulness to peoples of other cultures as well.

The Institution: Remembering Christ

For Christians the history of salvation naturally culminates in the coming of Jesus, his ministry, crucifixion, and miraculous resurrection. This provides a seamless transition into the Institutional Narrative where Jesus "institutes" the Eucharist. This version is from the Roman rite:

> The day before he suffered
> he took bread in his sacred hands

and looking up to heaven,
to you, his almighty Father,
he gave you thanks and praise.
He broke the bread,
gave it to his disciples, and said:
Take this, all of you, and eat it:
this is my body which will be given up for you.
When supper was ended, he took the cup.
Again he gave you thanks and praise,
gave the cup to his disciples, and said:
Take this, all of you, and drink from it:
this is the cup of my blood,
the blood of the new and everlasting covenant.
It will be shed for you and for all
so that sins may be forgiven.
Do this in memory of me.[92]

This prayer is most closely modeled on Matthew's version of the account,[93] but is nonetheless heavily embellished. Traditional Anglican Institutions are likewise paraphrased. But whether the exact texts are used (as many Protestants insist) or not, all Western liturgies agree that the Institutional Narrative is mandatory to the Eucharistic Prayer.

This is not so for the Eastern Orthodox. As we have seen, for Western Christianity it is the recitation of this short passage that effects the "change" in the elements. When Jesus says, "This is my body," and, "This is the cup of my blood," the transformation is believed to occur, and the simple elements of bread and wine are no longer as they seem. But for Orthodox Christians, it is the *epiclesis* (see below), a prayer inviting the transforming power of the Holy Spirit, that effects the change on the elements. Consequently many early Eucharistic prayers (such as the Didache) and some later Orthodox prayers (the Liturgy of Addai and Mari, for example) omit the Insitutional Narrative altogether.

The Institutional texts provide a number of difficulties for Western Christians. Far from merely being a retelling of a cozy meal with Jesus' friends, its language is filled with sacrificial import. Jesus hands bread and wine to his friends saying, "This is my body which will be given up for you.... Take this, all of you, and drink from it: this is the cup of my blood, the blood of the new and everlasting covenant. It will be shed for you and for all so that sins may be forgiven."

For many Christians, the sacrificial implications of the above text are every bit as unpalatable as the idea of eating flesh and drinking blood. Especially for women, who have been sacrificing their own flesh and blood for millenia, such ideas are not liberating or redemptive in any meaningful way.[94]

After much thought, the Festival of the Holy Names worked out the following paraphrase of the Institution account that we feel best illustrates what Jesus might have really meant:

> At the feast of Passover,
> Jesus and his friends met
> to celebrate their ritual meal.
> According to tradition,
> their rabbi picked up
> the unleavened bread to bless it,
> and surprised them instead with new words.
> Likening the bread to his own body
> about to be broken, he broke the bread,
> and passed it around the circle.
> When the time came
> for the final cup of wine to be shared,
> Jesus again spoke new words,
> and likened the wine to his own blood
> about to be spilled.

With this prayer we stand in a firm tradition of paraphrasing the scriptural Institutional texts, and also we honor both God and our consciences by *praying what we actually believe.*

It also occurred to us early on that, from the Orthodox perspective, the traditional Institutional Narrative is not even strictly necessary. So long as we include an *epiclesis*, we need not be tied to the four traditional (Biblical) accounts. This allows for a much broader repertoire of Institutional possibilities. Long-neglected texts, such as Jesus' "bread of life" discourse in John Chapter Six, has many possible uses, and has found its way into the Festival of the Holy Names' first Eucharistic prayer.[95] Other wonderful texts include John's prelude to the Lord's Supper: the footwashing scene,[96] and Luke's story of the two disciples on the road to Emmaus.[97] These texts can all be seen in Appendix D, Alternative Institutional Narratives.

Other possibilities abound, such as the Marriage Feast of the Lamb (Revelation) and the many post-resurrection mealtime accounts. A community need only approach these texts with imagination and an openness to what God is wanting to feed them to discover these and other rich Institutional possibilities. It is, simply, "remembering how Jesus fed us" and expressing the willingness to be fed in the present that creates a meaningful remembrance.

Another difficulty many Christians face with the more "traditional" Institution is the "change" that is supposed to be effected in the elements by the narratives. While Protestants have been content for centuries to dispense with the Aristotelian Transubstantiation doctrine of St. Thomas Aquinas, Roman Catholic theologians have been saddled with making sense of it as the accepted teaching.

This has been a particularly difficult albatross to bear. Some contemporary scholars, most notably Schoonberg and Schillebeeckx, have argued for a concept called "transignification." This name points to the locus of divine activity as being on the symbolic, psychological or even metaphysical level, rather than on any actual physical change in the elements. They seek to "remove this change and presence from the purely physical level to the specifically sacramental level, the level on which the inner meaning of ritual and liturgical language is the content of the power of the sacrament: the sacraments of the new law contain the grace which they signify."[98]

As Davies explains further, the being of things changes with a change of relationship

> For example, a colored cloth is simply decorative, but if a government declares that this is the national flag, its meaning has radically changed since it is the organ through which patriotism is expressed. Thus, a new meaning is given to the Eucharist, not by any [human being], but by the Son of God. Schillebeeckx argues that bread and wine, already useful to humanity in that they nourish physical life, have a further meaning in the human intercourse, for "bread is the symbol of life and wine is the symbol of joy."[99]

This new way of viewing the "change" that occurs has vast ecumenical potential. When the mother of a Baptist friend discovered I had become a Catholic, she reacted in horror that I might believe that the bread and wine actually turn into flesh and blood! I smiled upon hearing it, and I remember thinking, "Yes, but the change occurs in here (in my head), not out there." This very well may have been an explanation she could have received, perhaps even embraced, if I had had a chance to explain.

Though many Evangelical Protestants dismiss the Eucharist as "just a symbol," few people (even thoughtful Evangelicals) truly deny the power of psychological symbols in our daily lives. The phrase "just a symbol" is in fact, laughably oxymoronic—one might just as well describe the leader of the United States as "just the president" or Jesus as "just the Son of God," because in the lives of most of us, there are no greater powers than the psychological conditionings and symbolic and ritual patterns so deeply engrained in our imaginations and psyches.

Transignification is a powerful way of speaking about the "change" that takes place during the prayer. But like the early controversies of Part Two, it again asks us to think about exactly where the "change" is happening: is it in the bread and wine or in us? Transignification implies that it is in us, and in that it stands fully within the Orthodox understanding. American Jesuit Joseph Powers, an advocate of transignification, goes further, saying that the sacramental import has little to do with the "things" that are given, but everything to do with the "giving" itself:

> Bread and wine are thus given a new meaning by the Lord of the church, and so the words of consecration are directed not simply to the bread and wine, but to believers. And Christ is present sacramentally in an action that is the gift of himself. Christ is present, therefore, in a sign-act (not a thing, but an action of self-communication to other persons).[100]

Thus, for Powers (as for the Anglican reformer Thomas Hooker, whom we met in Part Two), the Eucharist is a verb! This is a very fruitful starting point for a community to evaluate the meaning of the Institutional Narrative for themselves. Is the power in a magical formula, or in the magic of the simple action of being fed by Christ? Few Christians today would affirm the former, but getting people to contemplate why the act is more powerful than the formula is difficult, as there is so much unexplained (and unexamined) tradition to wade through. With a broadened understanding of Institution and the concept of transignification, we are given two powerful tools to help us in our reevaluations and liturgical explorations of the remembering of Christ in the sharing of the Eucharistic elements.

The Epiclesis: Inviting the Spirit

Far more important to the Eastern Orthodox than the Institutional Narrative, the *epiclesis* is the prayer of invitation to the Holy Spirit. The Spirit is asked to visit and transform both the community and (in later prayers) also the bread and wine. This is the pivotal moment in the Orthodox liturgy, and it parallels the Orthodox insistance on the Resurrection as the redemptive moment in salvation history. While the West insists that it is Jesus' giving of his body and blood on the cross, symbolized in the giving of his body and blood in the Institutional Narrative, that is most important sacramentally and theologically, for the Orthodox it is the transforming power of the Spirit which quickened Jesus' dead body, and likewise rouses us from our sleep in the Eucharist.

Until the liturgical reforms of Vatican II, Roman usage has downplayed the importance of the *epiclesis*. But the scholarship of the liturgical movement has had profound and far-reaching influence: it is rare to find a Eucharistic prayer today in any liturgical church that lacks at least a brief *epiclesis*.

The 1979 Episcopal *Book of Common Prayer* gives the following *epiclesis*:

> We celebrate the memorial of our redemption, O Father, in this sacrifice of praise and thanksgiving. Recalling his death, resurrection, and ascension, we offer you these gifts.
>
> Sanctify them by your Holy Spirit to be for your people the Body and Blood of your Son, the holy food and drink of new and unending life in him. Sanctify us also that we may faithfully receive this holy sacrament, and serve you in unity, constancy, and peace; and at the last day bring us with all your saints into the joy of your eternal kingdom (363).

Like most *epicleses*, the twin petitions here to sanctify 1) the elements and 2) the community are expressed. This prayer offers a wonderful opportunity for a community to make clear (to God certainly, but most importantly to themselves) what their intentions are, both as Christians in general and in each particular Eucharist.

Yet there is one aspect of the prayer that may cause some difficulty: asking God to bless that which is already blessed. While most Christians affirm the reality of human sin, increasingly many are rejecting the notion that human sin has the power to "infect" the whole of Creation. The idea that "fallen humanity = fallen universe" is hubris to many theologians. The fact that humankind might have forgotten the steps to the cosmic dance in no way inhibits the cosmos from its soft-shoe and shuffle. As one colleague of mine put it, "Why do we need a consecration? When God said, 'It is good,' in the beginning, it was good enough for me."

Indeed, if the Holy Spirit indwells and suffuses the whole of Creation, why would we ask for something to be filled that is already brimming with divinity? This of course assumes a panentheistic[101] perspective, which has a solid place in orthodox Christian teaching, especially in the East. But even though we may affirm the Spirit's blessed ubiquity, we are, perhaps, less inclined to notice it. Thus, the *epiclesis* is an opportune time to redirect our awareness to the Spirit's immanent presence in our community, and even in the simple gifts of bread and wine on our altar.

One of the Festival of the Holy Names' *epicleses* does so explicitly:

> ...In this moment, through your bountiful Creation, you give us these gifts again. They are full of life and goodness, blessed and holy.
>
> Let us become aware of your presence in these gifts. For as your Spirit saturates and indwells all of Creation, O Christ, even so are these gifts—this bread, and this cup—brimming with divinity.
>
> Teach us to partake of them with due reverence, and in so doing, help us to go forth into the world with like reverence for all that we behold, for in you do all things consist and have their being.

Another of the Festival of the Holy Names' *epicleses* asks that we be made aware of God's presence in our community:

> Therefore we ask that, in the sharing of this bread, and in the drinking of this wine, our own eyes might be opened to behold you; in the glory of your Creation, in the Wisdom of your Word, and in the faces of our sisters and brothers gathered here in your name to celebrate an astounding love.

In such *epicleses* we affirm God's presence and the goodness of creation, while at the same time setting apart the elements for "sacred" use. Like the Buddhist who knows that all things have "Buddha nature" and that it is simply her blindness to it that propels her to seek enlightenment, so we affirm the holiness of all creation, and ask God in this prayer to awaken our senses to behold it, not only here in these elements, but in ourselves and the whole of the world.

This is probably one of the most useful aspects of sacramental worship when it is re-visioned: by setting off a certain area as "sacred space," we learn in a small environment what it means to step on holy ground. By setting apart certain objects as "sacred things," we learn the proper awe for them as we handle them, or in the case of the Eucharist, break, share, and consume them. Then when we turn our attention to the world at large and call it "holy," we know what that means. We know how to walk on the earth, because we know what it means to step on holy ground. We cherish the earth's gifts, because we know what holy objects are, and how they should be treated.

The *epiclesis* is one of the most vital elements of the Eucharistic prayer, and one that deserves close attention and careful wording. While the *anamnesis* is useful in calling to mind why it is we are grateful, it is the *epiclesis* that provides the shock of *satori* (enlightenment), which turns our attention from the particular to the universal and charges the temporal with eternity.

The Lord's Prayer

Our Father, who art in heaven,
hallowed be thy Name,
thy kingdom come, thy will be done,
on earth as it is in heaven.
Give us this day our daily bread.
And forgive us our trespasses
as we forgive those who trespass against us.
And lead us not into temptation,
but deliver us from evil.
For thine is the kingdom,
and the power and the glory forever and ever. Amen.

Not originally part of the Eucharistic prayer, the Lord's prayer eventually crept in, first among the churches of Africa in the early fourth century. Its use spread quickly, until by the end of the fourth century it was nearly universal. According to Augustine, it was placed after the fraction (the breaking of bread), but other early authorities place it after communion, then conclude with a doxology.[102]

While it is familiar to most folks, the radical nature of the Lord's prayer is often overlooked. The words are so familiar that for many they have become liturgical wallpaper: they provide a nice atmosphere but have little artistic or spiritual import of their own. This is in its own way tragic, since the Lord's prayer is one of the great and genuine treasures of the Western liturgical tradition. It asks that:

- God's Community (Kingdom) be realized
- We will have all that we need to live
- We be forgiven to the measure that we are willing to forgive
- We be delivered from danger

These are the simplest of needs, and yet as Balasuriay notes, this prayer is "a masterpiece of Jesus' revelation of the [intimate parent]hood of God and of human solidarity. It explains why Jesus contested all forms of evil prevailing in his day and helped in the integral liberation of persons."[103]

The prayer is radical for many reasons. First is the "shocking" way Jesus addresses God; not in the high and lofty terms the Jews were accustomed to, but almost irreverently, as "Abba," or "Daddy." Second, Jesus asks that the Community of God be made manifest here on earth, and then implies how this might be done: when all have enough for their basic survival, and when we have learned to forgive each other. This is a powerful and revolutionary document! Indeed, in the *content* of the prayer there is little that feminist and other contemporary believers might object to. Chiefly, the only objections raised have been the address of God as "Father" and the petition to not be led into temptation by God.

The "ecumenical" version found in the 1979 *Book of Common Prayer* addressses the latter concern aptly:

> Our Father in heaven,
> hallowed be your Name,
> your kingdom come,
> your will be done,
> on earth as it is in heaven.
> Give us today our daily bread.
> Forgive us our sins
> as we forgive those who sin against us.
> Save us from the time of trial,
> and deliver us from evil.

For the kingdom, the power
and the glory are yours, now and forever. Amen.

While the following version by Roman Catholic theologian Edward Gabriele partially succeeds in addressing the former concern by using the Aramaic "Abba." The word is still masculine in its original tongue, even though it is alien enough to us not to *feel* sexist:

Abba in heaven,
Your name is holy!
Your justice come,
Your will be done,
On earth as in the heavens.
Fill us this day
With all that we need.
Teach us to heal
As you have healed us.
Bring us not to the test
But deliver us always
from the power of evil.
You alone are God
And all belongs to you![104]

The issue of what to do with the reference to God as "Father" is a very difficult problem indeed. For if we were to simply substitute a gender-neutral name (such as "Creator") we lose Jesus' very point regarding God's familial relationship with us. At the Festival of the Holy Names, it seems, we are loathe to leave any stone unturned, and have dealt with this by referring to God using a gender-balanced strategy:

God our Father, God our Mother,
holy are your names.
May your community be realized,
and your desires manifest
on Earth even as in the heavens.
Grant us this day all that we require,
and as we have been forgiven by you,
help us to forgive others.
Walk with us through the paths of adversity,
stand firm with us in our times of suffering.
For yours are grace, justice, and love,
now and forever. Amen.

The Lord's Prayer (or "Jesus' Prayer" as we have titled it in the Festival liturgy) is a great starting point for a community interested in writing its own liturgy. It is familiar enough for everyone to understand what is at stake by reworking, and for everyone to experience the "shock value" inherent in changing familiar words. But it is also short enough that a small group just testing the waters can get their feet wet, and to discover what re-visioning liturgy is all about. It may well be the most important prayer a community will have to adapt, and caution is to be taken not to set a version in stone: different approaches will suggest themselves once a community begins to work with liturgy. A "Lord's Prayer of the Week" might begin appearing, which is a fine thing, especially if there is time provided for the community to discuss their feelings and impressions about the proffered texts.

Distribution of Communion

There is no clear historical consensus on how to call people to the table to receive communion. The most ancient form is probably the Orthodox, which is brief but beautiful: "Holy things for holy people!"

The current Roman Catholic usage in contrast is highly sacrificial in theme: "This is the Lamb of God who takes away the sins of the world. Happy are those who are called to his supper."

The 1979 *Book of Common Prayer* is simple and elegant, yet provides for a lengthening addition which hails from Zwingli's Eucharist service: "The Gifts of God for the People of God" (and may add: "Take them in remembrance that Christ died for you, and feed on him in your hearts by faith, with thanksgiving.")

At the Festival of the Holy Names we say simply: "All are invited to share this communion, for at God's table there is room for all. Come to the feast prepared for you from the foundation of the world."

Whatever text is used for the call to the table, it should be commensurate with the tone of the preceding prayers, and should be inviting to the people, rather than daunting (as in the Anglican "prayer of humble access.")[105]

After the call, the elements are distributed, usually with the words, "The Body of Christ," and, "The Blood of Christ," or some variation of the same. Since at the Festival we have remythologized the elements to be gifts other than Christ's body and blood, the words accompanying distribution differ with each Eucharistic prayer.

For our first Eucharistic prayer, where the bread symbolizes life and the wine joy, we offer them with the words, "The Bread of Life," and, "The Cup of Joy." Our second prayer is for liberation, and the elements represent the bodies and blood of all people everywhere, including Jesus, who have been the victims of injustice. Breaking the bread reminds us of the bodies, spirits and habitats that have been destroyed; pouring out the wine reminds us of their spilled blood. Therefore when distributing the bread we say, "We are all one body," and with the wine, "We are all one blood." In our fourth Eucharistic prayer, Christ in Community, it is the act of breaking bread together that makes us family, that makes us church. Therefore each element is distributed with the words, "Christ is here." The person receiving responds, "The Spirit is with us."

The Post-Communion Prayer

The use of a post-communion prayer is another fourth-century innovation. The Roman rite uses a short proper prayer recited by the priest alone, while for many Orthodox and Protestant churches, including Anglican and Lutheran, a corporate prayer of a fixed form is used. The standard text from the 1979 *Book of Common Prayer* is as follows:

> Eternal God, heavenly Father,
> you have graciously accepted us as living members
> of your Son our Savior Jesus Christ,
> and you have fed us with spiritual food
> in the Sacrament of his Body and Blood.
> Send us now into the world in peace,
> and grant us strength and courage
> to love and serve you
> with gladness and singleness of heart;
> through Christ our Lord. Amen (365).

While this is an adequate prayer, it is not terribly moving. Compare it with one from the British 1980 *Alternative Service Book*:

> Father of all, we give you thanks and praise, that when we were still far off you met us in your Son and brought us home. Dying and living, he declared your love, gave us

> grace, and opened the gate of glory. May we who share Christ's body live his risen life; we who drink his cup bring life to others; we whom the Spirit lights give light to the world. Keep us firm in the hope you have set before us, that we and all your children shall be free, and the whole earth live to praise your name; through Christ our Lord. Amen (144).

This prayer is one of the most inspiring and beautiful Post-Communion texts I have seen, and requires little adaptation. The first Post-Communion Prayer from the Lutheran *Book of Worship*, while not inspiring to my way of thinking, is at least brief and in little need of re-vision:

> We give you thanks, almighty God, that you have refreshed us through the healing power of this gift of life; and we pray that in your mercy you would strengthen us, through this gift, in faith toward you and in fervent love toward one another; for the sake of Jesus Christ our Lord. Amen.[106]

The Festival of the Holy Names' Post-Communion Prayer is panentheistic in theme:

> Living God, we thank you that in this feast you have given us yourself. Help us, as we go our myriad ways, to see you likewise given in all that we eat and drink, all that we meet, and all that we behold. Help us to live in this wonder, so nourishing our souls that we may see that we ourselves are the instruments of your grace and gifts to all the world. Amen.

The Post-Communion Prayer is another of those sections of the liturgy (like the Prayers of the People) where there is no dominating standard form. A community may be as free as they need be in writing a prayer that succeeds in wrapping up the thematic loose ends of their Eucharistic prayer, and—most importantly—turns the worshiper's attention from the comfort of the church community to his or her ministry in the larger world. Ideally, the Post-Communion prayer shifts us from words to action, from contemplation to commitment, from worship to work.

The Dismissal or Blessing

Finally, the Eucharist service concludes with a blessing. Again, this is a feature added to the liturgy in the fourth century, when the church was legalized and (with the advent of the Mystery thread) liturgies had become much more public and elaborate. The earliest of these liturgies provide for a blessing, but provide no text, suggesting that the blessing was either given extemporaneously, or was a form so well known that no one needed to write it down (such as the Aaronic blessing, below). For many years, the blessing was given by the bishop alone, but by mediaeval times, the parish priests were pronouncing them as well.

The 1552 *Book of Common Prayer* used the following blessing, which is continued in Anglican use today:

> The peace of God which passeth all understanding keep your hearts and minds in the knowledge and love of God, and of his Son Jesus Christ our Lord. And the blessing of God Almighty, the Father, the Son, and the Holy Ghost, be amongst you and remain with you always. Amen.

As beautiful as this text is, it is hardly inclusive; and for those coming from a Process Theology perspective, the adjective "Almighty" is problematic (and let's face it, "More mighty than anyone else" just doesn't have that liturgical ring to it). The simple form for the Roman Catholic liturgy, however, is easily adapted: "May almighty God bless you, the Father, and the Son, and the Holy Spirit" can be easily rendered "And may God bless you, Creator, Liberator and Comforter, now and forever," or something similar.

A fine adaptation can also be made of the Aaronic blessing: "May God bless you, and keep you. May God's gentle face shine upon you, and be gracious to you. May God rain down all blessings upon you and give you peace."

The Festival of the Holy Names makes use of a blessing written by United Church of Christ scholar Ruth Duck, which is actually less a blessing than a triumphant sending forth:

> Friends, continue your journey walking in love,
> Care for one another, care for the earth,
> Seek justice and make peace.
> Christ goes before you:
> live boldly, celebrate, and sing!
> Thanks be to God![107]

The blessing (or sending forth) might be seen as the liturgists' last chance to make their point in a thematic celebration, but most importantly it should create a segue into the parishioner's daily life, to carry over the blessings and commitments of this sacred space into the sacred space of our workaday lives. Duck's blessing is profound for this very reason; it reminds us to "continue our journeys," and then reminds us what it is we are supposed to be doing as people of faith in our world; finally reminding us that we do it neither alone nor under our own power nor do we do it gravely. We may go bravely because Jesus goes ahead of us, and he has met and embraced and overcome all adversity in his resurrection. And it is this power in which we make our way.

Summary

This analysis of the issues involved in reforming the liturgy of the Eucharist is far from comprehensive. Nearly every Festival of the Holy Names planning meeting surprises us with new objections to the traditional form that had not occurred to any of us before. Some might accuse us of becoming pickier, but it also may be that we are becoming more sensitive and aware by working and staying with this process.

Hopefully the most difficult issues—namely exclusive and hierarchical language and the theology of sacrifice—have been adequately discussed, if not solved to everyone's satisfaction. As it is impossible to be exhaustive in a treatise of this size, there are a number of additional issues which our congregation cares about that I have not been able to deal with here. Many of the specific gestures associated with our worship smack of dominance and imperialism, and these too must be critically evaluated. Is it appropriate, for instance, to genuflect in a church, since we no longer view God as a medieval monarch? Is bowing in direction of the altar a suitable substitute or is even this an inappropriate self-debasement? Does kissing the altar support the concept of sacrifice or can it not just as easily be a sign of affection for the place where our most intimate meals occur?

Similarly, communities need to discuss such rituals as the sign of the cross. Is this sign another glorification of sacrifice and self-immolation, or is it more, as in St. Patrick's breastplate, "binding to oneself the Trinity," an act of marriage of God to the heart? What about the sign of the cross over the elements or over the community in the corporate absolution? For some Christians such an act might be a gesture of inappropriate dominance on the part of the clergy. In the Festival of the Holy Names, for instance, our community has retained the absolution, but has re-visioned the sign of the cross itself, following the cross with an all-encompassing circle: ⊕. This creates the astronomical symbol of the earth—for our community the ultimate symbol of blessing and inclusivity.

Many communions, such as the Anglicans', no longer insist on signing the elements with the cross, but allow a simple laying on of hands during the consecration. This practice is also used by some in the Festival, and for many will be a fine compromise.

How to hold one's hands while presiding at liturgy also betrays some negotiable assumptions. In the standard "*orans*" position of the Eucharistic prayer, the celebrant stands with his or her hands facing outwards towards the congregation, parallel with the ears. But many celebrants tilt their hands towards heaven, suggesting a heaven-earth duality and an absentee-landlord God "away-up-there." Communities should discuss the implications of such gestures and should recommend to their clergy actions which are meaningful to them.

Another issue barely touched upon is that of silence during the liturgy. Except for Good Friday services, many congregants are uncomfortable with silence, and require their services to be as "never-a-dull-moment" active as their television shows. Communities should discuss the holy uses of silence, and how to use it intelligently and purposefully in their services.

One issue that is particularly painful for Roman Catholics is that of place, or exactly where the liturgy is celebrated. For many Roman Catholic liturgies, a consecrated church building is the only permissible venue, especially for sacraments such as the Eucharist and Holy Matrimony. What does it say about the world when we limit our definition of "sacred space" to the church building? Since the earliest of Christians shared the Eucharist in one another's homes, it seems that this simple practice at least should not be condemned. Yet other locations are wonderful and healing as well. Anyone who has gone on a church retreat and has experienced the Holy Eucharist beneath whispering arches of pine knows what a holy and special place this sort of cathedral can be. The Rev. Deborah Little, an Episcopal priest, currently celebrates an open-air Eucharist every Sunday on Boston Common, where suburbanites and street people stand and worship together.[108] I myself have even celebrated an Easter Mass at a Gothrock nightclub in San Jose (complete with a full band accompanying a new alt-rock setting for the Mass)! Perhaps we should be thinking more about taking our liturgies to where people already are or where they feel comfortable, rather than insisting they meet us on *our* turf.

The arrangement of church furniture is another topic that alone could fill a book, as the placement of nearly every pew, pulpit and other item has deep symbolic import that communities should not take for granted. Should pews be arranged in rows or in circles? Should the minister be elevated on his or her own platform, or should the minister lead while seated in the midst of the congregation? These and many other issues are vital points which fall outside the scope of this book and yet are important elements in the conduct of our corporate worship.

The most important point I would like to reiterate is the responsibility for each local community to decide for itself what it needs in a Eucharistic celebration, and to have the courage to pursue its vision, unhindered by our insecure need for a hierarchical imprimatur. The most important element in the process, in my opinion, is the community's willingness to experiment, to make "holy fools" of themselves on occasion, and to view liturgies that don't work and go by the wayside as learning tools rather than failures. It also takes energy and imagination, qualities not usually associated with liturgy. People are afraid of "doing it wrong," or they feel inadequate in their own skills at writing prayers. In this case, the process also requires courage.

It is my hope that this book will provide a basis for security, to give communities permission to "think outside of the box," to help them to see that they are not heretics for feeling the need for change in their liturgies, but that in fact, they stand firmly in the evolving tradition of the historical church. For if communities can feel empowered, if they feel that they have creative freedom, then soon this discussion of ways ahead will be hopelessly obsolete as new and creative solutions to the dilemmas described above are discovered and enacted.

EPILOGUE

A Vision of the 21st Century Church

One could say that the Jesus experiment failed. The Rabbi from Nazareth spoke the truth to the lowly and the powerful alike: God is no respecter of persons. The systems of hierarchy and exclusion that Jesus sought to overthrow—and did, in creating a community where all were accorded the dignity with which God views them—were put back in place with Constantine and the imperialization of the church. The church has ever since been to a large extent precisely the sort of institution against which Jesus railed, and the sort that would most likely see him crucified again. Even today, the very institution that should be liberating the oppressed in the name of Christ has become instead the watchdog of hierarchy and oppression, safeguarding the sin of patriarchy from the "threat" of relativism and feminism.

And for those who are asked to continue to celebrate a liturgy that supports and perpetuates their own oppression, doing so is becoming untenable for a growing number of persons, for whom such rites seem pointless or hypocritical. As Davies writes, "Without a real commitment against exploitation and alienation and for a society of solidarity and justice the Eucharistic celebration is an empty action, lacking any genuine endorsement by those who participate in it."[1]

Whether the church is in denial or defiance of the Gospel is for the hierarchs who keep these systems in place to decide. While they are deciding, however, the Gospel mandate that we "set free the captives" will not wait. The peoples of the Roman Catholic church have been discovering ever since Vatican II that *they* are the church, even while the heirarchy tries to take it back.

It cannot be taken back. Like the prisoner set free from Plato's cave, once people have seen that there is sunshine outside, they will never settle for life in a cave again. People of every denomination are waking up to the fact that the Christian tradition belongs to them, not exclusively to history, and certainly not to the heirarchs. And when one says, "This tradition belongs to me," one begins to make it one's own. This is an act of liberation, *the giving of God back to the common people*—this is the work of Christ.

What happens to Christian worship when everyday people take matters into their own hands? What happens when insightful pastors and priests celebrate the priesthood of all believers, and take instruction from their congregations instead of giving orders? What happens when women and men of faith and conscience say "no more!" and view the structure and worship life of their churches with the eyes of the liberating Gospel of Jesus?

If a community can pray a prayer together in perfect agreement, who is to say it isn't "correct"? We are not in search of the Holy Grail of inclusive liturgies. In this book I am hoping to inspire communities to be creative, to try things on for size, to think hard about how liturgy impacts one's life, and then to write liturgies that *impact life*, no matter how idiosyncratic or bizarre they might seem to those outside of the community. Even in the Episcopal Church, the days of a standard prayer book for the church are fading, as more and more communities turn to inclusive and more community-specific alternative liturgies. Back in 1976 Leonel Mitchell reported that "more Eucharistic *anaphoras* had been composed in the previous ten years than in the preceding millenium."[2] This is a trend to continue, but it need not be continued by "experts" or "scholars." This work must be done by ordinary souls who seek to make sense of their faith, and who demand that the words they pray make sense as well.

An Anglican monk told me that he feels that, "the Church needs to decide if it is there for all of God's children (especially the ones who need God's help most), or if it is there for the large benefactors who sit in the front pews. The Church needs to decide if it should be a vocal conscience for the people of God whose voices are not heard."

This decision will not be made overnight. Christianity is a religion of conversion, and conversion rarely (if ever) happens instantaneously. Yet the need is great, and growing. Schaffran speaks for a large population of the church's women and men when she writes,

> We are long overdue for a change, for movement from the too-often-sterile places and styles of prayer, devoid of any sign of a good and gracious God. We are long overdue for a change, for movement from the too-often-inhospitable places and styles of prayer, where "community" and "family" are far from the experience of the believers who gather. We are long overdue for a change, for movement from the too frequent uniformity of our worship to a profound sensitivity that acknowledges the exquisite beauty and mystery of our humanness, the richness of our diversity, and our capacity to manifest the power and glory of God.[3]

The change will come when the majority of the people are informed of their history and empowered to make the changes themselves. Married priest John Schuster suggests the following strategies for communities seeking self-empowerment and demanding justice in their liturgies and communal life. Though they are written specifically for Roman Catholics, Christians of other communions will find wisdom here as well:

1. Join a small community.
2. Study theology, Scripture, and church history.
3. Donate your "collection money" to a renewal effort.
4. Ask an ordained woman priest to celebrate Mass, a baptism, or a wedding in your home.
5. Create a safety net for religious [monks and nuns] and priests who want to transition to a family lifestyle.
6. Contact your local newspaper religion editors.
7. Join and support organizations that are committed to Church renewal.
8. Organize a demonstration at your church/cathedral calling for women's ordination.

9. Write to your bishop and ask for a written response to your concerns.
10. Organize a Day of Spirituality for dialogue with married priests.
11. Ask a married priest to celebrate Mass, a baptism, or a wedding in your home.
12. Start a religious education program.
13. Develop a community outreach program and identify yourself.
14. If you are a married priest, "go public."[4]

Change will only happen when women and men of faith make it happen. Those in power inevitably seek to retain it. Those who have been disempowered must empower themselves. In the case of our churches, it is the people in the pews, not the clergy, who should be leading the way.

In the parish where I serve we pastors practice what we call the "political celibacy" of the clergy. We lead liturgies, visit the sick, teach classes, and nothing else. Administration of the church is left entirely in the hands of the laity and we clergy take instruction from them. Bishops serve our parish by providing pastoral care to the priests, but have no administrative power over the congregation itself. We believe this is a model of church polity with great import for the church of the future, especially for episcopal churches (Catholic, Orthodox, and Anglican) that have so abused their power in the past.

The laity need to see themselves as the final decision-makers in terms of how the church is run, who will serve as pastors, and what liturgies will be celebrated. Laypersons of both genders must become informed participants in guiding the evolution of their tradition, and each community needs to make their own decisions in these matters. The time of the monarchy is over; the age of democracy is only now truly dawning around the world. Post-modernism reveals to us that reality is a plurality of truths and potentialities, and our churches will inevitably come to embrace this plurality in worship, theology, and polity.

I have a dream of a new kind of church in the twenty-first century, a church where rebirth and life are celebrated instead of sacrifice and self-immolation, where the people of God embrace their tradition as belonging truly to them, to do with as the Spirit moves, where all people are honored, regardless of their race, gender, sexual preference or social standing, and where power-over is a receding memory, a nightmare which fades in the morning.

It is my belief that the church exists as the forward-moving tip of human evolution, enshrining in its scriptures and ancient rites creative leaps that have yet, after two thousand years of struggle, bloodshed and shame, to be fully understood. It is my prayer that the laity of our churches will be empowered to take responsibility, to consciously guide this evolution as we spiral into the next millenium, to become, perhaps for the first time in our tradition's history, the Community of God upon earth.

APPENDICES

Appendix A

DIDACHE EUCHARIST

9:1 But as touching the Eucharistic thanksgiving
give ye thanks thus.

2 First, as regards the cup:
We give Thee thanks, O our Father,
for the holy vine of Thy son David,
which Thou madest known unto us through Thy Son Jesus;
Thine is the glory for ever and ever.

3 Then as regarding the broken bread:
We give Thee thanks, O our Father,
for the life and knowledge
which Thou didst make known unto us
through Thy Son Jesus;
Thine is the glory for ever and ever.

4 As this broken bread was scattered upon the mountains
and being gathered together became one,
so may Thy Church be gathered together
from the ends of the earth into Thy kingdom;
for Thine is the glory and the power
through Jesus Christ for ever and ever.

5 But let no one eat or drink of this Eucharistic thanksgiving,
but they that have been baptized into the name of the Lord;
for concerning this also the Lord hath said: Give not that
which is holy to the dogs.

10:1 And after ye are satisfied thus give ye thanks:

2 We give Thee thanks, Holy Father, for Thy holy name,
which Thou hast made to tabernacle in our hearts,
and for the knowledge and faith and immortality,

which Thou hast made known unto us
through Thy Son Jesus;
Thine is the glory for ever and ever.

3 Thou, Almighty Master,
didst create all things for Thy name's sake,
and didst give food and drink unto men for enjoyment,
that they might render thanks to Thee;
but didst bestow upon us spiritual food and drink and
eternal life through Thy Son.

4 Before all things we give Thee thanks
that Thou art powerful;
Thine is the glory for ever and ever.

5 Remember, Lord, Thy Church
to deliver it from all evil
and to perfect it in Thy love;
and gather it together from the four winds—
even the Church which has been sanctified—
into Thy kingdom which Thou hast prepared for it;
for Thine is the power and the glory for ever and ever.

6 May grace come and may this world pass away.
Hosanna to the God of David.
If any man is holy, let him come;
if any man is not, let him repent.
Maran Atha. Amen.

7 But permit the prophets to offer thanksgiving as much as
they desire.

Appendix B

CREEDS

The Apostles' Creed

I believe in God, the Father almighty,
maker of heaven and earth;

And in Jesus Christ his only Son our Lord;
who was conceived by the Holy Ghost,
born of the Virgin Mary,
suffered under Pontius Pilate,
was crucified, died, and was buried.
He descended into hell.
The third day he rose again from the dead.
He ascended into heaven,
and sitteth on the right hand of God the Father almighty.
From thence he shall come to judge the quick and the dead.

I believe in the Holy Ghost,
the holy catholic Church,
the communion of saints,
the forgiveness of sins,
the resurrection of the body,
and the life everlasting. Amen.

Nicene Creed

We believe in one God,
the Father, the Almighty,
maker of heaven and earth,
of all that is, seen and unseen.

We believe in one Lord, Jesus Christ,
the only Son of God,
eternally begotten of the Father,
God from God, Light from Light,
true God from true God,
begotten, not made,
of one Being with the Father.

Through him all things were made.
For us and for our salvation
he came down from heaven:
by the power of the Holy Spirit
he became incarnate from the Virgin Mary,
and was made man.
For our sake he was crucified under Pontius Pilate;
he suffered death and was buried.
On the third day he rose again
in accordance with the Scriptures;
he ascended into heaven
and is seated at the right hand of the Father.
He will come again in glory to judge the living and the dead,
and his kingdom will have no end.

We believe in the Holy Spirit, the Lord, the giver of life,
who proceeds from the Father and the Son.
With the Father and the Son he is worshiped and glorified.
He has spoken through the Prophets.
We believe in one holy catholic and apostolic Church.
We acknowledge one baptism for the forgiveness of sins.
We look for the resurrection of the dead,
and the life of the world to come. Amen.

The Creed of Saint Athanasius

Whosoever will be saved, before all things it is necessary that he hold the Catholic Faith. Which Faith except everyone do keep whole and undefiled, without doubt he shall perish everlastingly.

And the Catholic Faith is this: That we worship one God in Trinity, and Trinity in Unity, neither confounding the Persons, nor dividing the Substance. For there is one Person of the Father, another of the Son, and another of the Holy Ghost. But the Godhead of the Father, of the Son, and of the Holy Ghost, is all one, the Glory equal, the Majesty co-eternal. Such as the Father is, such is the Son, and such is the Holy Ghost. The Father uncreated, the Son uncreated, and the Holy Ghost uncreated. The Father incomprehensible, the Son incomprehensible, and the Holy Ghost incomprehensible. The Father eternal, the Son eternal, and the Holy Ghost eternal. And yet they are not three eternals, but one eternal. As also there are not three incomprehensibles, nor three uncreated, but one uncreated, and one incomprehensible. So likewise the Father is Almighty, the Son Almighty, and the Holy Ghost Almighty. And yet they are not three Almighties, but one Almighty. So the Father is God, the Son is God, and the Holy Ghost is God. And yet they are not three Gods, but one God. So likewise the Father is Lord, the Son Lord, and the Holy Ghost Lord. And yet not three Lords, but one Lord. For like as we are compelled by the Christian verity to acknowledge every Person by himself to be both God and Lord, so are we forbidden by the Catholic Religion to say, There be three Gods, or three Lords. The Father is made of none, neither created, nor begotten. The Son is of the Father alone, not made, nor created, but begotten. The Holy Ghost is of the Father and of the Son, neither made, nor created, nor begotten, but proceeding. So there is one Father, not three Fathers; one Son, not three Sons; one Holy Ghost, not three Holy Ghosts. And in this Trinity none is afore, or after other; none is greater, or less than another; But the whole three Persons are co-eternal together and co-equal. So that in all things, as is aforesaid, the Unity in Trinity and the Trinity in Unity is to be worshipped. He therefore that will be saved is must think thus of the Trinity.

Furthermore, it is necessary to everlasting salvation that he also believe rightly the Incarnation of our Lord Jesus Christ. For the right Faith is, that we believe and confess, that our Lord Jesus Christ, the Son of God, is God and Man; God, of the substance of the Father, begotten before the worlds; and Man of the substance of his Mother, born in the world; Perfect God and perfect Man, of a reasonable soul and human flesh subsisting. Equal to the Father, as touching his Godhead; and inferior to the Father, as touching his manhood; Who, although he be God and Man, yet he is not two, but one Christ; One, not by conversion of the Godhead into flesh but by taking of the Manhood into God; One altogether; not by confusion of Substance, but by unity of Person. For as the reasonable soul and flesh is one man, so God and Man is one Christ; Who suffered for our salvation, descended into hell, rose again the third day from the dead. He ascended into heaven, he sitteth at the right hand of the Father, God Almighty from whence he will come to judge the quick and the dead. At whose coming all men will rise again with their bodies and shall give account for their own works. And they that have done good shall go into life everlasting; and they that have done evil into everlasting fire.

This is the Catholic Faith, which except a man believe faithfully, he cannot be saved.

Appendix C

INSTITUTIONAL NARRATIVES: TRADITIONAL

Mark 14:22-24

While they were eating, he took a loaf of bread, and after blessing it he broke it, gave it to them, and said, "Take; this is my body." Then he took a cup, and after giving thanks he gave it to them, and all of them drank from it. He said to them, "This is my blood of the covenant, which is poured out for many."

Matthew 26:26-28

While they were eating, Jesus took a loaf of bread, and after blessing it he broke it, gave it to the disciples, and said, "Take, eat; this is my body." Then he took a cup, and after giving thanks he gave it to them, saying, "Drink from it, all of you; for this is my blood of the covenant, which is poured out for many for the forgiveness of sins."

Luke 22:19-20

Then he took a loaf of bread, and when he had given thanks, he broke it and gave it to them, saying, "This is my body, which is given for you. Do this in remembrance of me." And he did the same with the cup after supper, saying, "This cup that is poured out for you is the new covenant in my blood."

1 Corinthians 11:23-25

For I received from the Lord what I also handed on to you, that the Lord Jesus on the night when he was betrayed took a loaf of bread, and when he had given thanks, he broke it and said, "This is my body that is for you. Do this in remembrance of me." In the same way he took the cup also, after supper, saying, "This cup is the new covenant in my blood. Do this, as often as you drink it, in remembrance of me."

Appendix D

INSTITUTIONAL NARRATIVES: ALTERNATIVE

Luke 24:13-16, 27, 30

Now on that same day two of them were going to a village called Emmaus, about seven miles from Jerusalem, and talking with each other about all these things that had happened. While they were talking and discussing, Jesus himself came near and went with them, but their eyes were kept from recognizing him. Then beginning with Moses and all the prophets, he interpreted to them the things about himself in all the scriptures. When he was at the table with them, he took bread, blessed and broke it, and gave it to them. Then their eyes were opened, and they recognized him; and he vanished from their sight.

John 6:32-35

Then Jesus said to them, "Very truly, I tell you, it was not Moses who gave you the bread from heaven, but it is my Father who gives you the true bread from heaven. For the bread of God is that which comes down from heaven and gives life to the world." They said to him, "Sir, give us this bread always." Jesus said to them, "I am the bread of life. Whoever comes to me will never be hungry, and whoever believes in me will never be thirsty."

Jn. 13:1-5, 12-17, 20

Now before the festival of the Passover, Jesus knew that his hour had come to depart from this world and go to the Father.... And during supper Jesus, got up from the table, took off his outer robe, and tied a towel around himself. Then he poured water into a basin and began to wash the disciples' feet and to wipe them with the towel that was tied around him. After he had washed their feet, had put on his robe, and had returned to the table, he said to them, "Do you know what I have done to you? You call me Teacher and Lord— and you are right, for that is what I am. So if I, your Lord and Teacher, have washed your feet, you also ought to wash one another's feet. For I have set you an example, that you also should do as I have done to you. Very truly, I tell you, servants are not greater than their master, nor are messengers greater than the one who sent them. If you know these things, you are blessed if you do them. Very truly, I tell you, whoever receives one whom I send receives me; and whoever receives me receives him who sent me."

Appendix E

FESTIVAL OF THE HOLY NAMES LITURGY

Liturgy of the Word

All portions identified by an asterisk (*) are optional. The service may begin with a processional. All circle and stand around the altar.

Greeting/Invocation

Presider 1 Blessed is our God,
Creator, Liberator, and Comforter;
People **And blessed is Creation, now and forever. Amen.**

Call to Worship/Introit*

Gathering Collect

This or another invocation may be used.
Presider 1 Holy and Living God, in you we are born,
in you we move, in you we have our being.
Anoint us now with your Holy Wisdom;
enrich our hearts—dine and dance with us—
as we with glad hearts celebrate your holy names. Amen.

Gathering Dance

All **Gather here in the mystery of the hour**
Gather here in one strong body
Gather here in the struggle and the power
Spirit draw near[1]

Blessing with Water/Asperges*

Presider 2 Dear friends,
this water will be used to remind us of our origins,
of the waters of the womb from which we were born,
and of the waters of the Earth that refresh and sustain all beings.
May God bless me as I perform this service.
With the Earth's hallowed waters do I consecrate
this holy altar and sanctuary.

And bless also this people who gather to
celebrate an astounding love.

Silence

Presider 1 We will now spend the next few minutes in silence. You may use this time to review the theme and the readings in your bulletin.

Theme and Opening Prayer/The Collect

Presider 1 Please be seated. Today/Tonight, we celebrate....
Let us pray....

Litany*

Readings

The Crucifer processes with the cross to the appointed place, and holds the cross aloft over the head of the Reader.

Cantor Open your ears, O faithful people
Open your ears, and hear God's Word
Open your hearts, O royal priesthood,
God has come to you.

One or two readings, from various sources, at least one of them from scripture, the reader first saying:
A Reading from —. *Then.* Here ends the reading.

After each reading, a bell may be struck thrice to initiate a brief period of meditation. A single stroke ends the meditation. When the scripture has been read, the Cantor sings:
God has spoken to the people, Hallelujah!
And the words are words of wisdom, Hallelujah!

People **Hallelujah!**
God has spoken to the people, Hallelujah!
And the words are words of wisdom, Hallelujah!

Sharing the Gospel

Presider 2 We have heard the scripture of our tradition. Now we invite you to share from the scripture of your life. We open ourselves to hear your personal truth without judgment or interruption.

Statement of Faith/Credo*

Prayers of the People

Cantor Shema Israel, Adonai Elohenu, Adonai Echod!
People **Hear all the world, your God is one God!**

Prayers may be offered for all people of faith, for the Earth, for justice and peace, for the sick and suffering, and for wisdom. Praises may also be offered.

Confession/Confiteor

This or another form may be used.
Cantor For my resistance to being
all I'm created to be
For my denial of life, of life abundantly
For the discord I bring into the harmony
I beg the indulgence of Earth, sky and sea,
Of All-that-I-Am, of All Who Are, of All in All in All.

People **For my resistance to being**
all I'm created to be
For my denial of life, of life abundantly
For the discord I bring into the harmony
I beg the indulgence of Earth, sky and sea,
Of All-that-I-Am, of All Who Are,
of All in All in All.

Affirmation/Absolution

Presider 2, singing Shalom, Shalom, + Shalom, Shalom

Shalom Dance

Presider 2 Let us now each turn to a partner, and extend our right hands in peace as we begin our dance...

Exchanging the Peace/Pax

Presider 2 Peace be with you!
People **And also with you**

Presider 2 Let us share with one another
a sign of God's Peace.

Time may be taken for blessings, artistic presentations, and announcements: planning meetings, socials, etc.

Offertory and Offertory song/Offertorium*

Presider 1 At this time we invite you to share what God has given to you. If you have brought food for the food bank, please place it on the side altar. Let us with gladness present the fruits of our life and labor unto God and one another.

A song may be sung or played as the gifts are offered and, with the drink and the bread, presented at the altar. See Eucharistic Prayer II for instructions specific to this prayer.

Liturgies of the Table

Eucharistic Prayer I + Life and Joy

Presentation of the Gifts

Presider 1 Blessed are you, God of all creation.
Through your goodness
we have this bread to offer,
which earth has given
and human hands have made.
It will become for us the Bread of Life.
People **Blessed be God forever.**

Presider 2 Blessed are you, God of all creation.
Through your goodness
we have this drink to offer,
fruit of the vine and work of human hands.
This will become our Cup of Joy.
People **Blessed be God forever.**

Presider 1 Please join us around God's table.

Introductory Dialogue/Sursum Corda

Presider 1 Christ is here.
People **The Spirit is with us.**

Presider 1 Open your hearts.
People **We offer them to God.**

Presider 2 Let us give thanks to the Infinite One.
People **We rejoice to give thanks and praise.**

Presider 2 It is a right and good and joyful thing in all ways and everywhere to give thanks to you, O God...

Presider may say a proper preface (an introductory prayer concerning the day's theme.)

Therefore we join in the chorus of praise
that rings throughout eternity, with angels and archangels,
prophets and martyrs, creatures of earth, sea and sky
and all the holy women and men of every culture and age.
Together with rocks, hills, waters, mountains,
suns, moons, and stars, we magnify you as we sing/say:

Holy, Holy, Holy/Sanctus

All **Holy, holy, holy, God of love and power,**
All Creation speaks of your glory, O God-with-us.
Blessed are we who come in the name of our God!
Hosanna, Hosanna from our hearts!

Thanking the Creator/Anamnesis

Presider 1 Sacred and Immortal One,
throughout the history of the world,
it has always been your way
to bestow rich blessings upon your children:

In the ongoing weaving of the world, O God,
you give to us life.
In the gift of our communities and families,
you give to us joy.
In Jesus of Nazareth
you give to us an example of genuine living.
In his death and resurrection,
you give us the hope of eternal life.
Through the gift of your Holy Spirit,
you give us the courage and the power
to remake the world.

Indwelling of the Spirit/Epiclesis

Presider 2 And in this moment,
through your bountiful Creation,
you give us these gifts again.
They are full of life and goodness,
blessed and holy.

Let us become aware
of your + presence in these gifts.
For as your Spirit saturates and indwells
all of Creation, O Christ,
even so are these gifts—this bread, and this cup—
brimming with divinity.

Teach us to partake of them
with due reverence, and in so doing,
help us to go forth into the world
with like reverence for all that we behold,
for in you do all things consist
and have their being.

Remembering Christ/Institution

Presider 1, lifting up the bread
When once he walked among us
as a human being, Jesus said to his friends,
"I am the bread of life," and indeed,
Divinity is our substance and our sustenance.
"Anyone who follows my teaching,
though they have nothing,
yet never shall they hunger."

Presider 2, lifting up the chalice
Jesus likewise said
"I am the True Vine..." and indeed,
Divinity is the source of our hope and our joy.
"...Those who abide in me, and I in them,
shall bring forth much fruit."

Breaking of Bread/Fracture

Presider 1 From the One . . . Come the many . . .
And the many become One.

Jesus' Prayer/Pater Noster

Presider 2 Therefore, as Jesus taught us, let us pray:

All **God our Father, God our Mother,**
holy are your names.
May your community be realized,
and your desires manifest
on Earth even as in the heavens.
Grant us this day all that we require,
and as we have been forgiven by you,
help us to forgive others.
Walk with us through the paths of adversity,
stand firm with us in our times of suffering.
For yours are grace, justice
and love, now and forever. Amen.

Presider 1 And we break bread for those we love not present, especially . . .

The Communion/Communicatio

Presider 1 We have named these gifts
the Bread of Life and the Cup of Joy,
because life and joy are gifts which continually flow
from the gracious hand of our God.
But may these gifts also be for you
whatever it is you need
for God to feed you in this moment.

Presider 2 Life and Joy. These are the gifts of God.
All are invited to share this communion;
for at God's table there is room for all.
Come to the feast prepared for you
from the foundation of the world.

The bread is distributed, saying, "The Bread of Life."
The cup is distributed, saying, "The Cup of Joy."

A brief period of meditation may follow reception of communion. An a capella song or chant may be sung/said by all.

Post-Communion Prayer

Presider 1 Let us pray.
All **Living God, we thank you**
that in this feast you have given us yourself.
Help us, as we go our myriad ways,
to see you likewise given
in all that we eat and drink,
all that we meet, and all that we behold;
Help us to live in this wonder,
so nourishing our souls
that we may see that we ourselves
are the instruments of your grace
and gifts to all the world. Amen.

Communion Dance

Blessing/Benediction

This or another benediction may be used.

Presider 2 Friends, continue your journey walking in love,
Care for one another, care for the earth, seek justice and make peace.
Christ goes before you: live boldly, celebrate, and sing! Thanks be to God![2]
People **Thanks be to God!**

Eucharistic Prayer II + Liberation

The table is set with bread, an empty chalice and a cruet of wine.

Presentation of the Gifts

Presider 1 With this bread, O Christ,
we place here all the creative action of the peoples
of the Earth, their aspirations, their joy,
their achievements, and their work.

Presider 2 With this wine, we behold the sorrows,
the pain and the suffering of all your Creation.

Presider 1 Into this offering of the world we would gather those closest to us, our beloved and those at enmity with us, and with these we unite the great multitude of souls in Creation. With deepest compassion we join ourselves with the ceaseless journey of the universe, past, present and future, with its joys and sorrows, hopes and fears, that we may be one with it all.

Presider 2 We draw into this offering every form of life, animals and plants, rocks and fire, planets and stars, winds and waters; and we offer ourselves, all we have and all that we are. Let all existence be now placed here on our altar, that with joy and gratitude we may offer it to you.[3]

Presider 1 Please join us around God's table.

Introductory Dialogue/Sursum Corda

Presider 1 Christ is here.
People **The Spirit is with us.**

Presider 1 Open your hearts.
People **We offer them to God.**

Presider 2 Let us give thanks to the Infinite One.
People **We rejoice to give thanks and praise.**

Presider 2 It is a right and good and joyful thing in all ways and everywhere to give thanks to you, O God . . .

Presider may say a proper preface

Therefore we join in the chorus of praise
that rings throughout eternity, with angels and archangels,
prophets and martyrs, creatures of earth, sea and sky
and all the holy women and men of every culture and age.
Together with rocks, hills, waters, mountains, suns, moons,
and stars, we magnify you as we sing/say:

Holy, Holy, Holy/Sanctus

All **Holy, holy, holy, God of love and power,**
All Creation speaks of your glory, O God-with-us.
Blessed are we who come in the name of our God!
Hosanna, Hosanna from our hearts!

Thanking the Creator/Anamnesis

Presider 1 We thank you, O God,
that in every time and place
you have made your home
with the poor and the powerless.
With your hand you led your people Israel
out of bondage from Egypt.
Through your prophets
you taught your people to do justice,
to love mercy and to walk humbly
in your Spirit.

Presider 2 In Jesus of Nazareth
you made your home with us,
and taught us that it is the meek
who shall inherit the earth;
that those who suffer for what is right
are blessed in your eyes.
Through him you lived and died as one of us,
preaching the Good News of liberation
to the poor and the oppressed.
And even now you embrace us in love,
and give us strength to bring this Good News to all.

Remembering Christ/Institution

Presider 1 At the feast of Passover,
Jesus and his friends met
to celebrate their ritual meal.
According to tradition,
their rabbi picked up
the unleavened bread to bless it,
and surprised them instead with new words.
Likening the bread to his own body
about to be broken, he broke the bread,
and passed it around the circle.
When the time came
for the final cup of wine to be shared,
Jesus again spoke new words,
and likened the wine to his own blood
about to be spilled.

Consecration/Epiclesis

Presider 2 In the same way, therefore,
we offer to you, O holy God,
this simple bread and this wine:
Bless them now + that they may become for us
symbols of love and liberation,
as we praise you saying:

Breaking of Bread/Fracture

Presider 2, elevating the bread
Blessed are you,
Eternal Sustainer of the Universe;
for through your miraculous creation,
you bring forth grain from the Earth.
As these kernels were scattered upon the mountains
and were gathered and made one loaf,
even so do you make us one, for we are children of one Earth,
and partake of one bread.
The bread is broken
Therefore, when the bodies, spirits,
and homes of others are broken, we are broken.

Presider 1, elevating the cruet
Blessed are you,
Eternal Sustainer of the Universe;
For through your miraculous creation,
you bring forth the fruit of the vine.
As the fruit of many vines are put into
one press to be crafted into one vintage,
even so you have made us all one family,
sharing one blood.

Filling the cup Therefore, when the life-blood
of any creature spills, our blood is spilled.

Today/Tonight, we break bread for the suffering of the Earth,
for those whose habitats have been destroyed,
for those who struggle for justice,
who have paid the price for freedom
with their own flesh and blood,
and for the millions who suffer oppression,
sickness, and distress.

And we break bread for those we love, especially . . .

Jesus' Prayer

Presider 2 Present with each other,
and with all the world in spirit,
we share this simple meal together as one family,
offering this bread and this cup as signs of struggle and hope
for all creatures, praying as Jesus taught us:

All **God our Father, God our Mother,**
holy are your names.
May your community be realized,
and your desires manifest
on Earth even as in the heavens.
Grant us this day all that we require,
and as we have been forgiven by you,
help us to forgive others.
Walk with us through the paths of adversity,

stand firm with us in our times of suffering.
For yours are grace, justice
and love, now and forever. Amen.

The Communion

Presider 1 All are invited to share this communion;
for we are all one people. Come to the feast prepared for you
from the foundation of the world.

Communion proceeds in silence, or with the following words:
"We are all one body." "We are all one blood."

Post-Communion Covenant

All **Therefore we covenant with one another**
to work until bodies are broken no more,
To act until blood is no more spilled,
To practice peace until all can dance on the land
beneath the sun, eating their grain with joy
And drinking the fruit of the vine with a merry heart.
One day there shall be peace!
One day all — *All* — shall rejoice![4]

Communion Dance

Blessing/Benediction

This or another benediction may be used.

Presider 2 Friends, continue your journey walking in love.
Care for one another, care for the earth, seek justice and make peace.
Christ goes before you: live boldly, celebrate, and sing!
Thanks be to God![2]
People **Thanks be to God!**

Eucharistic Prayer III + Servants & Priests

Presentation of the Gifts

Presider 1 With this bread, O Christ,
we place here all the creative action of the peoples
of the Earth, their aspirations, their joy,
their achievements, and their work.

Presider 2 With this wine, we behold the sorrows,
the pain and the suffering of all your Creation.

Presider 1 Into this offering of the world we would gather those closest to us, our beloved and those at enmity with us, and with these we unite the great multitude of souls in Creation. With deepest compassion we join ourselves with the ceaseless journey of the universe, past, present, and future, with its joys and sorrows, hopes and fears, that we may be one with it all.

Presider 2 We draw into this offering every form of life, animals and plants, rocks and fire, planets and stars, winds and waters; and we offer ourselves, all we have, and all that we are. Let all existence be now placed here on our altar that with joy and gratitude we may offer it to you.[5]

Presider 1 Please join us around God's table.

Introductory Dialogue/Sursum Corda

Presider 1 Christ is here.
People **The Spirit is with us.**

Presider 1 Open your hearts.
People **We offer them to God.**

Presider 2 Let us give thanks to the Infinite One.
People **We rejoice to give thanks and praise.**

Presider 2 It is a right and good and joyful thing in all ways and everywhere to give thanks to you, O God...

Presider may say a proper preface

Therefore we join in the chorus of praise
that rings throughout eternity, with angels and archangels,
prophets and martyrs, creatures of earth, sea and sky
and all the holy men and women of every culture and age.
Together with rocks, hills, waters, mountains, suns, moons,
and stars, we magnify you as we sing/say:

Holy, Holy, Holy/Sanctus

All **Holy, holy, holy, God of love and power,**
All Creation speaks of your glory, O God-with-us.
Blessed are we who come in the name of our God!
Hosanna, Hosanna from our hearts!

Thanking the Creator/Anamnesis

Presider 1 Holy God, we bless you for your Creation,
for beauty that astounds us
and for goodness that humbles us;
for the canopy of stars that blankets this blue-green jewel
and for the deliciousness of fruit and cool-running water.
In every way you have made our home a blessing to us,
and charged us with responsibility to care for and nurture it.

Presider 2 We confess that we have not always
been kind to your Creation,
we have sullied the waters and air,
and taken life that was not ours to decide.
Time and again we tried to build
towers to reach the heavens,
setting up dominions for ourselves,
pretending to be rulers over the earth,
enlsaving the peoples, abusing our families,
and exploiting the poor.

All **We forgot that we were a holy people,**
servants of this earth and of one another,
And we forsook our holy duty
to make justice and teach peace to the nations.

Presider 1 But you did not forget us: in your compassion
you brought forth Jesus of Nazareth;
who taught us to dream of a community
where none are seen as diseased or forgotten,
where power is forsaken for intimacy
and where the presence of God is radiant.

Remembering Christ/Institution

Presider 2 When they met to celebrate the passover,
Jesus said to his friends,
"You who would be the greatest amongst you
must be the servant of all."
And then their reverend teacher wrapped himself
in a towel, and carefully washed their feet.

Presider 1 Still a dispute arose among them
as to which one of them
was to be regarded as the greatest.
But he said to them,
"The rulers of the Gentiles exercise power over them
but it shall not be so with you;
rather the greatest among you must become
like the least, and the leader like one who serves.
For who seems greater, the one who is
at the table or the one who serves?
Is it not the one at the table?
But I am among you as one who serves."

Presider 2 And then while they were
eating the meal of the covenant,
Jesus used the familiar symbols of bread and wine,
to celebrate a new relationship
between God and the earth;
A relationship of grace and friendship,
with the potential to remake the world.

Recognizing the Spirit/Epiclesis

Presider 1 Eternal God,
make your Holy Spirit known in our midst.

In the sharing of this meal make of us
a community of friends, a discipleship of equals,
teaching us to be servants and priests
one to another, proclaiming the Good News
of the Community of God amongst us.

Jesus' Prayer/Pater Noster

Presider 2 Therefore, as Jesus taught us, let us pray:

All **God our Father, God our Mother,**
holy are your names.
May your community be realized,
and your desires manifest
on Earth even as in the heavens.
Grant us this day all that we require,
and as we have been forgiven by you,
help us to forgive others.
Walk with us through the paths of adversity,
stand firm with us in our times of suffering.
For yours are grace, justice
and love, now and forever. Amen.

Call to the Table

Presider 2 We are a beloved priesthood,
a holy community, God's own.
We are called to proclaim the wondrous acts of the one who
brought us through the darkness into light.

Presider 1 Let us serve one another with grace, washing each other's hands, feeding one another, and proclaiming Christ's presence wherever two or more are gathered. Come to the feast prepared for you from the foundation of the world.

A celebrant takes the first communicant and leads him or her by the hand to the table, where the celebrant washes his or her hands, and offers the bread and wine in silence, while the congregation drums and dances. When the communicant has dined, the music stops, and s/he turns to the congregation, and proclaims: Christ is here!
The people reply: **The Spirit is with us!**

Then the first communicant leads the second communicant to the table and repeats the rite.

Post-Communion Prayer

All **Blessed are you, God of all Creation,**
for you have given us a meal
to celebrate community one with another.
May we who eat this bread
be sustanance to those in need,
may we who drink this cup testify
to the wonder of this Creation
and may we delight in our bodies and minds,
calling others into joy and life and wholeness.
Give us opportunity to take these gifts to our neighbors, courage to speak truth and build community,
and wisdom to enjoy our eternal life. Amen.

Communion Dance

Blessing/Benediction

This or another benediction may be used.

Presider 2 Friends, continue your journey walking in love,
care for one another, care for the earth,
seek justice and make peace.
Christ goes before you: live boldly, celebrate, and sing!
Thanks be to God![2]
People **Thanks be to God!**

Eucharistic Prayer IV + Christ in Community

Presentation of the Gifts

Presider 1, elevating the bread
Blessed are you, our Creator,
for the life and wisdom and transforming love
that you have made known to us
through your child, Jesus.
People **Glory to you forever!**

Presider 2, elevating the wine
Blessed are you, our Creator,
for you have called us to be branches
of the true vine which you have made known to us
through your child, Jesus.
People **Glory to you forever!**

Presider 1 As the grains of wheat once scattered
were gathered to become one bread,
so may all your people from the ends of the earth
be gathered into your community.[6]

Presider 2 Beloved, this is the joyful feast
of the people of God.
Come from the East and the West,
and from the North and the South,
and gather about the table of God.[7]

Introductory Dialogue/Sursum Corda

Presider 1 Christ is here.
People **The Spirit is with us.**

Presider 1 Open your hearts.
People **We offer them to God.**

Presider 2 Let us give thanks to the Infinite One.
People **We rejoice to give thanks and praise.**

Presider 2 It is a right and good and joyful thing in all ways and everywhere to give thanks to you, O God . . .

Presider may say a proper preface

Therefore we join in the chorus of praise
that rings throughout eternity, with angels and archangels,
prophets and martyrs, creatures of earth, sea and sky
and all the holy men and women of every culture and age.
Together with rocks, hills, waters, mountains, suns, moons
and stars, we magnify you as we sing/say:

Holy, Holy, Holy/Sanctus

All **Holy, holy, holy, God of love and power,**
All Creation speaks of your glory, O God-with-us.
Blessed are we who come in the name of our God!
Hosanna, Hosanna from our hearts!

Thanking the Creator/Anamnesis

Presider 1 Eternal God,
from before the times of our reckoning,
we have celebrated with a holy meal
the family you have made of us.

You have come to us in many ways:
to the children of Abraham and Sarah,
you came in manna, the life-giving bread
that appeared as dew upon the ground,
nourishing and giving witness to your faithfulness
day after day.

To the disciples, you came in Jesus, the Bread of Life,
feeding the souls of all who have ears to hear;
to Christians you have come in the bread of Eucharist,
uniting a family of faith, now and forever more;
and to people of compassion everywhere
you have come in your life-giving Spirit
to provide a soulful feast for the whole of the Earth.

Remembering Christ/Institution

Presider 2 Christ, we remember that on the day when you
emerged from the violence and despair of death
two disciples journeyed to a village called Emmaus.
While they were talking, you yourself came near
and went with them, but their eyes were kept
from recognizing you.
Later, when you were at the table with them,
you took bread, blessed and broke it and gave it to them.

The bread is broken Then their eyes were opened,
and they recognized you.

Blessing of the Spirit/Epiclesis

Presider 1 Therefore we ask that,
in the sharing of this bread,
and in the drinking of this wine,
our own eyes might be opened to behold you
in the glory of your Creation, in the Wisdom of your Word,
and in the faces of our sisters and brothers
gathered in your name to celebrate an astounding love.

Jesus' Prayer

Presider 2 Therefore as Jesus taught us, let us pray...

All **God our Father, God our Mother,
holy are your names.
May your community be realized,
and your desires manifest
on Earth even as in the heavens.
Grant us this day all that we require,
and as we have been forgiven by you,
help us to forgive others.
Walk with us through the paths of adversity,
stand firm with us in our times of suffering.
For yours are grace, justice
and love, now and forever. Amen.**

Presider 2 May our sharing in this bread and cup
be a sign of our faith: in the ongoing goodness of a God who journeys with us; in the power of love to move any barrier
within and among us; in the mystery of the call given to each one of us; to make food and peace abundant for everyone.

Presider 1 These are the gifts of God for the family of God.
Let us share this bread and wine as Jesus taught us,
knowing that our lives are forever changed
by this and every breaking of bread.

The bread is distributed with the words: "Christ is here."
The wine is distributed with the words: "The Spirit is with us."

Post-Communion Prayer

All **Good and gracious God,**
You are the bread of the poor, the bread of our lives.
May we recognize you
every time we join someone on a journey;
every time we share a meal;
every time we take bread into our hands.
May this recognition create in us such hope and joy
that we might live consciously
in your transforming presence.
May you create such a longing for truth in us
that we will never be satisfied
until the whole earth experiences
your justice and peace.[8]

Blessing/Benediction

This or another benediction may be used.

Presider 2 Friends, continue your journey walking in love,
Care for one another, care for the earth,
Seek justice and make peace.
Christ goes before you: live boldly, celebrate, and sing!
Thanks be to God![7]
People **Thanks be to God!**

Prayers of the People I

We believe that silence and dance are appropriate forms of prayer. Therefore with all our hearts, minds, and bodies, let us pray to our Creator in word, song, silence, and movement, singing:

Inhabit our prayer, O God.
or this **God hear our prayer.**

Reader For the peace of the world, for the welfare of the holy Church of God, and for the unity of all peoples,
let us pray to our Comforter. **R.**

Reader For our President, for the leaders of the nations, and for all in authority, that they might be granted compassion and insight,
let us pray to our Sustainer. **R.**

Reader For the good Earth which God has given us, and for the foresight and will to conserve it, let us pray to Holy Wisdom. **R.**

Reader For the strength to bear all manner of adversity,
let us pray to our Deliverer. **R.**

Reader That we may end our lives in faith and hope, meeting our passage with grace and dignity, let us pray to the Lover of our souls. **R.**

Reader Let us now offer up our own needs to God....

Reader Let us now offer up to God our praises and thanksgivings, singing:

Inhabit our praise, O God!...
or **God, Hear our praise!**

Reader Ever present and eternal God,
hear the prayers and praises of your people.
Help us to live in hope, to build your community,
and to be bearers of grace to all. **R. Amen.**

Prayers and Praises of the People II

We believe that silence and dance are appropriate forms of prayer. Therefore with all our hearts, minds, and bodies, let us pray to our Creator in word, song, silence, and movement, singing:

Inhabit our prayer, O God.
or this **God hear our prayer.**

Reader For the cleansing, healing and rest of the Earth and all her creatures, the waters, soil and air,
we pray . . . **R.**

Reader For a world-wide awakening to justice, liberation, and love, we pray . . . **R.**

Reader For increasing accountability and integrity of leaders in the church, the nations, and local social and political positions of power, we pray . . . **R.**

Reader For creative justice in our personal and public lives, for the helpless, for the downtrodden, for the betrayed, abused, and afflicted, we pray . . . **R.**

Reader For courage to confront evil, to live true to our divine natures, for the ability to hear God's voice,
we pray . . . **R.**

Reader For the healing of all creatures sick and suffering, poisoned, disrespected and dying in our midst, known and unknown to us, we pray . . . **R.**

Reader For the welcoming of the Christ Spirit with every breath we breathe, we pray . . . **R.**

Reader Let us now offer up our own needs to God . . .

Prayers commemorated by sounding a bell and/or lighting a candle.

Reader With all our hearts, minds and bodies, let us praise our Creator, singing:

Inhabit our praise, O God!
or **God, Hear our praise!**

Reader For the times we have been aware of your presence in our lives, we are grateful! **R.**

Reader For the wonder, intricacy, beauty and mystery of Creation and of the sacredness of our own existence, we are exuberant! **R.**

Reader For the true existence of love and compassion in the midst of suffering and evil, we acclaim your presence! **R.**

Reader For the growing awareness worldwide of our selfishness to this Earth and for the actions being taken to heal her and repent, we thank you! **R.**

Reader For creativity, beauty, justice, variety, emotion, ritual, sensuality, rivers, rocks and trees, love, solitude, change and trust, we are amazed! **R.**

Reader Let us now offer up our individual praises and thansgivings.

Praises are offered and are commemorated by cymbals and bells and/or lighting a candle.

Reader Ever present and eternal God,
hear the prayers and praises of your people.
Help us to live in hope, to build your community,
and to be bearers of grace to all. **R. Amen.**

NOTES

INTRODUCTION

1. For the sake of clarity, the word "church" in this book refers to all who call themselves Christian (unless otherwise noted, such as the Gnostics in section One)—Catholic, Protestant, and Orthodox—and will be spelled with a lower case "c". "Church" with an upper case "C" will refer to a specific church (i.e. "The Roman Catholic Church" or "The Presbyterian Church (USA)").
2. William A. Gerrard, III, "Mainline Protestant Churches in Crisis," *Lexington Theological Quarterly*, April 1992, 27:44.
3. Elizabeth Schüssler Fiorenza, "Tablesharing and the Celebration of the Eucharist," in *Can We Always Celebrate the Eucharist?* Mary Collins, and David Power, eds. (New York: Seabury Press, 1982), 4.
4. Helen M. Wright, "Diversity of Roles and Solidarity in Christ," in *Women Priests: A Catholic Commentary on the Vatican Declaration*, Arlene Swidler, and Leonard Swidler, eds. (New York: Paulist Press, 1977), 247.
5. This is especially painful for women seminarians and clergy concerning the Eucharist, since they do not have the option of remaining silent during offensive sections when they are presiding.
6. Contemporaneously, the Quakers and the Salvation Army.
7. Charles Williams developed a theology of "co-inherence" in his many novels and theological treatises, especially *Descent Into Hell* (Grand Rapids: Eerdmans, 1970).
8. See www.apocryphile.org/interview.html for interview form.
9. See Gregory Dix, *The Shape of the Liturgy* (London: Dacre, 1945).
10. Gary Macy, *The Banquet's Wisdom: A Short History of the Theologies of the Lord's Supper* (New York: Paulist Press, 1992), 58.

11. As Jarislov Pelikan has nicely documented in his fine *Jesus Through the Centuries* (New Haven: Yale University, 1985).
12. I have my undergraduate philosophy professor Wayne Swindall to thank for this insight.
13. Raymond Firth, "The Plasticity of Myth," in *Sacred Narrative: Readings in the Theory of Myth*, Alan Dundes, ed. (Berkeley: University of California Press), 216.
14. Th. P. Van Baaren, "The Flexibility of Myth" in Dundes, 223.
15. Marjorie Procter-Smith, *In Her Own Rite: Constructing Feminist Liturgical Tradition* (Nashville: Abingdon, 1990), 59.
16. Horton Davies, *Bread of Life & Cup of Joy: Newer Ecumenical Perspectives on the Eucharist* (Grand Rapids: Eerdmans, 1994), 233.

PART ONE

1. Marion J. Hatchett, *Commentary on the American Prayer Book* (New York: Seabury Press, 1981), 290. The similarities of this pattern with even modern Eucharistic practice is obvious; the contemporary Roman Catholic Presentation of the Gifts uses the above prayers in only a slightly altered form.
2. Mark 2:15-19
3. William R. Crockett, *Eucharist: Symbol of Transformation* (New York: Pueblo Publishing Company, 1992), 5.
4. Matthew 8:11-12
5. 1 Corinthians 10:16-17
6. Galatians 3:26-29.
7. 1 Corinthians 11:18-22, 27-29
8. Especially John Chapter 6.
9. Exodus 24:4-11
10. Hebrews 2:17-3:1
11. Hebrews 9:24-10:1
12. Crockett, 20.
13. Jeremaiah 31:31-34

14. Hans Lietzmann, *Mass and Lord's Supper* (Leiden: EJ Brill, 1979), 196-203; Gunther Bronkamm, *Early Christian Experience* (London: SCM Press 1969), 136-137.
15. John Shelby Spong, *Rescuing the Bible from Fundamentalism* (San Francisco: HarperSanFrancisco, 1991), 217-226.
16. Donald Bridge and David Phypers. *Communion: The Meal that Unites?* (Wheaton: Harold Shaw, 1981), 30.
17. Macy, 30.
18. Justin Martyr, First Apology (http://www.knight.org/advent/fathers/)
19. Macy, 30.
20. www.knight.org/advent/fathers/
21. Macy, 29.
22. Macy, 26-7.
23. Robert D. Linder, "The Christian Centuries," in *Eerdman's Handbook to the History of Christianity,* Tim Dowley, ed. (Grand Rapids: Eerdmans, 1977), xiii.
24. Crockett, 5.
25. White, James F. *Documents of Christian Worship* (Louisville: John Knox Press, 1992), 186-7. Emphasis mine.
26. *The Apocryphon of John.* James M. Robinson, ed. *The Nag Hammadi Library* (San Francisco: Harper & Row, 1978), 104-123.
27. Bridge and Phypers, 50.
28. Compare, for instance, James' soteriology with Paul's.
29. Bridge and Phypers, 51.
30. Quoted in Crockett, 86.
31. John. D. Zizioulas, "The Early Christian Community," in *Christian Spirituality: Origins to the Twelfth Century,* Bernard McGinn and John Meyendorff, eds. (New York: Crossroad, 1987), 36.
32. Bridge and Phypers, 51.
33. Hugh Wybrew, "The Byzantine Liturgy from the *Apostolic Constitutions* to the Present Day," in Jones, 249.

34. Macy, 50.
35. Bridge and Phypers, 62.
36. *Ibid.*, 61-62.
37. E.J. Yarnold, S.J. "The Liturgy of the Faithful in the Fourth and Early Fifth Centuries," in Jones, 241.
38. *Ibid.*, 238.
39. *Ibid.*, 239.
40. Macy, 27.
41. Max Thurian, *The Mystery of the Eucharist: An Ecumenical Approach* (Grand Rapids: William B. Eerdmans, 1984), 68.
42. Crockett, 80.
43. Macy, 43.
44. Joanne Carlson Brown and Rebecca Parker in *Christianity, Patriarchy, and Abuse: A Feminist Critique*, Brown, Joanne Carlson, and Carole R. Bohn, eds. (Cleveland: Pilgrim Press, 1989), 5.
45. *Ibid.*
46. *Ibid.*, 6-7.
47. Davies, 151-152.
48. Saint Hilary of Poitier, *The Trinity*, translated by Stephen McKenna, CSSR (The Fathers of the Church, vol. 25), (New York: The Fathers of the Church, Inc., 1954), 285.
49. "Athanasius' Creed," *The Book of Common Prayer* (New York: Oxford University Press, 1979), 864. (See Appendix B.)
50. Wybrew, 250.
51. Macy, 49.
52. Chadwick, Henry. *The Early Church* (New York: Penguin, 1967), 127. This happened later, under Theodosius I (379-395).
53. Quoting the Orthodox Easter Troparions.
54. Davies, 264.
55. John Meyendorff, *Byzantine Theology: Historical Trends and Doctrinal Themes* (New York: Fordham University Press, 1987), 29.

56. Ernst Benz, *The Eastern Orthodox Church: Its Thought and Life* (Chicago: Aldine Publishing Company, 1983), 34.
57. Quoted in Davies, 156.
58. *Ibid.*, 153.
59. *Ibid.*, 166.
60. Myendorf, 357.
61. Myendorf, 359-60.
62. Thurian, 27.
63. Bridge and Phypers, 53.
64. *Ibid.*, 48-49.
65. Macy, 29.
66. Bridge and Phypers, 63.
67. *Ibid.*
68. In the words of the Roman rite.
69. *Ibid.*, 53.
70. Thurian, 12.
71. Anselm, *Cur Deus Homo*, Chapter Nine, quoted in Brown and Bohn, 7.
72. Brown and Parker, 7-8.
73. Hebrews 13:11-12
74. Hebrews 10:1-13
75. Crockett, 95.
76. Bridge and Phypers, 65.
77. *Ibid.*, 64.
78. *Summa Theologiae* 3a. 75,2; quoted in Crockett, 121.
79. Macy, 57.
80. Crockett, 123.
81. *Ibid.*, 124.
82. *Ibid.*
83. Radbertus, *On the Body and Blood of the Lord* 1.2, quoted in Crockett, 108.
84. *Ibid.*

85. *Ibid.* 19:15, quoted in Thurian, 40.
86. Macy, 87-88.
87. Quoted in Macy 119.
88. Lanfranc, *On the Body and Blood of the Lord*, quoted in Crockett 110-111.
89. Macy, 80.
90. Guitmond d'Aversa, *De Corporis et Sanguinis Christi*, quoted in Thurian, 42.
91. Macy, 84.
92. *Ibid.*, 199-200.
93. *Ibid.*, 106.
94. *Summa Theologiae* III, Qu.75, Art. 4, quoted in Thurian, 44.
95. Thomas Gilby, ed., *St. Thomas Aquinas: Theological Texts* (London: Oxford University Press, 1955), 620.
96. Quoted in Macy, 125. As a matter of fact, Aquinas' formulation wasn't even particularly good Aristotle — only in the Aristotelianism of Catholic theology does one find substance divorced from its accident!
97. Macy, 120.
98. *Ibid.*, 121.
99. Quoted in Bridge and Phypers, 80.
100. John Dillenberger, ed., Martin Luther, *Selections from His Writings* (New York: Doubleday, 1961), 270.
101. Martin Luther, *W.XXVI, 445, 462*, quoted in Thurian, 44.
102. Quoted in Bridge and Phypers, 90.
103. Thurian, 61.
104. Quoted in Bridge and Phypers, 90.
105. See Matthew Fox, "The Great Scandal of Protestantism," *Creation*, July-August 1985.
106. Crockett, 151.
107. *Ibid.*, 152.
108. *Ibid.*, 151.

109. J.K. Reid, ed., *Calvin: Theological Treatises* (Philadelphia: Westminster Press, 1954), 151.

110. Crockett, 158.

111. *Ibid.*, 154.

112. Quoted by Crockett, 160.

113. Quoted in Bridge and Phypers, 106.

114. *Ibid.*, 106.

115. Thomas Cranmer, *True and Catholic Doctrine and Use of the Sacrament of the Lord's Supper* (London: Chas. J. Thynne, 1907), 20-21.

116. Crockett, 176.

117. *Ibid.*, 177.

118. *Ibid.*, 178.

119. *Ibid.*

120. Bridge and Phypers, 127.

121. *Ibid.*

122. Macy, 79.

123. *Ibid.*, 73.

124. *Ibid.*, 76.

125. *Ibid.*, 77.

126. *Ibid.*

127. *Ibid.*, 86.

128. *Ibid.*, 87.

129. H. Wayne Pipkin, ed., *Huldrych Zwingli, Writings* (Volume 2) (Allison Park: Pickwick Publications, 1984), 135.

130. Bridge and Phypers, 116.

131. Crockett, 138.

132. *Ibid.*, 139.

133. Bridge and Phypers, 116.

134. *Ibid.*

135. D.H. Tripp, "Protestantism and the Eucharist" in Jones, 295.

136. Davies, 3.

137. Heard innumberable times by anyone who has grown up in an evangelical environment: I quote scores of pastors and evangelists of my childhood experience.
138. Bridge and Phypers, 83.
139. Bridge and Phypers, 137.
140. Seaburg, Carl, ed. *The Communion Book* (Boston: Unitarian Universalist Ministers Association, 1993), 293.
141. Seaburg, 11.
142. Bridge and Phypers, 115.
143. Colin Buchanan, *Encountering Charismatic Worship* (New York: Grove Books, 1977), 17.
144. Procter-Smith, 28-29.
145. Davies, 129-130.
146. Bridge and Phypers, 160.
147. As the Vatican II documents insensitively call all non-Roman Catholic Christians, including female ones.
148. Bridge and Phypers, 160.
149. *Ibid.*, 176.

PART TWO

1. 1 Corinthians 11:3. All scripture quotations are from the *New Revised Standard Version of the Bible.*
2. Matthew 19:30
3. Isaiah 40:4
4. Rosemary Radford Ruether, *Sexism and God-Talk* (Boston: Beacon, 1983), 33.
5. *Ibid.*
6. Charlotte Perkins Gilman, *His Religion and Hers* (New York: Century, 1923), 46.
7. *Ibid.*, 46-47
8. In the following pages I shall refer several times to "women's experience," by which I mean, as Procter-Smith describes it, "that historical and present reality which has been and continues to be ignored or distorted because of women's enforced

silence and lack of access to education and positions of authority. It is collective experience, and it is objectively available to any who wish to study it, as men's experience has always been. Thus the feminist movement's concern with women's experience is neither ahistorical nor antitraditional *per se*; it is simply concerned with recovering our own history and our own tradition." Procter-Smith, 32-33.

9. Procter-Smith, 14-15.

10. Ruether, 16-17.

11. Mary Catherine Hilkert, "Experience and Tradition — Can the Center Hold?" in *Freeing Theology: The Essentials of Theology in Feminist Perspective,* Catherine Mowry LaCugna, ed. (San Francisco: HarperSanFrancisco, 1992), 12-13.

12. Susan A. Ross, "God's Embodiment and Women" in LaCugna, 199.

13. *Ibid.*

14. *Ibid.*

15. Bruce Cockburn, "Free to Be," *Circles in the Stream* (Toronto: True North Records, 1978).

16. Ross, 195.

17. "It is very good..." Genesis 1:10.

18. J.D. Crichton, "A Theology of Worship," in Cheslyn Jones, Geoffrey Wainright, Edward Yarnold, SJ and Paul Bradshaw, *The Study of Liturgy* (New York: Oxford University Press), 1993.

19. Macy, 193-4.

20. Ross, 199.

21. Ruther, 31-2.

22. Elisabeth Schüssler Fiorenza, *A Discipleship of Equals* (New York: Crossroad, 1993).

23. See Ruether, *Ibid.*, 18-9.

24. *Ibid.*, 23.

25. Procter-Smith, 85-6.

26. Mary Daly, *Beyond God the Father* (Boston: Beacon Press, 1973), p. 19.

27. Karen L. Bloomquist, "Sexual Violence: Patriarchy's Offense and Defense," in *Christianity, Patriarchy, and Abuse: A Feminist Critique,* Joanne Carlson Brown, and Carole R. Bohn, eds. (Cleveland: Pilgrim Press, 1989), 67.
28. See LaCugna, Catherine Mowry. "God in Communion with Us: The Trinity" in LaCugna, 92.
29. Procter-Smith, 69.
30. See Bloomquist, 67.
31. Hardesty, Nancy A. *Inclusive Language in the Church* (Atlanta: John Knox Press, 1987), 92.
32. *Ibid.*, 14-15.
33. *Ibid.*, 2.
34. *Ibid.*
35. *Ibid.*, 62-3.
36. Procter-Smith, 61.
37. Ruether, 19-20.
38. Hardesty, 15.
39. Jann Aldredge-Clanton, *In Search of the Christ-Sophia* (Mystic: Twenty-Third Publications, 1995), 29.
40. Arianism, condemned at Alexandria in 320.
41. LaCugna, 84.
42. Janet Schaffran, *More Than Words: Prayer and Ritual for Inclusive Communities.* (New York: Crossroad, 1994), 6.
43. Hardesty, 10, 56.
44. *Ibid.*, 56.
45. Luke 24.
46. John Shelby Spong, *Rescuing the Bible from Fundamentalism.* (San Francisco: HarperSanFrancisco, 1991), 169.
47. Procter-Smith, 33-34.
48. *Ibid.*, 100.
49. Hardesty, 15.
50. See 1 Cor 11:3 and many other Pauline references where women are afforded lesser status than men.

51. Ruether, 32-33.
52. Hardesty, 102.
53. *Ibid.*, 12.
54. *Ibid.*, 58.
55. "Blessing for a Birthday," 1928 *Book of Common Prayer*, p. 597.
56. Prayer of Humble Access, *Ibid.*, p. 82.
57. Easter Vigil Lections, Years A, B and C.
58. Juan M.C. Oliver, "Language Shaped and Shaping," in *How Shall We Pray? Expanding Our Language about God,* Myers, Ruth A,. ed. (New York: The Church Hymnal Corporation, 1994), 148-9.
59. See the *Divinization Thread* in Section One.
60. Anselm, *Cur Deus Homo*, Chapter Nine, quoted in Brown and Bohn, 7.
61. Beverly W. Harrison and Carter Heyward, "Pain and Pleasure: Avoiding the Confusions of Christian Tradition in Feminist Theory," in Brown and Bohn, 153.
62. Elizabeth Johnson, "Redeeming the Name of Christ," in LaCugna, 124.
63. Rita Nakashima Brock, "And a Little Child Will Lead Us: Christology and Child Abuse," in Brown and Bohn, 52-53.
64. Shiela Redmond, "Christian 'Virtues' and Recovery from Childhood Sexual Abuse," in Brown and Bohn, 74.
65. Joanne Carlson Brown and Rebecca Parker, "For God So Loved the World?" in Brown and Bohn, 23.
66. Carter Heyward, *The Redemption of God.* (Washington, DC: University Press of America, 1982), 58.
67. Brown and Parker, 8.
68. *Ibid.*, 9.
69. Sheila Collins, *A Different Heaven and Earth* (Valley Forge: Judson Press, 1974), 88-89.
70. Daly, 77.
71. Brown and Parker, 4.

72. Ruth Duck, "Sin, Grace, and Gender in Free-Church Protestant Worship," in Marjorie Procter-Smith and Janet R. Walton, eds. *Women at Worship: Interpretations of North American Diversity* (Louisville: Westminster/John Knox Press, 1993), 61.
73. Procter-Smith, 151.
74. Heyward, 58.
75. Harrison, Beverly and Heyward, Carter. "Pain and Pleasure: Avoiding the Confusions of Christian Tradition in Feminist Theory," in Brown and Bohn, 145.
76. Brown and Parker, 18.
77. Harrison, Beverly Wildung, *Making the Connections.* (Boston: Beacon Press, 1985), 18-19.
78. Fortune, Mary F. "The Transformation of Suffering: A Biblical and Theological Perspective," in Brown and Bohn, 146-7.
79. Ruether, 137.
80. Ruether, 215.
81. Ross, 119.
82. The second coming of Christ.
83. Rauschenbusch, Walter. *A Theology for the Social Gospel.* (New York: Abingdon Press, 1917), 174. Quoted in Brown and Parker, 8.
84. Ruether, 85.
85. See "The Divinity Thread" in Section One.
86. Aldredge-Clanton, 47.
87. See Hardesty, 41
88. Hardesty, 41.
89. *Tao Te Ching* Poem 16.
90. Albert Nolan, *Jesus Before Christianity* (Maryknoll: Orbis, 1985), 39.
91. Ray Overholt, "Ten Thousand Angels," in *Favorites Volume Five* (Grand Rapids: Zondervan, 1961), 22.
92. Ruether, 30.
93. Procter-Smith, 31.

94. Ruether, 209-210.
95. *Ibid.*, 207.
96. See Bloomquist, 68-69.
97. Fortune, 101.
98. Bloomquist, 68.
99. Ruether, 208-209.
100. Hilkert, 20.
101. *Ibid.*
102. Brock, 55.
103. Redmond, 85.
104. Brock, 53.
105. Women should be silent in the churches. For they are not permitted to speak, but should be subordinate, as the law also says." 1 Corinthians 14:34
106. Ross, 190.
107. *Ibid.*, 204.
108. *Ibid*, 204-205.
109. Aldredge-Clanton, 12.
110. Rosemary Radford Ruether, *Women-Church* (San Francisco: Harper & Row, 1985), 5.
111. Luke 1:48-53
112. Matthew Fox, *Meditations with Meister Eckhart* (Santa Fe: Bear and Co, 1983), 81.

PART THREE

1. Ralph N. McMichael, "How Are We to Name the Trinity in Our Eucharistic Prayers?" in Myers, 115.
2. Kyle Wiseley (Portland, Oregon)
3. Spong, 236.
4. *Ibid.*, 237.
5. Richard Norris, "Inclusive Language Liturgies," in Myers, 38.

6. Stephen Mitchell, trans. *The Enlightened Mind* (New York: HarperCollins, 1991), 10.
7. Spong, 231.
8. Procter-Smith, 34.
9. *Ibid.*, 13.
10. McMichael in Myers, 115-116.
11. Mark 2.
12. Hilkert in LaCugna, 72.
13. *Ibid.*
14. *Ibid.*, 74.
15. Ruether, *Women-Church*, 15.
16. Jay C. Rochelle, *Create and Celebrate!* (Philadelphia: Fortress Press, 1971), 19-20.
17. Procter-Smith, 22.
18. *Ibid.*
19. Gail Ramshaw-Schmidt, *Christ in Sacred Speech* (Philadelphia: Fortress Press, 1986), 4.
20. McMichael in Myers, 115.
21. Procter-Smith, 135.
22. Ellen K. Wondra, "O For a Thousand Tongues to Sing," in Meyers, 7.
23. LaCugna in LaCugna, 108.
24. For an example, see John E. Skoglund and Nancy E. Hall, *A Manual of Worship* (Valley Forge: Judson Press, 1993).
25. Procter-Smith, 31.
26. Quoted in Bridge and Phypers, 154.
27. Davies, 259.
28. *Ibid.*
29. Acts 2:46
30. Appendix D.
31. Edward Schillebeeckx, *The Catholic Tradition* (New York: Consortium, 1979), 305.

32. Quoted in Davies, 92.
33. Davies, 92.
34. *Ibid.*, 93.
35. *Ibid.*, 33.
36. *Book of Common Prayer*, 370.
37. Davies, 180.
38. *Ibid.*, 185.
39. Quoted in Davies, 192.
40. Davies, 193.
41. *Ibid.*, 197-198.
42. Adapted for Festival use from *The Abraxis Eucharist,* in Seaburg, 250-251.
43. Gustavo Gutiérrez, *The Theology of Liberation* (Maryknoll: Orbis Books, 1973), 262-263.
44. Mary Collins, "Is the Eucharist Still a Source of Meaning for Women?" *Origins* 21 (Sept. 12, 1991), 228.
45. Quoted in Davies, 141.
46. Davies, 211.
47. Procter-Smith, 82-83.
48. Sheila Redmond, "Remember the Good, Forget the Bad: Denial and Family Violence in a Christian Worship Service," in Marjorie Procter-Smith and Janet R. Walton, eds. *Women at Worship: Interpretations of North American Diversity* (Louisville: Westminster/John Knox Press, 1993), 77.
49. Festival, Eucharistic Prayer III. See Appendix E for the full text of the Festival's Eucharistic prayers.
50. Davies, 85.
51. This mythology is little more than two hundred years old and does not reflect the historical teaching of the church.
52. Jürgen Moltmann, *The Theology of Hope* (New York: Harper & Row, 1967), 33.
53. Quoted by Davies, 116.
54. *St. Joseph's Sunday Missal* (New York: Catholic Book Publishing Co., 1985), 546.

55. Brian Wren.
56. Schaffran, 4.
57. See Patricia Wilson-Kastner, "Dialogue or Disputation: The Character of the Debate about Inclusive Language," in Meyers, 129.
58. Ruth A. Meyers, "Principles for Liturgical Language," in Myers, 93-94.
59. Margaret Moers Wenig, "Reform Jewish Worship: How Shall We Speak of Torah, Israel, and God?" in Procter-Smith and Walton, 38-39.
60. Procter-Smith, 52.
61. Redmond, in Procter-Smith and Walton, 74.
62. Aldredge-Clanton, 5.
63. Johnson, in LaCugna, 120-121.
64. Paula S. Datsko Barker, "Lord, Teach Us to Pray: Historical and Theological Perspectives on Expanding Liturgical Language," in Myers, 41.
65. *Ibid.*
66. Barker, in Myers, 50.
67. Johnson, in Procter-Smith, 107.
68. *Supplemental Liturgical Materials* (New York: The Church Hymnal Corp., 1991), 39-40.
69. Schaffran, 12.
70. Ware, in Procter-Smith and Walton, 104.
71. Richard Fabian, *Worship at Saint Gregory's* (San Francisco: All Saints' Company, 1995), 29.
72. *The Liturgy According to the Use of the Liberal Catholic Church* (London: St. Alban's Press, 1983), 204.
73. *St. Joseph's Missal*, 548.
74. Susan J. Clark, Celebrating Earth Holy Days (New York: Crossroad, 1992), 127.
75. Confession by Lawson Barnes, from the Liturgy acccording to the use of the Festival of the Holy Names.

76. For a more complete treatment of these competing ways of viewing the universe, see Inna Jane Ray, "Sacred or Scared," in *Feast,* Vol. I, No. 2.
77. *Service Book of the Holy Orthodox Catholic and Apostolic Church* (Antiochian Orthodox Christian Archdiocese, 1971), 101.
78. "The M. Scott Peck Interview," *The Door,* Vol. 20, No. 2, 10.
79. Procter-Smith, 132.
80. Fabian, 25-26.
81. *Ibid.*, 26.
82. *Book of Worship,* 511.
83. Fabian, 30.
84. Justin, *Apology* 1.67.6
85. Fabian, 30.
86. *Sunday Missal,* 555-556.
87. M. C. Godby, *A Creation Eucharist* (Wembley Downs, 1991), 7-8.
88. Alternative Service Book (Oxford: Oxford University Press, 1980), 119.
89. Fabian, 45
90. *The Sunday Missal,* 559.
91. *A Book of Services* (Edinburgh: The Saint Andrew Press, 1980), 34-35.
92. *Sunday Missal*, 560-561.
93. All four traditional institutional passages can be found in Appendix D.
94. See, for example, Rita Nahashima Brock's *Pathways of the Heart: A Christology of Erotic Power.*
95. See the Festival of the Holy Names' first Eucharistic prayer, the "Life and Joy" liturgy, Appendix E.
96. See the Festival of the Holy Names' third Eucharistic prayer, "Servants and Priests" for an example of an Institution from this source, Appendix E.
97. See the Festival of the Holy Names' fourth Eucharistic prayer, "Christ in Community," Appendix E.

98. Joseph M. Powers, quoted in Davies, 222.

99. Davies, 223.

100. *Ibid.*, 227.

101. "Panentheism" is a term coined by K.C.F. Krause (1781-1832) for his own theological studies. The insertion of the Greek preposition "*en*" denotes that, unlike pantheism, where God is all, in panentheism God is *in* all. Wheras in classic pantheism, to subtract God from the universe would leave nothing, with panentheism subtracting the universe from God would still leave God in all of God's transcendence.

102. Yarnold, in Jones, et. al., 233.

103. Davies, 189.

104. Edward F. Gabriele, *Act Justly, Love Tenderly, Walk Humbly* (Winona: St. Mary's Press, 1995), i.

105. This ghastly prayer may be found in the American *Book of Common Prayer* on page 337.

106. Lutheran *Book of Worship*, 94.

107. Ruth Duck, *Flames of the Spirit* (Cleveland: The Pilgrim Press, 1985), 93.

108. Nan Cobbey, "An Unusual, Yet Common, Congregation," in *Episcopal Life*, April 1997.

107. Ruth Duck, *Flames of the Spirit* (Cleveland: The Pilgrim Press, 1985), 93.

EPILOGUE

1. Davies, 219.

2. *Ibid.*, 259.

3. Shaffran, 10.

4. John Shuster, *Shaping the Church of the Future* (Port Orchard: New Church Publications, 1994), 22-27.

APPENDIX E

1. Phillip A. Porter, *Singing the Living Tradition* (Boston: Unitarian Universalist Association, 1993), 389.

2. Duck, 93.
3. Godby, 7-8.
4. Seaburg, 293.
5. Godby, 7-8.
6. *Didache*.
7. *Ibid*.
8. Marietta Fahey, SHF from Schaffran's *More than Words*.

BIBLIOGRAPHY

Aldredge-Clanton, Jann. *In Search of the Christ-Sophia.* Mystic: Twenty-Third Publications, 1995.

Arnold, Eberhard, ed. *The Early Christians.* Grand Rapids: Baker, 1970.

Astell, Ann W. *Divine Representations: Postmodernism and Spirituality.* Mahwah: Paulist Press 1994.

Benz, Ernst. *The Eastern Orthodox Church: Its Thought and Life.* Chicago: Aldine Publishing Company, 1983.

Bridge, Donald and David Phypers. *Communion: The Meal that Unites?* Wheaton: Harold Shaw, 1981.

Bronkamm, Gunther. *Early Christian Experience.* London: SCM Press 1969.

Brown, Joanne Carlson, and Bohn, Carole R., eds. *Christianity, Patriarchy, and Abuse: A Feminist Critique.* Cleveland: Pilgrim Press, 1989.

Buchanan, Colin. *Encountering Charasmatic Worship.* New York: Grove Books, 1977.

Carr, Anne E. *Transforming Grace: Christian Tradition and Women's Experience.* San Francisco: Harper & Row, 1988.

Chadwick, Henry. *The Early Church.* New York: Penguin, 1967.

Cherry, Kittredge and Sherwood, Zalmon, eds. *Equal Rites: Lesbian and Gay Worship, Ceremonies, and Celebrations.* Louisville: Westminster/John Knox Press, 1995.

Clark, Susan J. *Celebrating Earth Holy Days.* New York: Crossroad, 1992.

Cobbey, Nan. "An Unusual, Yet Common, Congregation" in *Episcopal Life*, April 1997.

Cockburn, Bruce. "Free to Be," from *Circles in the Stream*. Toronto: True North Records, 1978.

Coll, Regina A. *Christianity & Feminism in Conversation*. Mystic: Twenty-Third Publications, 1994.

Collins, Sheila. *A Different Heaven and Earth*. Valley Forge: Judson Press, 1974.

Cranmer, Thomas. *True and Catholic Doctrine and Use of the Sacrament of the Lord's Supper*. London: Chas. J. Thynne, 1907.

Crockett, William R. *Eucharist: Symbol of Transformation*. New York: Pueblo Publishing Company, 1992.

Crossan, John Dominic. *Jesus: A Revolutionary Biography*. San Francisco: HarperSanFrancisco, 1994.

Daly, Mary. *Beyond God the Father*. Boston: Beacon Press, 1973.

Davies, Horton. *Bread of Life & Cup of Joy: Newer Ecumenical Perspectives on the Eucharist*. Grand Rapids: Eerdmans, 1994.

de Waal, Esther. *Every Earthly Blessing*. Ann Arbor: Servant Publications, 1991.

Dillenberger, John, ed. *Martin Luther, Selections from His Writings*. New York: Doubleday, 1961.

Dix, Gregory. *The Shape of the Liturgy*. London: Dacre, 1945.

Dowley, Tim, ed. *Eerdman's Handbook to the History of Christianity*. Grand Rapids: Eerdmans, 1977.

Duck, Ruth. *Flames of the Spirit*. Cleveland: The Pilgrim Press, 1985.

Fabian, Richard. *Worship at Saint Gregory's*. San Francisco: All Saints' Company, 1995.

Fiorenza, Elisabeth Schussler. *A Discipleship of Equals*. New York: Crossroad, 1993.

Fox, Matthew. *Meditations with Meister Eckhart*. Santa Fe: Bear and Co, 1983.

Fulkerson, Mary McClintock. *Changing the Subject: Women's Discourses and Feminist Theology*. Minneapolis: Fortress Press, 1994.

Gabriele, Edward F. *Act Justly, Love Tenderly, Walk Humbly*. Winona: St. Mary's Press, 1995.

Gilby, Thomas, ed., *St. Thomas Aquinas: Theological Texts*. London: Oxford University Press, 1955.

Gilman, Charlotte Perkins. *His Religion and Hers*. New York: Century, 1923.

Godby, M.C. *A Creation Eucharist*. Wembley Downs, 1991.

Grey, Mary. *Feminism, Redemption, and the Christian Tradition*. Mystic: Twenty-Third Publications, 1990.

Gutiérrez, Gustavo. *The Theology of Liberation*. Maryknoll: Orbis Books, 1973.

Guzie, Tad W. *Jesus and the Eucharist*. Mahwah: Paulist Press, 1974.

Haddon, Genia Pauli. *Uniting Sex, Self & Spirit*. Scotland: Plus Publications, 1993.

Hardesty, Nancy A. *Inclusive Language in the Church*. Atlanta: John Knox Press, 1987.

Harrison, Beverly Wildung. *Making the Connections*. Boston: Beacon Press, 1985.

Hatchett, Marion. *Commentary of the American Prayer Book.* New York: Seabury Press, 1981.

Heyward, Carter. *The Redemption of God.* Washington, DC: University Press of America, 1982.

Saint Hilary of Poitier. *The Trinity*, translated by Stephen McKenna, CSSR. *The Fathers of the Church, vol. 25.* New York: The Fathers of the Church, Inc., 1954.

Hosmer, Rachel and Jones, Alan. *Living in the Spirit.* New York: Seabury, 1979.

Johnson, Elizabeth A. *She Who Is: The Mystery of God in Feminist Theological Discourse.* New York: Crossroad, 1992.

Jones, Cheslyn; Wainright, Geoffrey; Yarnold, Edward, SJ; and Bradshaw, Paul. *The Study of Liturgy.* New York: Oxford University Press, 1993.

Kimel, Alvin F. *Speaking the Christian God: The Holy Trinity an the Challenge of Feminism.* Grand Rapids: Eerdmans, 1992.

LaCugna, Catherine Mowry, ed. *Freeing Theology: The Essentials of Theology in Feminist Perspective.* San Francisco: HarperSanFrancisco, 1992.

Layton, Bently. *The Gnostic Scriptures.* New York: Doubleday, 1987.

Lietzmann, Hans. *Mass and Lord's Supper.* Leiden: EJ Brill, 1979.

Lossky, Vladimir. *The Mystical Theology of the Eastern Church.* Crestwood: St. Vladimir's Seminary Press, 1976.

Mabry, John R. *God As Nature Sees God.* Rockport: Element Books, 1994.

Macy, Gary. *The Banquet's Wisdom: A Short History of the Theologies of the Lord's Supper.* New York: Paulist Press, 1992.

Martin, Francis. *The Feminist Question: Feminist Theology in the Light of Christian Tradition*. Grand Rapids: Eerdmans, 1994.

McBrien, Richard P. *Catholicism*. San Francisco: HarperSanFrancisco, 1981.

McGinn, Bernard and Meyendorff, John. *Christian Spirituality: Origins to the Twelfth Century*. New York: Crossroad, 1987.

Meyendorff, John. *Byzantine Theology: Historical Trends and Doctrinal Themes*. New York: Fordham University Press, 1987.

Mitchell, Stephen, trans. *The Enlightened Mind*. New York: HarperCollins, 1991.

Moltmann, Jürgen. *The Theology of Hope*. New York: Harper & Row, 1967.

Myers, Ruth A,. ed. *How Shall We Pray? Expanding Our Language about God*. New York: The Church Hymnal Corporation, 1994.

Naumann, James R. "Creation Imagery in the Early Eucharistic Prayers." Thesis: Graduate Theological Union, 1991.

Neu, Diann L., & Hunt, Mary E. *Women-Church Sourcebook*. Silver Spring: WATER, 1993.

Neu, Diann L. *Women-Church Celebrations*. Silver Spring: WATER, 1985.

——*Women and the Gospel Traditions*. Silver Spring: WATER, 1989.

Nolan, Albert. *Jesus Before Christianity*. Maryknoll: Orbis, 1985.

O'Collins, Gerald. *A Concise Dictionary of Theology*. Mahwah, Paulist Press, 1991.

Oden, Amy. *In Her Words*. Nashville: Abingdon, 1994.

Pipkin, H. Wayne, ed. *Huldrych Zwingli, Writings* (Volume 2). Allison Park: Pickwick Publications, 1984.

Power, David N. *The Sacrifice We Offer*. New York: Crossroad, 1987.

Procter-Smith, Marjorie and Walton, Janet R., eds. *Women at Worship: Interpretations of North American Diversity.* Louisville: Westminster/John Knox Press, 1993.

Procter-Smith, Marjorie. *In Her Own Rite: Constructing Feminist Liturgical Tradition.* Nashville: Abingdon, 1990.

Ramshaw-Schmidt, Gail. *Christ in Sacred Speech.* Philadelphia: Fortress Press, 1986.

Reid, J.K., ed. *Calvin: Theological Treatises*. Philadelphia: Westminster Press, 1954.

Remsberg, John E. *The Christ*. Amherst: Prometheus Books, 1994.

Richard, Lucien, OMI. *What Are They Saying About the Theology of Suffering?* Mahwah: Paulist Press, 1992.

Robinson, James M., ed. *The Nag Hammadi Library*. San Francisco: HarperCollins, 1978.

Rochelle, Jay C. *Create and Celebrate!* Philadelphia: Fortress Press, 1971.

Ruether, Rosemary Radford. *Sexism and God-Talk.* Boston: Beacon, 1983.

——*Women-Church*. San Francisco: Harper & Row, 1985.

——*Shaping the Church of the Future: An Action Plan for Roman Catholic Renewal.* Port Orchard: New Church Publications, 1994.

Schaffran, Janet. *More Than Words: Prayer and Ritual for Inclusive Communities*. New York: Crossroad, 1994.

Skoglund, John E. and Nancy E. Hall. *A Manual of Worship.* Valley Forge: Judson Press, 1993.

Spong, John Shelby. *Rescuing the Bible from Fundamentalism.* San Francisco: HarperSanFrancisco, 1991.

Stevenson, Kenneth. *The First Rites: Worship in the Early Church.* Collegeville: The Liturgical Press, 1989.

Thompson, Brad. *Liturgies of the Western Church.* Philadelphia: Fortress Press, 1961.

Thurian, Max. *The Mystery of the Eucharist: An Ecumenical Approach.* Grand Rapids: William B. Eerdmans, 1984.

Thurian, Max and Wainwright, Geoffrey. *Baptistm and Eucharist: Ecumenical Convergence in Celebration.* Grand Rapids: WCC/Eerdmans, 1983

Underhill, Evelyn. *Mysticism.* Oxford: One World Press, 1993.

Watkins, Keith. *Celebrate with Thanksgiving.* St. Louis: Chalice Press, 1991.

Wessels, Anton. *Images of Jesus.* Grand Rapids: Eerdmans, 1986.

White, James F. *Documents of Christian Worship.* Louisville: John Knox Press, 1992.

Williams, Charles. *Descent Into Hell.* Grand Rapids: Eerdmans, 1970.

Wright, Helen M. "Diversity of Roles and Solidarity in Christ," in *Women Priests: A Catholic Commentary on the Vatican Declaration,* Swidler, Arlene and Swidler, Leonard, eds. New York: Paulist Press, 1977.

Alternative Service Book. Oxford: Oxford University Press, 1980.

The Book of Common Prayer. New York: Oxford University Press, 1979.

A Book of Services. Edinburgh: The Saint Andrew Press, 1980.
Book of Worship: United Church of Christ. New York: UCC Office for Church Life and Leadership, 1986.

Catechism of the Catholic Church. Washington D.C.: United States Catholic Conference, 1994.

The Liturgy According to the Use of the Liberal Catholic Church. London: St. Alban's Press, 1983.

Lutheran Book of Worship. Minneapolis: Augsburg, 1978.

Service Book of the Holy Eastern Orthodox Catholic and Apostolic Church. Antiochian Orthodox Christian Archdiocese, 1971.

St. Joseph's Sunday Missal. New York: Catholic Book Publishing Co., 1985.

Supplemental Liturgical Materials. New York: The Church Hymnal Corp., 1991.

www.ingramcontent.com/pod-product-compliance
Lightning Source LLC
Chambersburg PA
CBHW032036080426
42733CB00006B/99

* 9 7 8 0 9 7 4 7 6 2 3 8 8 *